Metaphorical Ways of Knowing

Metaphorical Ways of Knowing

The Imaginative Nature of Thought and Expression

Sharon L. Pugh
Indiana University

Jean Wolph Hicks
Indiana University and
University of Louisville

Marcia Davis
Indiana University

National Council of Teachers of English
1111 W. Kenyon Road, Urbana, Illinois 61801

Manuscript Editor: Julie Bush
Production Editor: Rona S. Smith
Cover Design: Loren Kirkwood
Interior Design: Doug Burnett

NCTE Stock Number: 31514-3050

Permissions acknowledgments appear on page 214.

Library of Congress Cataloging-in-Publication Data
Pugh, Sharon L.
    Metaphorical ways of knowing: the imaginative nature of thought
    and expression / Sharon L. Pugh, Jean Wolph Hicks, Marcia Davis.
        p.   cm.
    Includes bibliographical references and index.
    ISBN 0-8141-3151-4 (pbk.)
    1. English philology—Study and teaching—Theory, etc. 2. English
language—Composition and exercises—Study and teaching—Theory,
etc. 3. English language—Rhetoric—Study and teaching—Theory, etc.
4. Interdisciplinary approach in education. 5. Pluralism (Social sci-
ences) 6. Language arts (Education) 7. Multicultural education.
8. Thought and thinking. 9. Knowledge, Theory of. 10. Imagination.
11. Metaphor. I. Hicks, Jean Wolph, 1953– . II. Davis, Marcia,
    1956– . III. Title.
PE65.P85   1997
420' .7—dc21   96-47982
                                                                      CIP

Contents

Preface   vii

Acknowledgments   ix

Introduction: Language, Thought, and Imagination   3

I. Metaphor and Learning

1. Metaphor and Meaning   13
2. Ways of Knowing: Metaphor and Learning   34
3. Reimagining Ourselves   48

II. Multiple Perspectives: Metaphors and New Outlooks

4. Experiencing Other Lives   69
5. Change   84
6. Time   95
7. Exploring Cultures through Traditions   109

III. Imagining Language

8. English as a Metaphor for Multiculturalism   129
9. World Literatures in English   142

IV. Making Sense: The Experience of Metaphor

10. Seeing and Hearing with the Imagination   157
11. Metaphors of Taste and Smell   170
12. The Imagination of the Body: Movement and Touch   180

V. Conclusion and References

Conclusion   195

References   197

Permissions Acknowledgments   214

Index   215

Authors   221

Preface

In this volume, three of the authors of *Bridging: A Teacher's Guide to Metaphorical Thinking* return to the subject we felt we had barely begun in our first book. Here we have focused on metaphorical and imaginative thinking as tools for learning, captured in the phrase *ways of knowing*.

Learning is an act of discovery. Language is the main equipment that human learners take on this expedition. Because of the uncharted nature of the territory ahead in the quest for new knowledge, learners need not only the right apparatus but also the skill and imagination to use it in versatile ways. Our aim in this book is to emphasize imagination in using language for thought and expression.

As English teachers, we value precision, structure, and clarity in language, attributes that students certainly need in order to function in a communicative society. However, we should not let these values obscure the equally important values of experimentation, originality, and playfulness. Traditionally, school instruction has emphasized accurate transmission of information and ideas. Too often, we complain that students aren't hearing what we say, that is, they aren't understanding us; and they aren't saying what we expect to hear, which is to say they aren't being clear. These concerns are valid, but we should be just as concerned with whether students are using language for exploration and invention.

Too often, imagination gets squeezed. It is still functioning—it has to be for language to work at all—but it is operating in a very small space. The well-known demise of creativity in many children throughout the school years is one consequence of this compression. Like anything that is alive, imagination needs room, freedom, and stimulation to grow and be healthy.

We have written this book especially for teachers of grades 5–14 who are interested in integrating the development of language and thinking into a reading-writing curriculum. We also reach out to teachers who are attempting an even broader integration, that of English and social studies into a humanities block. By offering a theoretical basis for viewing metaphor as a way of knowing, and by suggesting many avenues through which this way of knowing may be explored and developed, we hope to promote the cause of the imagination so that it will be given the kind of attention that rational, scientific knowledge has received for centuries.

Sharon L. Pugh
Jean Wolph Hicks
Marcia Davis

Acknowledgments

We wish especially to thank the librarians of the Monroe County (Indiana) Public Library, the Louisville (Kentucky) Free Public Library, and the Indiana University Library who put their expertise to work for us in locating obscure citations and materials. We also thank Julie Chen and Mayumi Fujioka, IU doctoral students, for contributing a number of Chinese and Japanese name origins, and Bhupender K. Sharma, who kindly shared Hindi names with us.

We appreciate the time taken by teachers to read and respond to our work, including Anne Greenwell of Ahrens High School (adult education) in Louisville; Brenda Overturf of Mt. Washington (Kentucky) Middle School; Danna Morrison of Hebron Middle School (Bullitt County, Kentucky); and the teachers in the Louisville Writing Project's Advantage classes.

Special thanks also go to photographer Dave Staver and computer expert David Hicks for their contributions to our work.

Metaphorical Ways of Knowing

Introduction: Language, Thought, and Imagination

The whole story of humanity is basically that of a journey toward the Emerald City, and of an effort to learn the nature of Oz.

Loren Eiseley, *The Unexpected Universe*

L anguage is an act of the imagination, a means by which we construct in our minds images (or, to use a related word, imitations) of each other's thoughts and experiences. Unlike the dances of bees, the songs of whales, or the scents of moths, our messages have meanings on multiple levels, so that the human language user is more poet than information processor. When a person speaks the simplest sentence, ten listeners may interpret it ten different ways, and yet we understand each other well enough to communicate, cooperate, or quarrel in amazingly complex ways.

We believe that the English class is a place where students should learn a great deal about their own creative powers as language users and makers, destined to understand and express themselves in original yet communicative ways throughout their lives. At the heart of these creative language and meaning processes, we believe, is the imaginative logic of metaphorical thinking, defined in our previous book, *Bridging,* as "drawing parallels between apparently unrelated phenomena to gain insight, make discoveries, offer hypotheses [and] wage arguments" (Pugh et al. 1992, 2). To be a metaphorical thinker, as we all are, is to be "a constructive learner, one who actively builds bridges from the known to the new" (5).

Metaphorical thinking and knowing begin early in the life of a language user. In *Mental Leaps* (the title itself a metaphor for understanding analogies), Holyoak and Thagard (1995) tell the story of Neil, a four-year-old who tried to establish the significance of a tree to a bird by comparing the bird's experience with his own. At first he called the tree the bird's chair, because it is where the bird sits, but then decided that it was more like the bird's yard, because it is where the bird's nest—or "house"—is located. An even earlier example, described by Johnston (1993), is a two-and-a-half-year-old child's comparison of his training pants to a stop sign, both meaning "don't go." Gibbs (1994), in a chapter entitled "The Poetic Minds of Children," supports his claim that young children have significant ability to think in figurative terms with numerous examples, including the use of metonymy by a two-and-a-half-year-old who told his mother "don't broom my mess" (423) and a ten-line poem composed by a seven-year-old projecting herself into the experience of a raindrop.

In their work using therapeutic metaphors with children, Mills and Crowley (1986) equate telling a story with telling a metaphor, which they believe accounts for the "natural receptivity to metaphor" in children. Defining metaphor as "the critical substance of change," they compare its power in children with putting a flame to a candle, "igniting the child's imagination to its brightest valence of strength, self-knowledge, and transformation" (xix).

Throughout childhood, adolescence, and adulthood, we can revisit virtually any fairy tale and see how its meaning continues to develop for us. We may decide, as Shel Silverstein (1974) did in his poem "The Little Blue Engine," that "The Little Engine Who Could" holds up a sometimes unreachable ideal of self-reliance and fails to acknowledge that often we need each other to succeed. Or as Toni Morrison (1977) suggests in *Song of Solomon*, adults may still act like Hansel and Gretel, drawn to their doom by the powerful forces of hunger or desire. We may know a Cinderella, waiting passively to be rescued from an unsatisfactory life, or a Gingerbread Man, running away from those who love and care about him into the jaws of fate. We may also use metaphorical understanding to reject damaging premises. Why should the young woman in "The Three Spinners" (Grimm 1966) look for supernatural ways to accomplish the impossible feats set by a demanding future spouse? Why not just say, as did Bartleby the Scrivener in Melville's parable of resistance, "I would prefer not to" ([1853] 1990, 57)?

In a course on critical and creative thinking across the curriculum, a prospective teacher, Jennifer Kuhn, used the lead character from Eric Carle's *Mixed-Up Chameleon* (1984) to reflect on her learning. In this story, a chameleon tries to emulate an admirable characteristic in every animal he meets. He grows pink wings to be elegant like the flamingo, a bushy tail to be smart like the fox, a big head and trunk to be strong like the elephant, and so on. In the end, he decides that he prefers being himself, but knows it was important for him to go through all the changes he experienced. From this story, Jennifer draws a personal metaphor:

> I am definitely not saying that I wanted to be, or think, like other people in the class. However, I did appreciate hearing what everyone else had to say. It helped me look at issues and problems in my own everyday life that I may never have thought about before. In addition, I gained insight into some of the biased thinking that I now

admit I do sometimes. Instead of going through physical changes, I went through mental changes. My attitude toward critical thinking and the approaches I take have, in my opinion, become much more advanced. Going back to the chameleon, this animal and many others take on the color of their surroundings. Yes, this is usually to hide from a predator; however, I wish to focus on how these animals adapt to the circumstances surrounding them. While the animals remain entirely what they are, in every aspect a chameleon, or rabbit, or any other animal, each knows how to survive in the wild—they adapt. I would say this is what critical thinking is: The act of adapting to the current environment.

While I can retain my own individuality, my thoughts and opinions, I can also keep an open mind and allow others around me to express their personal opinions. I can also read or interpret materials and attempt to understand where the author is coming from, whether or not I tend to agree. Perhaps by adapting to my "surroundings," I will sometimes change my ideas, or form new opinions, or discover that, perhaps, I was wrong about something. (Kuhn 1995)

The chameleon metaphor has its risks, as it is often used to signify either deviousness or acquiescence to a prevailing view. But Jennifer steers it in another direction. "Adapting to the current environment" does not, for her, mean a self-protective conformity. It has the much more powerful meaning of understanding the present environment as deeply as possible by projecting herself into the viewpoints and experiences of others who share it with her. And like a chameleon, she can change without losing either her identity or her integrity. In the end, Jennifer's metaphor has not only represented her as active and in charge but has also perhaps altered our stereotype of chameleons.

Because language is inherently metaphorical, its transformations into new meanings never end. What we understand via language we understand, in some sense, metaphorically. This is true in disciplinary knowing as well as in literature whenever we understand the unfamiliar in terms of forms and images derived from what we know. In the field of psychology, for example, Sternberg (1990) proposes a taxonomy of theories of intelligence based on their central metaphors. The geographic metaphor assumes that a theory of intelligence should provide a map of the mind, while the computational metaphor compares the mind to computer software operating in the hardware of the brain. Sternberg compares these concrete metaphors to metaphors based on academic disciplines, including psychology, biology, and sociology, and then he compares these with what he calls "the systems metaphor," which is cross-disciplinary, the metaphor of metaphors.

Almost a half century ago, the scientist R. W. Gerard (1952) identified two central challenges to education: to "teach rigor while preserving imagination," and to "preserve open-mindedness while teaching current systems" (258–59). To illustrate these principles in relation to each other, he developed the metaphor of the river and its bed: "The river carves its bed, and the bed controls its waters; only by their continual interplay can a particular system develop" (257). This image, evoking the notion of guided but free energy, captures our idea of the English classroom. It is a place where teachers and students together carry forward the processes by which the language changes and grows, all having a creative license to stretch, bend, rearrange, and shape English in new ways.

English is a very rich medium for combining rigor and imagination, open-mindedness and knowledge of a current system. It has the most extensive vocabulary of any language in the world. The *Oxford English Dictionary* contains over a half million definitions, with five thousand added in each new supplement. Where do all these words come from? Only about half the English vocabulary stems from its original Old Germanic parentage. The rest is imported, largely from Greek, Latin, and French, but also from virtually every other part of the linguistic world, including Arabic, Russian, Sanskrit, Hindi, Persian, Japanese, Chinese, Hawaiian, Malay, Native American and African languages, and many more. And English is a tough medium, one that cannot be damaged by our experiments whether they succeed or fail. The damage, rather, would come in leaving it alone, neglecting its possibilities, denying it the energy of our imaginations.

In our previous book we used the image of the bridge to characterize metaphorical thinking as the process of crossing from the known to the new. And once we have crossed a bridge, the journey goes on. Hence the present volume, which takes up where we left off before, draws on the image of the map to extend our notion of metaphorical ways of knowing. Just as a bridge epitomized the metaphor's function of meaningfully joining separate phenomena, a map epitomizes the idea of going somewhere, which we find inherent in the concept of *ways* of knowing.

The map is an especially rich metaphor from the perspective of the constructivist claim that "knowledge is 'right' or 'wrong' in light of the perspective we have chosen to assume" (Bruner 1990, 25). Both the map and the globe from which it is projected incorporate particular perspectives. Even though the planet is a sphere in space and so has no top or bottom, conventional maps represent north as the top and south as the bottom of a two-halved ball, with north as "up" and south as "down." We northerners may take this representation for granted and even imagine an "up" and "down" in the universe, but it is quite annoying to those in the Southern Hemisphere who get tired of being on the bottom rather than the top of the earth. This point was brought home to the authors, who had made reference to the weather "down there" in a letter to linguist Donald S. McDonald in South Australia. In his response, he retorted, "We're not 'down there'—you are the ones in the Antipodes!" (1994). Later, on the wall of a restaurant called The Laughing Planet (in Bloomington, Indiana), we discovered a map produced in New South Wales—the Down Under Map of the World—that in fact showed south as "up" and north as "down." And there was Australia, nearly at the top, along with New Zealand, most of South America, and southern Africa, while the United States occupied a position halfway to the bottom.

The Mercator Map, the one we are used to seeing, spreads out the curved surface and in so doing enlarges the land areas near the poles; since there is more land toward the north, the Northern Hemisphere is represented as disproportionately large. For example, Alaska looks three times larger than Mexico when in fact it is smaller. Construing this particular distortion as a metaphor for the domination of the European worldview, German historian Arno Peters (1990) constructed an alternative, the New World Map, which distorts the shapes of continents but keeps land areas in accurate proportions. Given their inevitable distortions in order to achieve particular accuracies, the two maps together give us a better picture of the world than either one alone and demonstrate the power of multiple perspectives.

Maps of cities, continents, the earth, and the universe have in various ways embodied humanity's view of itself as the index of reality. The 1991 PBS series *The Shape of the World* shows how the enterprises of exploration, science, mathematics, religion, and philosophy collaborated in the development of geographical knowledge. The first program, "Heaven and Earth," traces the flat-to-round-earth controversy from the oldest surviving world map, a Babylonian clay version of a flat earth, through the Greeks' scientific view of the earth as a sphere, back to the medieval Christian conviction of flatness, and then to the Renaissance's reaffirmation, once and for all, of the global form. We can see in this vacillation not only an academic debate but also a chart of the evolution of human knowledge. The flat disk, fixed in space with a definite center and edge, has yielded to the constantly moving sphere, which has no inherent edge, top, or bottom, although we assign these features to it, anchoring it to a position and a frame.

The tension between the apparent certainty of the representation and the uncertainty that characterizes knowledge is at the heart of language, a system constantly striving to surpass itself.

Metaphorical ways of knowing endeavor to press established relationships between language and meaning into new fields through imaginative comparison. This book is intended as a resource for English teachers who want their students to experience language as a creative medium for thought and expression. Part I, Metaphor and Learning, begins with an exploration of the uses of metaphor in constructing meaning, including its function in symbol-making, exploring the unknown, discovering underlying knowledge, and formulating positions or arguments. It then looks at learning as change and how this quality is captured in the popular media as well as in literature and the creative work of students. Finally, the lens focuses on the generation of the self and how metaphors can be powerfully involved in this process.

Part II emphasizes the multiplicity of reality and the dynamics of dialogical reasoning, which is reasoning from alternative perspectives. Such reasoning, or knowing, is based on empathy and the ability to experience other lives. Fundamental human concepts such as that of time, as well as cultural perspectives, can be illuminated by dialogical reasoning, which opens up possibilities often ignored in a monological worldview.

Part III centers on the English language, exploring ways in which its history and current status as the most powerful world language make it the linguistic equivalent of a map of multiculturalism. This metaphor is developed in both the English vocabulary and the world literatures of English. Part IV is about metaphors themselves as vehicles for expressing and elaborating sensory experience. Each part combines discussion with a number of teaching/learning ideas to help the teacher transform the conceptual content of this book into classroom practice.

Suggestions for Using This Book

Like any piece of professional literature, this book is meant to focus attention on a particular aspect of the field. We hope *Metaphorical Ways of Knowing* will engage you in a dialogue with us about the imaginative use of language and thought in the classroom. We have suggested possibilities and shared our strategies and resources that are consistent with the theoretical perspective we explore in this volume.

We see this book as serving several audiences. It will provide background information for practitioners and preservice teachers who want to consider the implications of metaphorical thinking and teaching. It will provide teaching suggestions appropriate for students in grades 5 through 14, including in many cases an array of resources that will inspire additional learning activities.

For a teacher who uses a workshop approach, there are numerous excerpts from literature that will suggest mini-lesson ideas, as well as short activities for demonstrations of reading and writing strategies. One of our favorites is the retelling of a Native American story, "Salmon Swims Up the River," in Chapter 4. Several examples of mini-lesson ideas for using metaphor in persuasive writing and in developing editorial cartoons appear in Chapter 1; Chapter 3 features guided imagery as a tool for discovering writing ideas; and Chapter 11 suggests a strategy for drafting "found" poems. The plethora of exercises in Part IV on using the senses will help students explore their writing styles and discover their voices, but may be best used in a workshop environment for practice rather than for a graded assignment. Chapter 12 in particular provides several passages useful in helping young writers learn from authors' models. In other chapters are models that may help students develop pieces on topics of their own choosing and suggestions to help them find authentic contexts for writing about their experiences and feelings. See, for example, "Revisiting the Self" in Chapter 3.

For a teacher who uses a unit approach, chapters are thematically organized. For example, Chapters 1 and 2 deal with persuasive and informative writing, while Chapters 10, 11, and 12 provide many ways to help writers use sensory language. Chapter 7 will be useful in developing a genre study about myths. Chapter 8 focuses on language study, and Chapter 9 on multicultural and cross-cultural literature.

Several chapters are especially appropriate for use in interdisciplinary thematic unit planning, such as Chapter 5 on change, Chapter 6 on time, and Chapter 7 on cultural values. We think the suggestions on time will be especially "timely" as the year 2001 approaches and the twenty-first century begins. Simply sharing the perspectives of authors from different epochs on the nature of time will provide discussion stimuli.

Many of the topics and activities we have included here are relevant to subject areas besides language arts. Below we suggest some chapter linkages with social studies, history, science, art, music, theater arts, and physical education:

> *Social studies:* Introduction, section on map imagery; Chapter 5, "Change"; Chapter 6, "Time"; Chapter 7, "Exploring Cultures through Traditions"
>
> *History:* Chapter 8, "English as a Metaphor for Multiculturalism"
>
> *Science:* Chapter 2, "Ways of Knowing"; Chapter 4, "Experiencing Other Lives," Chapter 5, "Change"
>
> *Art and Music:* Chapter 10, "Seeing and Hearing with the Imagination"
>
> *Theater Arts and Physical Education:* Chapter 12, "The Imagination of the Body"

In fact, teachers of any subject who enjoy sharing daily quotes and short literary passages with students will find a new supply of material in nearly every chapter of the book. Many are by authors who have little exposure in traditional literature anthologies.

Our fondest hope in writing this book is to capture the imaginations of English teachers everywhere and stimulate them to look at the language they teach in new ways.

I Metaphor and Learning

Metaphors offer a ready perspective for comprehending something new. They are particularly useful at an early stage of learning: They provide a starting place; they make connections to that which is already well-understood; they suggest possibilities for further exploration.

Howard A. Peelle, *Computer Metaphors*

Metaphor and Meaning

To talk of metaphor is to talk of tropes, those figures of speech that operate on the meaning (the "signified") rather than the form (the "signifier") of words.

J. David Sapir and J. Christopher Crocker,
The Social Use of Metaphor

Which came first, the metaphor or the meaning? It's almost as difficult to sort out as the old chicken-or-the-egg riddle. A metaphor that has to be explained has no meaning, at least initially. And a metaphor that has meaning has departed from conventional meaning. As Ortony and his colleagues (1983) have argued, "When people use a metaphor, meaning and use become about as remote from one another as is possible in the course of successful communication" (6). The curious part, Ortony notes, is that when we're not *saying* what we mean, literally speaking, people *understand* what we mean, figuratively speaking.

"Today's metaphor is tomorrow's literal sense" (Moore 1982, 3). If you say someone was *sacked* (fired), you are using a term that originated from the practice of handing workmen their tool sacks upon discharging them (Rosenthal and Dardess 1987). If you *sack* the quarterback by tackling him (or her) behind the line of scrimmage, you're relying on a different metaphorical origin. It comes from the *sack* that means to loot and pillage, presumably because it was in sacks that one carried away the loot. And if you "hit the *sack,*" you are using a World War II expression for going to bed, which for a soldier was often a bedroll or sleeping bag—a "sack" (Chapman 1987). That is why we say that metaphor is inextricably meshed with the meanings we attach to the words we use. Because our language is metaphorical, metaphor and meaning are inseparable. Words can be symbols because of metaphor. Words can be arguments because of metaphor. Words can be tools of discovery because of metaphor.

That discovery may be possible because at the root of metaphor is experience. Our experiences shape us and shape our language; they are the core of our ability to construct knowledge. Because we have seen, heard, and felt, we can imagine things we have not seen, heard, or felt. Because we have lived inside our lives, we can imagine what it might be like to live outside our lives, or to reinvent ourselves to become what we dream of being.

There are three major theories as to how metaphor operates: substitution, comparison, and interaction. Those who argue that metaphor is a matter of substitution portray it as remedying a gap in our vocabulary; a figurative expression is substituted for a literal one. Others interpret metaphor as an implicit comparison. In the third model, metaphor is viewed as interacting with its topic to produce a new, emergent meaning. Typically, some combination of these models finds its way into most discussions of metaphor; the theories are not considered to be mutually exclusive (Ortony et al. 1983; Pollio et al. 1977).

The interaction model laid the groundwork for the work of Lakoff and Johnson (1980). They differentiate between *conventional metaphors,* such as *sack,* which "structure the ordinary conceptual system of our culture [and are] reflected in our everyday language," and *imaginative metaphors,* which "are capable of giving us new meaning to our pasts, to our daily activity, and to what we know and believe" (137). They argue that both "old" and "new" metaphors make sense of our experiences, providing coherent structure and highlighting some aspects while hiding others.

In this chapter we will emphasize imaginative metaphors rather than conventional metaphors (which we will define as words having metaphorical roots) and the ways in which they can function as symbols. We will suggest how this occurs and offer two ways that these imaginative metaphorical symbols are used: to give insight by helping us discover commonalities and to present or imply arguments.

Relationship between Symbol and Metaphor

As we first argued in *Bridging: A Teacher's Guide to Metaphorical Thinking, metaphor* for us is a broad term, subsuming many of the traditional terms relating to figurative language. Our position was inspired by others, including Lakoff and Johnson (1980), who portray the representation of reality as metaphor, and Best (1984), who construes metaphor broadly to include simile, allegory, analogy, parable, anecdote, fable, song—"anything that transfers and translates the abstract into the concrete, thus making the abstract more accessible and memorable" (165). Best believes that learners are initially hostile to abstraction and must be approached by way of the concrete, which is the function of metaphor. This goes far beyond the schoolchild's traditional definition, which focuses more on distinguishing metaphor from simile: a comparison between two unlike objects that *doesn't* use *like* or *as.* (For a complete discussion of the form and function of metaphor, please see our first volume.)

Symbol is one such term that is entangled in the notion of metaphor. Symbols, in the language of semiotics (the study of signs), are "signs that bear an arbitrary relationship to that which they stand for" (Suhor 1991, 1). Whereas symbols do not entail comparisons (the cross is not *like* redemption; the color yellow does not *resemble* Chinese royalty), they often "derive their extra meaning from some sort of likeness on the level of emotional or ideological abstraction" (Burroway 1992, 281). Thus, the cornucopia symbolizes abundance; scales represent justice; the oak tree stands for strength and long life (Cirlot 1971). In our speech, however, we use these symbols as metaphors. We say, for example, that the scales are tipped in the defendant's favor. There are no real scales in most courtrooms; we are speaking metaphorically.

Metaphorical expressions are also symbolic, carrying their own connotations and often very different degrees of intensity. There is symbolically more emotion behind *raking a student over the coals* than in *taking her down a peg.* The first reflects British kings' practice of dragging victims slowly over a bed of burning coals for punishment; the second is merely an eighteenth-century British navy custom of raising or lowering the ship's flags via ropes tied to pegs according to the degree of honor being conferred (Rosenthal and Dardess 1987).

In our use of language, we employ such symbols all the time, consciously or unconsciously, to convey our intended meanings. When we rely on metaphorical expressions, the symbolic root may be a generation or two away. During World War I, the Air Service (forerunner of the U.S. Air Force) popularized a slang expression for dropping a bomb, *laying an egg,* from the shape of some bombs. In the theater, failing miserably was the equivalent of bombing, so it is no surprise that performers soon were said to be "laying an egg" when their acts flopped (Urdang, Hunsinger, and LaRoche 1991).

Burroway (1992) contends that symbols are unavoidable in literature because they are unavoidable in life. We humans function symbolically all the time: "We must do so because we rarely know exactly what we mean, and if we do we are not willing to express it, and if we are willing we are not able, and if we are able we are not heard, and if we are heard we are not understood. Words are unwieldy and unyielding, and we leap over them with intuition, body language, tone, and symbol" (283).

She interprets the following dialogue to make her point:

"Is the oven supposed to be on?" he asks. He is only peripherally curious about whether the oven is supposed to be on. He is really complaining: *You're scatterbrained and extravagant with the money I go out and earn.* "If I don't preheat it, the muffins won't crest," she says, meaning: *You didn't catch me this time! You're always complaining about the food, and God knows I wear myself out trying to please you.* "We used to have salad nicoise in the summertime," he recalls, meaning: *Don't be so damn triumphant. You're still extravagant, and you haven't got the class you used to have when we were young.* "We used to keep a garden," she says, meaning: *You're always away on weekends and never have time to do anything with me because you don't love me anymore; I think you have a mistress.* "What do you expect of me!" he explodes, and neither of them is surprised that ovens, muffins, salads, and gardens have erupted. When people say "we quarreled over nothing," this is what they mean. They quarreled over symbols. (281)

We all have symbols in our lives. Often they are objects that represent people, places, emotions, and other times that now are gone. It might be a quilt that Great-Grandma made, the teddy bear you carried around everywhere, a favorite book that you read over and over, a comfortable bathrobe, a mug of cocoa with just the right number of marshmallows, or a bowl of homemade potato soup.

What do all of these images have in common? In some cultures, they are associated with feelings of nurturing and comforting. Perhaps that's because most of these items can be connected with times when we were young or ill and received some extra attention, or with memories of times past. The objects capture the essence of those times for us, providing a feeling of security.

Objects tend to store our memories and emotions. We go about our daily lives without particularly thinking about someone from our past, until we catch a glimpse of an item that he or she often used, admired, or perhaps gave to us. Then the feelings and faces flash back. Sometimes this is pleasant; sometimes it is heart-wrenching. Other times it can be scary.

We may deal with our emotions by attaching them to the object. The object then becomes a symbol of the event that triggered the emotion. Ann Landers, the advice columnist, once printed a letter from a woman whose husband had been killed in a military plane collision. She tried to go on with her life but often woke up shaking in the middle of the night. At first she thought she was merely cold and found herself drawn to her husband's terry-cloth robe, packed away. It was ratty and old, but its warmth solved both her physical need and an emotional one that she had not admitted, even to herself. She wrote that putting on the robe helped her express her grief for her husband and gave her the strength to tell her daughter that Daddy wasn't just away on a trip. She eventually married an understanding man "who knows that in the back of my closet hangs a tattered terry-cloth robe that I still wear from time to time" (Landers 1988).

Symbols in Our Lives and in Our Literature

Activity 1: Stories for Symbols

Trying It Out

The tattered robe described above was more than a possession of the woman's husband. It became a metaphor—an image of comfort, of times past, and as time went on, perhaps also for acceptance of loss. Sharing her story and bringing in an object that has become a symbol to you will help get your students thinking and writing about the symbols in their own lives. Time for writing in journals or writers' notebooks will help them explore the source and significance of the symbolic meaning and their feelings, then and now.

One of the authors has an old sugar bowl, another example of an object that became a symbol. The bowl is brown with age. The glaze is crackled and the lid is gone. It was crudely made, its handles looking like the fat snakes children roll out of clay. She treasures it, though, because it has come to represent perseverance and endurance to her. Exactly 145 years ago, a fifteen-year-old girl snatched this sugar bowl off her grandparents' kitchen table and hid it in her apron. She carried it there as she walked behind her family's wagon from North Carolina to Kentucky, and then from Kentucky to Oregon—and then back again to Kentucky a few years later. The family had wintered in Kentucky on the way to Oregon, then returned there to settle when Oregon wasn't what they were hoping it would be. Not all artifacts have such unusual stories behind them, but this one illustrates how the symbolic meaning becomes attached to the object. The admiration for the girl who took such care of this tangible piece of her past lives on in the families of her descendants, people who never knew her but who feel connected to her and share her desire to feel connected to home and family.

Activity 2: Learning Literary Devices through Storybooks

Susan Hall has compiled a resource book for teachers and librarians, *Using Picture Storybooks to Teach Literary Devices* (1990). It is specifically designed for use with both adolescents and elementary students. Hall provides several pages of suggested books to teach numerous devices such as foreshadowing, point of view, and symbolism. She also provides a rationale for using picture books and storybooks with older students (Elleman 1983; McNamara 1984; Watson 1978). Simple, clearly illustrated examples of literary devices will prepare students for understanding and recognizing these devices in more difficult literary texts.

An afternoon at the public library will help you locate many charming picture books that can introduce the devices you want your students to examine, although Hall's book will certainly streamline the process. For example, to teach symbolism, she recommends using *Rose Blanche* by Roberto Innocenti and Christophe Gallaz (1985). The illustrations and text tell a story of a German girl who discovers a concentration camp near her town. She sneaks food to the starving children. Her red hair bow and the red swastika arm bands of the Nazis become contrasting symbols of kindness and cruelty. The book does not answer all the "why" questions, but neither does it hide the dark side of the Holocaust and war. Using the point of view of a child, we see the tragedy as she might have.

The Man Who Could Call Down Owls, by Eve Bunting (1984), is a tale of good and evil, with good represented by the Owl Man in his snowy cape and evil by the stranger who tries to steal his power. He cannot, however, for the Owl Man's power is love. The destruction of the stranger is graphic; in both of these books, the expected maturity level of the readers is higher than what may have been typical a decade or more ago.

Knots on a Counting Rope is based on a metaphor for the passage of time and for the growing maturity a blind Indian boy evidences as he overcomes obstacles in his life. Written by Bill Martin Jr. and John Archambault (1987), it is a simple but touching conversation between the boy and his grandfather. The grandfather uses the knots on the rope to recount the boy's successes; each knot symbolizes a dark mountain that the boy has learned to cross.

Metaphor as Heuristic

A metaphor has a way of helping us see through the surface to the deep-level meanings of both experiences and communications. It raises subtle or hidden commonalities. It can organize our experiences and give them a structure that was not apparent in the living of the moment but that rings true upon reflection. Metaphor becomes, then, a device for exploring the unknown in terms of the known, for helping us to discover and understand new knowledge. It is a tool of insight. It provides us with a perspective for comprehending something unknown by comparing it to familiar objects and experiences. That is key; metaphors based on experiences we *haven't* had will have limited value, if any. For example, in using the domino effect as a metaphor to explain cause and effect, one must ascertain that students do indeed know what dominoes are, how they can be stacked on edge, and what happens if the first domino is jarred or knocked over (Allen and Burlbaw 1987).

When we say that metaphor is a heuristic device, we mean that it leads us to discovery—in particular, the discovery of new knowledge and new understandings. Anderson and Sunstein (1987) found that writing improved when students were taught to use metaphor to think their way through scientific topics. One student wrote about the nervous system as two-way traffic flow. A second student wrote about tonsils as a platoon of soldiers stationed at the mouth of a river. Another described the stance of the writer as shifting psychologically from participant to spectator when moving from expressive to poetic writing. Metaphor served a heuristic function for these writers; by pursuing the implications of their metaphors and extending them consistently, students became more aware of their thought processes.

In helping us to discover new knowledge, metaphor builds on our prior knowledge and thus has great potential in improving both teaching and learning. All contemporary learning theories emphasize the importance of connecting new information to what the learner already knows; comparisons are a primary way of achieving this connection. As Peelle notes (1994): "Myths, imagery and figurative language served to cut between the known and the unknown. For instance, constellations of stars were seen as familiar animal and human forms, and celestial motions were believed to influence activities on earth. Until astronomers developed more advanced notions, such metaphorical views were important in navigation, agriculture and religion—buffering the staggering incomprehensibility of the cosmos" (2).

Not surprisingly, scientists have long used metaphorical comparisons to explain their discoveries in terms that others can understand. Consider the following, from a book called *The Economy of Vegetation*, written over two centuries ago:

> High-towering palms, that part the Southern flood
> With shadowy isles and continents of wood,
> Oaks, whose broad antlers crest Britannia's plain,
> Or bear her thunders o'er the conquer'd main,
> Shout, as you pass, inhale the genial skies,
> And bask and brighten in your beamy eyes;
> Bow their white heads, admire the changing clime,
> Shake from their candied trunks the tinkling rime;
> With bursting buds their wrinkled barks adorn,
> And wed the timorous floret to her thorn;
> Deep strike their roots, their lengthening tops revive,
> And all my world of foliage wave, alive.
>
> (Darwin 1791, 1.475–85)

Although the language may now seem stilted to us, Erasmus Darwin was creating pictures of trees with words. If we try, we can see palms in a wide and shallow swamp that seems more like a flood than a permanent body of water, and oak trees whose high, spreading tree crowns (a metaphorical term in itself) resemble antlers. In personifying the trees, Darwin helps us see their "white heads" in winter bowing, shaking off in the March winds the thin coating of ice (rime) that has covered their branches, with blossoms and foliage covering their wrinkled limbs and bringing them back to life. He has used imaginative ways of knowing to share scientific observations.

Darwin was famous in his day as a physician, educator, scientist, and poet.[1] *The Botanic Garden* is a book-length poem in which he combines his interests in science and literature. Darwin's conception of the book may seem all the more novel when one learns that these poems were published in 1789 and 1791. We expect poetry elsewhere, as in Emily Dickinson's description of the bat's

> small Umbrella quaintly halved
> Describing in the Air
> An Arc . . .

in poem #1575, "The Bat is Dun with Wrinkled Wings" (1876 in Johnson 1960, 653). But we need to open ourselves to other possibilities, to go beyond traditional literary forms, as Darwin did, in order to use metaphors heuristically.

Other early scientists may not have been as taken with the poetic form, but they also used imagery in recording their observations of flora and fauna. Linnaeus, an eighteenth-century Swedish naturalist, described buds and bulbs as "the winter-cradles of the plant" (in Darwin [1791] 1973, pt. 1, n. 14). Modern scientists have discovered anew the power of metaphor to illuminate; now "cradles" give way to "incubators" in describing processes that involve dormancy and regeneration.

Even somewhat illogical or "deviant" metaphors serve a strong heuristic purpose in the scientific community: "They forge . . . alternative schemes of reference and formulate relationships before unsuspected. Such expressions often present us with a discordant view that assails the bastions of accepted meaning and makes those who still accept it either defend or capitulate" (Muscari 1988, 426). Muscari explains that these metaphors eventually become what Lakoff and Johnson (1980) termed "conventional." Muscari argues that conventional metaphors are not supposed to stay fresh, at least in the realm of science. "Good" scientific metaphors, he says, lose elasticity as they gain a technical meaning. We don't think of chemical *messengers, charm,* or *antimatter* as metaphorical terms, and yet they are. "For a metaphor to stay metaphorical in science is almost a dereliction of duty and a forfeit of purpose" (Muscari 1988, 426).[2]

In the English classroom, we probably cannot imagine ourselves taking a similar stance. We rail against the cliché and encourage students to develop their own metaphors. We want them to emulate the scientists whose original insight captured an unlikely commonality. Sharing scientific metaphors may help our students understand that developing a metaphor is not a random act of word-grabbing but a craft that combines reflection and ingenuity.

We can take a lesson from the scientists, who have used metaphors both to understand concepts and processes and to invent them. Luria (1985) "intuited the distribution of bacterial mutants from the seemingly irrelevant contemplation of a slot machine in action" (158). Dawkins described genes as "selfish," stating that an organism is the gene's "survival machine, and it so programs the machine that it will turn out gene copies at a maximum rate, regardless of personal cost" (in Curtis and Barnes 1985, 369). In this metaphor, genes are personified while organisms, including people, are rendered as machines, a twist that effectively dramatizes the dynamics of evolution.

Conversely, computers frequently are described using anthropomorphic metaphors—they have memory, language, and intelligence; perform jobs; and get "bugs" and viruses (Peelle 1984). We readily accept these metaphors because they help us understand and deal with complex technology in more "natural" ways. The ability to use the natural world as a metaphorical inspiration for the technological world is similarly evident in the invention of the plastic twist-top cap. The action of turning to open and then to close as it dispenses sticky substances like glue makes the twist-top self-cleaning. The generating metaphor? The horse's rectum (Honeck and Hoffman 1980).

While this particular picture may not be as pleasing as some other metaphors, it graphically illustrates the power of the metaphor to communicate. We as teachers of writing have long focused on communicating, and metaphor is a familiar term in our classrooms. The ability to create pictures with words is something we should strive for in all types of writing, however. We need to help our students improve their writing *outside* our walls as well as within them.

Trying It Out

Metaphors in the Content Areas

Activity 1: Metaphors in Content-Area Learning

The stereotypical view of content-area writing—writing in science, math, social studies, industrial arts, language, and so on—is that it is utilitarian and pretty flavorless. This need not be, especially if we use metaphor to help students *write to learn*. We need to remember, as Mahood states (1984), that "metaphors give form to abstractions and help us make sense of the world around us. In the classroom these models can help students make the leap from the known to the unknown, to accommodate new information rather than simply to assimilate it" (13).

Asking students to look for metaphors in their textbooks and having them practice explaining terms from other subject areas using metaphors could turn into a project that positively and permanently affects students' abilities to write and to learn. One source of metaphors in learning is *Studying for History* by David Pace and Sharon L. Pugh (1996). They use metaphors to help students take stances as learners in a history class: "Many students experience history courses as if they had been shipwrecked in the wilderness. They feel they are lost in a vast continent of dates, events, and concepts. They have no idea how to chart a path across the new territory or how to make use of the resources around them. When their first efforts to deal with their surroundings fail, they give up or hope that some miraculous insight will save them" (2). The guide they have developed provides strategies and tools that will help students become independent learners who are able to orient themselves and chart paths in this unfamiliar territory. Pace and Pugh suggest three enabling metaphors to help students think like historians: historians as detectives, judges, and lawyers. They provide scenarios that feature these enabling metaphors in a format which will help students understand how to be more intentional or strategic in their reading and studying of history texts.

Activity 2: Using Metaphors in Content-Area Writing

The focus in many examples in Chapters 1 and 2 is on metaphors that teach us. The suggestions that follow may be used to help students explore the value of metaphorical language in describing the realities of the topics they are studying.

Perhaps you've enjoyed the homework misadventures of the cartoon character Calvin of Bill Watterson's "Calvin and Hobbes." Calvin epitomizes the student who sees no value in report writing and who puts nothing of himself into it. His assignments are always postponed to the last minute, and his research is often fabricated. In one particular comic strip episode, Calvin ceremoniously places his work into a shiny plastic folder, certain that his teacher will, to paraphrase a cliché, judge the report by its cover (Watterson 1989).

Content-area writing traditionally has focused on the formal school report as a vehicle for sharing factual information. It is not always a satisfactory method for either students or teachers because, as Calvin demonstrates, in such formats, form can obscure content. We are dissatisfied with students' efforts when they conform to the letter rather than the spirit of the research assignment, offering a slick exterior in lieu of a solid piece of writing. Students who aren't invested in the project will put little of themselves into it. If it has all the "parts," we can imagine some students thinking, maybe the teacher won't notice that it really doesn't say anything. With increased availability of reference materials and documents that can be downloaded via computer CD and the Internet, it is especially important that we explore ways to help our students learn to research and synthesize information. Not only do we want to make it difficult for them to recycle someone else's work as their own, of course, but we also want them to learn how to use data from a variety of sources to create something that is uniquely theirs.

In the following activity, we suggest both a broader view of the ways factual information can be shared and a strategy for helping English students move into nonfiction writing by using Erasmus Darwin's "poetry that teaches" as a model. Using the discipline of science to show that metaphors can be heuristic, that is, can lead us to the discovery of knowledge, may give students a new understanding of metaphor's heuristic nature in more abstract forms of literature and language. Good nonfiction writing depends on careful observation, detailed research, and sometimes personal experience. The poetry of Randall Jarrell (1914–65) is especially useful in demonstrating the value of observation and research in developing images. Toward the end of his life, he wrote especially for children. Read, for example, the opening lines from "Bats":

> A bat is born
> Naked and blind and pale.
> His mother makes a pocket of her tail
> And catches him. . . .

(1969, 314)

Ask students to visualize the metaphors. Does thinking of the mother bat's tail as a pocket give us an understanding of the flexibility of her body and an image of how she carries her baby with her? Later Jarrell describes the bat's erratic flight as "dancing." Does that word give its flight more intentionality than humans might initially perceive? If metaphors help us understand something that before might have been either unclear or just invisible to us, then they have functioned as heuristics, devices that lead us to knowledge.

You may wish to share the entire poem and to discuss with students Jarrell's crafting of it. In particular, students could be asked which details from the poem they could gather by reading reference books and which they could gather by observing bats for an evening or so. Where do they think Jarrell discovered the information and images in the poem?

To show that experience is the best teacher, you may also wish to share the following journal entry, made by a spelunker after a trip to Lava Beds National Monument:

> I found a brown ceiling that breathed with [bats] in the deep tonsils of a cave, much further in than I would have expected. I admired the expanse of the little brown variety—their numbers

camouflaged by their tight clusters, like little arrowheads jutting out from the bull's-eye they formed. I watched in awed open-mouthed, wide-eyed silence, eager for Jim to catch up, so I could share the discovery. . . .

Bat fact: Before flight, bats always relieve themselves to make themselves lighter. I learned an interesting fact about guano today. It is beneficial when used as fertilizer. But I did not feel any improved quality to my growth from the guano as 500 eager producers showered me with it! (Davis n.d.)

Another form for nonfiction writing can then be shared: the feature story. Feature stories appear in newspapers and magazines and differ from news stories in their timeliness. News stories generally impart information that is immediate—things that have just happened, possibly that very day. To print "news" a few days or weeks later would make it stale and unnecessary. Features certainly may have a timely focus but generally do not depend on being published *today*. You may want to obtain a copy of "Outdoors South: Navigators of the Night" by Steve Bender (1991), published in *Southern Living* magazine. This one-page feature story is full of facts but clearly uses experience and observation to enhance the telling of those facts. He begins by placing himself in the scene; his description is both rich and informative. Then in a later part of the article, he writes:

Pregnant and nursing females gather by the thousands to form huge nurseries in these subterranean chambers. Hanging by sharp claws to the cave's ceiling, they pack so closely together that at times the entire roof seems alive. Such extreme gregariousness may seem repulsive to us, but it's a matter of survival to the bats. Bats don't build nests, so baby bats depend on the combined body heat of the adults around them to keep warm. (27)

Students could be asked to compare the above excerpts to the last nine or ten lines of the Jarrell poem. Which version uses the most positive image? How does the author give that effect? Are the images in each "bat" piece strong ones? Why or why not? Does each impart similar information?

Students may wish to do their own research on some type of living creature. They should start with careful observation and note-taking. While some might arrange to observe an animal at the zoo, others might choose to document the appearance, actions, and habitat of their own pets. Backyards, city parks, and even alleys are full of life, from birds and squirrels to cockroaches and moths. Students may know of an unusual species in their own neighborhoods. The campus of the University of Louisville, for example, has protected many generations of albino squirrels. Local lore has it that their progenitors were released years ago by the science department.

Like Davis and Bender, students should also record their own thoughts and feelings as they watch their creatures. After one or more observation periods, students then can gather some unusual facts about their creatures, using reference books and other library resources. They should focus particularly on facts that they don't think everyone knows. For instance, we found the information on "bat nurseries" quite interesting because it explained the real story behind a familiar image, that of large groups of bats hanging together in caves. (A model of this prewriting process, along with a final draft of a poem, appears in the next chapter.)

Some students may want to try a feature story. Others may wish to imitate Jarrell's style in a poem. Or you might bring in the work of other poets, such as "The Bat" by Ruth Herschberger, to show how a student might use the voice of the creature in describing itself. The poem ends in a delightful turn of perspective:

> And if the human family finds me odd,
> No odder they, locked in their crazy yards.

> (in Dunning, Lueders, and Smith 1966, 30)

Content-area writing is sometimes difficult for students because of the narrow view they have of what form it must take. Sharing examples like these may help your students discover that scientific writing—and, by extension, writing in any subject area—can be a rich, image-based form of nonfiction literature.

Metaphor as Way of Presenting an Argument

In the Holocaust Museum in Washington, D.C., there is a display of shoes that were last worn more than fifty years ago by Jewish men, women, and children before they were killed in the gas chambers of Nazi Germany. These shoes stand as a silent testimony to the horrors of the Holocaust and as an argument against all who would claim that the genocide stories are a hoax. The symbol of the empty shoes is such a powerful one that it is already being used in other arguments. Helen Casey of Louisville, Kentucky, organized The Silent March, a march on Washington in a "motionless parade of empty shoes representing Americans who have died by gunfire. A voiceless lineup . . . Shoes without anyone to fill them: It is a poignant image, and a compelling way to protest" (Aprile 1994b).[3]

As we discussed earlier, metaphors become symbols when we attach positive or negative attitudes and emotions to them. Schools and athletic teams, for example, have long used mascots and other symbols to focus spirit and goodwill. Of late, the associations behind these symbols have been examined with an increasingly fine lens. Organizations have been challenged to find new mascots to replace ones that have become politically sensitive. The use of the Confederate flag and insignia has been denounced as repugnant to African Americans, and the use of Indian names and likenesses has been protested as demeaning to Native Americans (Adams 1993). Those who claim that we as a nation are going overboard in the name of political correctness are generally not those whose ethnicity is being caricatured. Such symbols can be perceived as a nonverbal assault, whether the assault is made wittingly or not.

There is an implied argument in the metaphors we use because we are aiming for particular effects. We are making a statement with our statements, in other words. While we often think of arguments as confined to the political arena, they are part of our daily speech as well. Comforting a friend who has lost a boyfriend, we might suggest that she "give her wounds time to heal." This may imply that we believe her partner was at fault and guilty of hurting her feelings or damaging her psyche. Even though we are using medical metaphors in consoling our friend, it would not be equally appropriate to note that she was involved in a "sick relationship." Such a metaphor has far different connotations and would probably lead to another kind of argument!

The connotations a particular metaphor may have can be positive or negative, then, depending on one's stance. The associations become an argument, so to speak, implying a point of view. In the months following Hungary's cessation of communist rule, the American press referred to Hungary's economy as "goulash capitalism," a phrase that caught the interest of a Hungarian scholar studying cross-cultural communications and attitudes. The implied argument was that Hungary's capitalism was a homemade mishmash of ingredients. What if the Hungarian press came up with the phrase "hamburger democracy"? There is an argument in that metaphor as well. Consider the possible associations: fast-food restaurants (quantity but not quality), Popeye's hamburger-obsessed friend, Wimpy (gluttony), feedlot meat production (unfeeling exploitation), and rainforest destruction (selfish usurpation of the world's resources) (Molner 1990).

Cinnamond (1987) has found that metaphors are more useful in determining the point of view of the authors than in determining the meaning of the text. He concluded that this use of metaphor can obstruct reality. "The metaphors inform and create our notions of truth, and if used frequently enough, come to a position of acceptance as the reality rather than a description of it" (26). And that is how metaphor becomes a tool of propagandists, advertising agencies, politicians, and, indeed, anyone who wants to sway our opinions. Metaphor can be a powerful persuader. It creates a hyperbole that highlights the incompatibilities of our assumptions and the lapses in our logic. For example, in his review of a book on evolution, Dawkins (1989) argued that "to claim equal time for creation science in biology classes is about as sensible as to claim equal time for the flat-earth theory in astronomy classes, or as someone has pointed out, you might as well claim equal time in sex education classes for the stork theory" (34).

Often when we think of using metaphors as arguments, we are thinking of the persuasive use of examples and the building of a case through comparison. Consider, for instance, this passage from Chief Seattle's prescient message to the president of the United States in 1855: "The air is precious to the red man. For all things share the same breath—the beasts, the trees, the man. . . . [W]hatever happens to the beasts also happens to man. All things are connected. Whatever befalls the earth befalls the sons of the earth" (Seattle 1855). If the metaphorical argument has worked, we find ourselves taken aback by the fundamental truth of the comparison. Our minds quickly test the conclusion with various personal examples and validate it.

Consider also Wendell Berry's explanation of harmony as an argument for human morality. Have you ever known intuitively that something was wrong, just *wrong*, even though no one had told you so? Perhaps it was a situation you'd never even come across or previously thought about. Or perhaps you've noticed how, across cultures and ages, human societies that had little or no contact with one another still share many laws, norms, and mores. In the argument below, Berry relies on metaphor to suggest that such a similarity in moral beliefs is no accident:

> In a society addicted to facts and figures, anyone trying to speak for agricultural *harmony* is inviting trouble. The first trouble is in trying to say what harmony is. It cannot be reduced to facts and figures—though the lack of it can. It is not very visibly a function. Perhaps we can only say what it may be like. It may, for instance, be like sympathetic vibration: "The A string of a violin . . . is designed to vibrate most readily at about 440 vibrations per second: the note A. If that same note is played loudly not on the violin but near it, the violin A string may hum in sympathy." This may have practical exemplification in the craft of the mud daubers which, as they trowel mud into their nest walls, hum to it, or at it, communicating a vibration that makes it easier to work, thus mastering their material by a kind of song. Perhaps the hum of the mud dauber only activates that anciently perceived likeness between all creatures and the earth of which they are made. For as common wisdom holds, like *speaks* to like. And harmony always involves such specificities of form as in the mud dauber's song and its nest, whereas information accumulates indiscriminately, like noise.

Of course, in the order of creatures, humanity is a special case. Humans, unlike mud daubers, are not naturally involved in harmony. For humans, harmony is always a human product, an artifact, and if they do not know how to make it and choose not to make it, then they do not have it. And so I suggest that, for humans, the harmony I am talking about may bear an inescapable likeness to what we know as moral law—or that, for humans, moral law is a significant part of the notion of ecological and agricultural harmony. A great many people seem to have voted for information as a safe substitute for virtue, but this ignores—among much else—the need to prepare humans to live short lives in the face of long work and long time. (1988, 52–53)

In essays such as Berry's, the metaphor becomes an elegant tool of reason and persuasion. Equally persuasive, perhaps, but less elegant are the political and propagandistic statements that sway public opinion. What we once called slogans—such as Hoover's "a chicken in every pot" and FDR's "New Deal"—have now evolved into sound bites. Public figures strive to speak in quotable, pithy sentences that can stand alone and are likely to be featured on the evening news. To capture the attention of the media, and subsequently the public, words have to be concise and pack a wallop. Metaphor is likely to play an increasingly important role in both developing and interpreting sound-bite politics where allusions serve as arguments. No one has to ask what side you're on if you bring up corporate glass ceilings (beyond which women and minorities seem unable to advance) and now, in Japanese firms in the U.S., rice-paper ceilings (beyond which American executives seem unable to advance) (Rochelle Kopp in Ward 1995).

The danger in slogans and sound bites is that they may come to stand for much more than they really are, or, conversely, they may stand for nothing at all. As Wendell Wilkie said in 1938, "A good catchword can obscure analysis for fifty years" (Seldes 1983). "Outcome-based education" is a current bugaboo, in part because it has become symbolic of many things that go beyond the schoolhouse walls. To hear some radio talk-show hosts, one would think that outcome-based education is synonymous with the destruction of the country. As a term, it has traveled far from its origins and is now associated with Big Brother—test scores are one thing, but portfolios expose us in all directions, critics exclaim. Who will control what is in the collection? Who will determine who has access to it? "A student's mind is invaded in the sense that her skills, strategies, attitudes, beliefs, and opinions will be laid out for strangers to view" (Lahrson 1995).

Actually, "outcomes" have long been used to describe the student objectives that curriculum planners have in mind when they write course descriptions. The literal meaning of "outcome-based education" is education that focuses on abilities. Where do we want our students to be at the end of the course or instructional period? What do we want them to be able to do? It is a way of planning backwards so that the ends don't get obscured by the means. This is not a bizarre notion. It can help us determine how best to use the precious time students spend in our classes. If we unpack the term from the associations that opponents have heaped onto it, perhaps there will be room for dialogue on what the aims of education are or should be.

Mixed metaphors can also lead to faulty arguments. Our daily speech is no doubt a rich source of mixed or faulty metaphors, if only we were aware of it; if the poor metaphors were visible to us, we probably wouldn't use them. Purposefully examining such metaphors can illuminate the error in thinking that they entail and alert us to make our comparisons more carefully in the future. For example, a language arts teacher told her seventh graders to decide on their endings before they started writing a composition. They could change everything except that. This was to give them an "anchor" to work toward, saying that by holding to their original ending, students would know when they were finished. But consider the implications of that metaphor. To "work toward" an anchor is to take a dive or to sink. This mixed image certainly does not imply a direction that would get somebody somewhere. And for that matter, what does an anchor do? It stops motion, keeps a ship in one place. Even by itself, the anchor is a questionable metaphor for this writing task. Critiquing it as such may also help bring into question the value of being so inflexible regarding the story's ending. Such an anchor, while originally envisioned as an aid to young writers, may actually hold them back.

"Metaphors are not simply linguistic tools by which we try to understand something. Once expressed they also carry with them a hortatory dimension with power to fashion allegiances and to control attitudes," writes Herron (1982, 236). Columnist Ellen Goodman suggests that in our attempts to present arguments and fashion these allegiances, we sometimes abuse language. She has called for a moratorium on the use of the language of the Third Reich in anything but a historically accurate sense:

> The further we are removed from the defeat of the Nazis, the more this vocabulary seems to be taking over our own. It's become part of the casual, ubiquitous, inflammatory speech Americans use to turn each other into monsters. Which, if I recall correctly, was a tactic favored by Goebbels himself.
>
> Just in the past month, the NRA attacked federal agents as "jackbooted government thugs" who wear "Nazi bucket helmets and

black storm trooper uniforms." . . . [C]ongressmen have compared environmentalist agencies with Hitler's troops . . . [portraying] EPA officials as an "environmental Gestapo." . . . Anti-abortion groups talk about the abortion holocaust. . . . Rush Limbaugh likes to sprinkle the term "feminazis" across the airwaves. (1995)

She notes that many of the targets of this inflammatory language would have been targets of persecution under Hitler. The misuse of Nazi vocabulary insults the memory of Holocaust survivors and "diminishes the emotional power of these words should we need them." Crying Hitler, she suggests, may be the modern-day equivalent of crying wolf.

Metaphor is most often associated with the written and spoken word, but it is a powerful presence in image as well. Advertisers depend on this, as do cartoonists. The following activity allows students to explore both the notion of the metaphor as a unit of meaning and the editorial cartoon as a metaphorical way of knowing.

Trying It Out

Editorial Cartoons as Metaphorical Arguments

Editorial cartoonists combine visual and concrete ways of knowing with very abstract ways of knowing. Through metaphorical representation, they comment visually on the changing scene. Cartoonists rely on easily recognizable images and symbols to deliver their messages and make their arguments. Sometimes they create symbols that then make their way into the culture at large.

In this activity, students can learn how to identify the metaphorical arguments made by the editorial cartoonist. For other examples, try American history books, published collections, and materials available through your local "Newspapers in Education" program.

Activity 1: Identifying the Metaphor

Ask students to determine the political event depicted in Nick Anderson's political cartoon from 1991 (next page). Although now it might be interpreted as the dissolution of the Soviet Union, that had not yet occurred at the time the cartoon was printed.[4] At that point, it represented the move toward independence from the central Soviet government by various Soviet republics—but clearly indicated the cartoonist's opinion of what would ensue.

A discussion might focus on questions such as these:

- What is the visual metaphor that Anderson uses to express the change in the Soviet government? *(The change in government is like water going down a drain.)*

Figure 1.1.
Nick Anderson's
Political Cartoon

- How do we know that Anderson doesn't mean, literally, that water is going down the drain? *(The water takes the shape of a map outline and is labeled "USSR," which stands for United Soviet Socialist Republic.)*

- Look at a map of the U.S.S.R. What has Anderson done to make sure we will see the metaphor he implies? *(Islands, coasts, and borders are roughly suggested in the swirling water.)*

- What statement is Anderson making about the state of the Soviet Union in this cartoon? *(The union is literally dissolving; it's going down the drain.)*

- Note the date of the cartoon. It was printed more than three months before the Soviet Union ceased to exist. What might that imply about the nature of editorial cartoons to capture a society's mood, reflect national thought, or predict political events? Would the cartoon seem as effective to you now if the Soviet Union had not dissolved? Why or why not?

- Play with the metaphorical image in this cartoon further. What, for example, does the swirling water suggest? Would this cartoon have given a different message if the water had been flowing slowly? What other insights do you have about the implications of the drain metaphor? Your extension of the metaphor will reflect what you know of the current status of the Commonwealth of Independent States. *(Questions to consider: What will happen to this dissolved nation? Will the water go to a purification plant for cleaning and eventual reuse? If so, who or what might represent this purification plant? Or will the water be replaced as new streams rush in to fill the void? What if the basin dries up and remains barren?)*

Activity 2: Analyzing a Political Cartoon

Ask students to apply the same general questions used with the Anderson cartoon to an editorial cartoon that they select. If they are unfamiliar with the event or issue depicted, suggest that they read the major news stories and editorials for the date of the cartoon (and perhaps for a few previous days) or consult other resources, including people. Sample questions follow:

- What is the event or issue being depicted? How did you come to that conclusion? Explain the symbols being used and what each stands for. What, in other words, is the visual metaphor, and what is the literal interpretation of that metaphor? What comment is the cartoonist making about this issue or event? Do you agree or disagree? Explain.

- Evaluate the effectiveness of the imagery or metaphor that the cartoonist has chosen. Is it an interesting comparison? an enlightening one? a trite one? Explain. Extend the metaphor, if you can. What other implications do you see?

Activity 3: Finding Real Audiences

Ask students to identify an issue they believe in strongly, or to list needs they see in their school or community. After listing possible topics, students can brainstorm metaphors that could be used in an editorial cartoon about those issues. Suggest students choose one or more of their best ideas to sketch as editorial cartoons. In peer response groups (three or four students who will share their work with one another and provide each other with feedback), students can use questions such as those below to help determine whether their visual metaphors are effective in making the intended points.

- What event or issue do you think my cartoon depicts? What led you to that conclusion?

- What is the visual metaphor that I used? What symbols do you see in the different elements?

- What do you think my attitude toward that issue is?

- What do you find confusing?

- What labels, if any, would you suggest that I add?

- What symbols could you suggest that I might want to use in addition to or in place of the ones I chose?

Students should be warned not to give in to the temptation to explain their work. Cartoons should "speak" for themselves. If people are misinterpreting a cartoon, the cartoonist may want to sketch some other versions and get additional feedback. Students should be encouraged to select an appropriate publication (one that will be read by the intended audience) and to draft a letter explaining why they hope the editor will publish their cartoon. After asking for feedback from the peer response group and teacher, students can be asked to revise, edit, and mail their letters. An alternate way to publish student work is to cover a wall in your classroom, hallway, or cafeteria with butcher paper. Have students post copies of their political cartoons for others to see. (Rather than draw them freehand, students may wish to use a photocopying machine with an enlarging feature, or an opaque projector.) Students may wish to invite graffiti responses on issues they raise.

In the next chapter, we will move from metaphor as a carrier of meaning and focus on the role of metaphor as what has become popularly described as a *way of knowing*. This term may stem from the fact that *knowing* is *seeing*. When words for *see* entered our language, they eventually all came to mean "know" (Lakoff 1990). We all have different perspectives from which we see or know our world. We believe that metaphor informs those perspectives and as such becomes a vehicle for learning.

Notes   1. Erasmus Darwin recognized and accepted the "survival of the fittest" before his grandson Charles, the famous evolutionist, was even born.

2. As Muscari (1988) and Hoffman (1980) note, acceptance of the metaphor in science has waxed and waned. Some scientists still scoff at the notion of couching a theory in metaphorical terms, in "fantasies." Only recently has the awareness that the world is not very much apart from the symbol system we use, Muscari says, led to a reawakening of interest in metaphors in science.

3. Her husband, Dr. John Patrick Casey, was killed by a patient wielding a hand gun in 1990.

4. The flag of the Soviet Union, the hammer and sickle, last flew over the Kremlin on December 31, 1991 (Stanglin 1991).

2 Ways of Knowing: Metaphor and Learning

Midway between the unintelligible and the commonplace, it is a metaphor which most produces knowledge.

Aristotle, *Rhetoric III*

How do we "know" or learn our world? How do we construct knowledge? At one time, academicians might have replied that we discover knowledge only through empirical means— "hypothesis plus test equals proof." Specialists in more and more fields, however, are finding that alternative perspectives may be useful in the discovery of knowledge. Objective facts can be sterile or even meaningless when divorced from their subjective contexts. True understanding often depends on the "invisibles" of "the internal world of experience: emotion, sensation, hunch, belief, and dream" (Wolf 1992, 954).

In the public health field, for instance, there is recognition that untrained but interested private citizens have ways of knowing that may be superior to trained experts' abilities in documenting environmental hazards and diseases (P. Brown 1993). In college education classes, students are sometimes given fictional texts in order to make pedagogical abstractions real. Fictional situations become representations or metaphors for theory and practice (Borman and O'Reilly 1992). Metaphor is finding its way into descriptions of research results as researchers call for increased attention to and valuing of different ways of knowing and move from objective measurement tools to more intuitive ways of interpreting observations.

Western Europeans may value scientific knowing, but other cultural groups value other ways of knowing. For example, Native American ways of knowing include the intuitive, the spiritual, and the personal (Barden and Boyer 1993). They also include story and the use of language. "The combination of song, prayer, and poetry is a natural form of expression for many Navajo people. A person who is able to 'talk beautifully' is well thought of and considered wealthy. To know stories, remember stories, and to retell them well is to have been 'raised right'" (Tapahonso 1993, 107).

There is also growing support for the notion that gender plays a role in the ways that we learn. In their widely acclaimed book *Women's Ways of Knowing*, Belenky, Clinchy, Goldberger, and Tarule (1986) identified five basic ways of knowing among women: silence, received knowledge, subjective knowledge, procedural knowledge, and constructed knowledge. These descriptions both rely on metaphor and provide new metaphors for understanding different kinds of learners. Women in *silence* fear the consequences of their words and therefore remain quiet. They don't trust language. *Received knowers* want the authority (teacher or text) to provide them with the answer; they haven't developed a voice of their own. As writers, they are likely to string quotes together rather than to state their own opinions. Women who are *subjective knowers* put their faith in their own experiences; they accept or reject what authorities say based on their own personal knowledge. They often make global generalizations and may become angry when faced with opinions different from their own. *Procedural knowing,* on the other hand, is objective and involves looking beyond intuition for evidence to support opinions. Some procedural knowers focus on learning procedures for developing an understanding of a subject. Others try to develop procedures for getting at other people's knowledge. Women who *construct knowledge* believe that all knowledge is created and that the knower is part of that knowledge. They synthesize knowledge and experiences using appropriate procedures, often transferring their classroom learning to their own lives (Ortman 1993; Nugent 1993).

The concept of "ways of knowing" as developed by Belenky and her colleagues has proved invaluable to educators who find limitations in "stage" theories yet seek a vocabulary for expressing the many variations in how humans learn and come to know. "Ways of knowing," moreover, is as conducive to synthesis as to analysis: one can employ different ways of knowing at different times and use them in relation to each other. This powerful concept emphasizes the complexity of human thought and steers away from the oversimplification that is often the result of strict categorizing. The educational community in general (and the authors of this book in particular) acknowledges the great service provided by Belenky, Clinchy, Goldberger, and Tarule in establishing "ways of knowing" as an alternative to hierarchical conceptions of thought and development.

The ways of knowing that Belenky and her colleagues propose provide a sort of map for understanding our students, whether female or male, as do the various learning styles inventories that have been developed to help students understand their own ways of learning as well as to help teachers devise experiences that will meet learners' needs.[1] In another ground-breaking book, *Frames of Mind: The Theory of Multiple Intelligences* (1983), Howard Gardner identifies seven different ways of knowing: linguistic, logical-mathematic, spatial, bodily- kinesthetic, musical, intrapersonal, and interpersonal.

Expanding the ways of knowing that we value may be reflected in the adoption of performance-based assessment in some school systems. Rather than measure all student learning through multiple-choice questions on standardized tests, schools are asking students to demonstrate, for example, that they can write for real purposes and to real audiences, that they can solve authentic problems using a variety of disciplinary tools, and that they can work cooperatively in groups to accomplish a task.

Expanding the ways of knowing should also help meet the needs of students who are not comfortable with or adept at learning verbally. By legitimizing other sign systems as tools of exploring, building, and demonstrating knowledge, we open new doors for students who may have been marginalized in the classroom. May (1993) suggests that we employ such diverse activities as painting, poetry, dancing, singing, computer graphics, drawing, playing musical instruments, composing on synthesizers, writing dialogue, acting in plays, architecture, sculpture, photography, and pottery. She raises a number of questions about what might happen to the students who typically are on the dropout track if

> we expanded the role of the arts in the teaching of reading or science in the fourth, fifth, and sixth grades . . . just when the famous reading slump begins for many students . . . [or in] the middle school years, when many students so dramatically lose interest in classroom activities? Would students attain new conceptual languages to organize and express their learning? Would their interest and commitment to learning increase by association? Would they feel immediately involved in their own learning activities and find instructional activities they can share with their peers? What would happen if the arts were a part of every high school class from English to science? Would students become more actively engaged in creative learning? (433–34)

Trousdale and Harris (1993) also argue that the literature classroom must provide an environment that is conducive to all learners and all ways of knowing. They suggest ways of going beyond verbal modes of written response and oral sharing to create opportunities for students to respond to literature, using Gardner's Seven Intelligences model. In particular, they studied the use of choral reading and reader's theater. They concluded that reader's theater is an "effective vehicle for aesthetic involvement in literature. As with choral reading, students are interpreting character, action, motivation, mood, and tone by doing and experiencing them, rather than by talking about them" (205). Staging, lighting, costumes, props, sets, and background music provide students with opportunities to use visual, aural, and spatial ways of knowing. Gestures and movement relate to bodily-kinesthetic ways of knowing. The lines themselves can be correlated with what Gardner calls linguistic intelligence, while writing and acting in the chorus as narrators or as characters relate to interpersonal and intrapersonal intelligences.

NCTE's October 1994 *Notes Plus* presents ideas for using other ways of knowing through transmediation. Students are asked to create multisign texts by "imaginatively translating one's understanding from one medium, often a written text, into another one" (7). In these activities, students use sounds, shapes, colors, and images to express their understandings of and responses to literature. High school students created a visual essay addressing the theme of war and peace to commemorate Memorial Day at their school after reading Remarque's *All Quiet on the Western Front* (Slagle 1994). Middle school students transformed printed words into aural form using a radio-script format (Reissman 1994). And elementary students created a mood museum to show colors and abstract shapes that reflected the moods of different chapters in L'Engle's *A Wrinkle in Time* (Rosengarten 1994).

In the remaining sections in this chapter, we present additional discussion and activity ideas that explore ways of knowing. We examine the nature of learning, defining it as a *change in conceptualization,* and invite you and your students to consider the metaphors for learning that help or hinder your intellectual growth. Using an example from the popular *Star Trek* series, we then consider metaphor as a way of knowing and learning that can lead us to alternative conceptualizations. We further explore learning through other ways of knowing—experience, observation, reflection, and research—in a cross-disciplinary activity.

Experience as a Way of Knowing: Learning for Conceptual Change

All of us have a base of knowledge that we carry around with us, metaphorically speaking, in our heads. That background knowledge is part of us and consists of experiences and learned information that we use to filter new experiences and information. Consider, for example, what you know about games. Your background knowledge of games probably includes ones that you've played at different stages of your life—peek-a-boo, Candyland™, baseball, poker, and so on. You know that games have players, rules, and outcomes. You may also know that games can be enjoyable or tedious, depending on how they are played and with whom. Because of your experience, you also have a schema, or framework, that you can use when learning new games.

As children, some of us initially had the experience of playing games with someone older—a parent or grandparent—who always let us win. This may have given us a false notion about games—that is, that we would always win them. When this false notion was finally tested and we came upon an opponent who outplayed us, it may have been frustrating and disillusioning. It may have taken us a long time to accept this new knowledge about games—and about ourselves. People who never accept this information are labeled as "poor sports." Even in the face of the evidence that they cannot always win, they refuse to adjust their background knowledge about games. They don't learn how to lose.

You can use this explanation of winning and losing games to help students understand what is going on in their minds when they learn new information in school. While experience is an excellent teacher, experience is not all-encompassing. It is one way of knowing. The following example reinforces the value—the necessity—of using multiple perspectives or ways of knowing in order to learn. This is true whether we wish to learn why the soup tastes funny or whether gravity exists in a vacuum. The account is based on the notion of teaching for conceptual change (C. Anderson 1987).

We all have background knowledge about many different subjects even before we begin our formal education, based on things that we have observed and learned informally. One example is the concept of day and night. We've all heard the words *sunset* and *sunrise.* For most of us, there was a time when we thought the sun actually moved through the sky, and that when it "set" in the west, it moved around to the other side of the earth. There finally came a time, however, when our incorrect assumption was challenged and we came to understand that the earth rotates on its axis, turning away from the sun (to create night) and turning toward the sun (to create day). As Anderson would say, we experienced *conceptual change.* In other words, we changed the way we understood a concept. That, in a nutshell, is learning.

The danger comes when we don't actively recognize the conflict between the old knowledge and the new knowledge. Then our brains are not really going to be able to use that new knowledge. Oh, we may remember enough of the wording from a text or a lecture to recognize key words and pass a test, but we won't be able to retain or use that new information.

Charles W. Anderson describes just such a situation in a science class about photosynthesis (Roth 1985a, 1985b; Roth and Anderson 1987; C. Anderson 1987). Students could read the chapter, answer the questions, and pass the test on the unit. Right afterward, however, when questioned in layman's terms rather than with technical terminology, they couldn't tell someone else how plants get their food. Many reverted to false or incomplete explanations, such as "they suck it up from water in the soil." They hadn't really *learned* the information after all. Because they hadn't tried to see how the new information might conflict with their previous assumptions, that new information remained unconnected—and was quickly lost. Students relied instead on their background knowledge, even though it was not an accurate explanation for how plants produced food. In effect, they completely ignored the information that they had been "taught" during this science unit.

In diagnosing our students' learning strengths and problems (and in helping them to do the same), it may be useful to see what kinds of things the science students above did instead of learning the new material. Students will probably recognize themselves in one or more of these scenarios (based on C. Anderson 1987):

- Students read to find a familiar idea and then filled in the explanation from their own background knowledge, never getting far enough to realize that they had selected the right answer, but for the wrong reason.

- They answered questions at the end of the chapter by finding bold-faced words, never really considering the definitions and information being given about those terms.

- They memorized isolated facts for a test, never trying to connect those facts to see the total picture, and therefore missing the key concept entirely.

- They expected new information to confirm their prior assumptions, never realizing that instead the information negated their prior assumptions.

On the other hand, students who *did* learn the new material were aware of the conflict between the text and their own assumptions and were willing to abandon misconceptions in favor of the new explanations.

The following questions may be used with students as journal prompts or as small-group discussion topics to further explore their own experiences with learning and conceptual change.

- When do you remember being aware of a conflict between your belief about something and its true explanation—like the idea of the sun's rising and setting versus the fact that the earth actually rotates? What caused you to change your understanding of the concept?

- Have you ever experienced such a conflict that did not lead to your changing your understanding? Why did you stick with your old beliefs?

- Have you ever had an experience like the science students who could pass a test about a subject but couldn't describe the concept correctly—even right after the test? How did that make you feel? Why did you think that happened?

- What is your understanding of the meaning of "learning as change"? What other metaphors have you heard used for learning? How do you view learning? For example, is it an adventure in uncharted territory, or is it forced labor? Do you talk about your brain as being "full" or "switched off"? Are your metaphors positive or negative? What effect might that have on your growth as a learner?

- How can you make sure your teachers are aware of your background knowledge about a given topic? How can you try to relate new knowledge to "old" knowledge?

- Judith A. Best (1984) says that "metaphor is sneaky; it creeps into the mind and grabs hold of something that is there. It stretches that thing, applying it to something new, pulling the mind along with it. Metaphor is like the Pied Piper or the Siren's song. It is difficult to resist" (166). Try to think of an example of a misconception you or others have had about a concept in math, social studies, or one of your other classes. How might you use metaphor to help someone else recognize the difference between his or her assumptions and the way the concept really works?

Trying It Out

Metaphor as a Way of Knowing: Learning from *Star Trek*

One type of learning involves cultural awareness—seeing beyond our own ways to understand ideas and attitudes that are foreign to us. "Darmok," an episode of the TV series *Star Trek: The Next Generation,* illustrates how learning about others can lead to change in perceptions and feelings (Lazebnik and Menosky 1991). If you are a *Star Trek* fan, the word *Darmok* may be enough to make you recall the episode in which Captain Jean-Luc Picard met the Tamarians. If it does, then you have just experienced the way words can be packed with images and thus become metaphors. When those metaphors are ones that are known by our audience, we are understood. When the metaphors are not shared, however, communication is blocked, as it often is when we ask our students to read classic works of literature full of unfamiliar allusions—and as it was when Dathon used metaphors that were unfamiliar to Picard. If you aren't a *Star Trek* aficionado, you may be feeling a communication block now, too, but please bear with us as we share the background of the story.

In the "Darmok" episode, the starship *Enterprise* crew finds that the Tamarian language is impossible for the computerized Universal Translator to decipher. It seems to be nothing but a string of proper names. (If English were similarly structured, we would be speaking only in phrases such as "Nixon at Peking," "Liberace, his suit gleaming," and "Grant and Lee at Appomattox.") Suddenly, Picard finds himself on El Adrel with the Tamarian captain, Dathon. Dathon seems to have planned this meeting, but Picard cannot determine why. It finally appears that they are to fight a luminous beast, although Picard had first assumed Dathon was his adversary instead.

To communicate, Dathon teaches Picard his language through concrete demonstrations. For example, Picard can't keep a fire going; Dathon throws him a burning stick and says, "Timba, his arms wide." Although he first thinks "timba" means "timber" or piece of wood, Picard finally realizes that "arms wide" indicates generosity. Picard truly sees the light now, realizing that his adversary-turned-companion is speaking in metaphor. He understands that the Tamarians have held him against his will so that the basis for an alliance can be formed. The message Dathon is trying to impart is that two strangers become comrades when faced with a common foe. Sharing a common experience is the basis for understanding.

Picard shares a metaphor of his own, telling the story of Gilgamesh and Enkido, who also became friends while battling a common enemy.[2] Enkido dies in battle. As the wounded Dathon closes his eyes, we realize the Gilgamesh metaphor is an apt one for what Picard and Dathon have experienced as well. Later, Picard averts war, now able to use Tamarian metaphors meaningfully to communicate with the Tamarians. The Tamarians mourn their leader's death and now have a new metaphor: Picard and Dathon at El Adrel—a leader sacrifices his life in exchange for peace.

Students may enjoy watching the episode and pausing to debate the meaning of various Tamarian metaphors, such as *Shaka, when the walls fell* (failure); *Darmok on the ocean* (alone); *Uzani, his army at Lashmere with fists open* (to lure enemy); *Uzani, his army at Lashmere with fists closed* (to fight); and *Kiasi's children, their faces wet* (grief, mourning).

Near the end of the episode, the crew members talk about metaphors based on Western literature, such as Romeo and Juliet. Ask students to consider "Juliet on the balcony." Proponents of cultural literacy such as E. D. Hirsch (1987) would call familiarity with this image a requirement for educated Americans. How important is it for the members of a particular culture to share a body of literary metaphors? In what ways is the concept of cultural literacy inclusive? exclusive? If we decide that there are pieces of information that all members of our cultural group should know, then who should decide what that information is?

In the closing scene of "Darmok," Picard is reading some of Homer's works. He says they contain some of the "root metaphors of our culture." Students may be invited to consider what that means and to read excerpts from *The Iliad* or other classics. Can they find metaphors that have become everyday expressions (and may not seem metaphorical at all now)? Are there expressions that resemble metaphors but carry no meaning for the students? If metaphors are no longer meaningful to readers, their enjoyment of the literature may be diminished. Most English teachers have had experience with this phenomenon. When the study of literature becomes the study of an artifact, our students' interest and response may sag. Perhaps the experience of dealing with unintelligible metaphors in "Darmok" can give us a perspective for examining the issue of which pieces of literature secondary students should be required to read.

Trying It Out

Multiple Ways of Knowing: Experience, Observation, Reflection, and Research

Literature is a way of knowing. Literature teaches us about ourselves, about our lives. It is an active process, one that requires us to construct knowledge: "[R]eading becomes an 'encounter' because it involves interpreting, and in the process of interpreting we find our own preoccupations addressed within the text. We are not passive in this process, for we read the text with a selective foregrounding of our own concerns and even make it address questions that were not present to its author" (Perkins 1988, 116).

Because we read through the filter of our own concerns, we relate to certain authors and characters who help us understand ourselves. And we hope that most of our students have had the experience of seeing themselves in the books that they read and learning about themselves in the pieces they write. Such readings and writings teach us. They lead us to discoveries, as readers and writers, that come from the process we undertake.

Other readings and writings are designed to teach others, to inform or persuade them. Editorials, brochures, letters of recommendation or complaint, and reports are typical vehicles for teaching others, but they are not the only ones. All of us are familiar with fables and stories with morals. Such pieces of literature clearly teach us as they entertain us. A genre such as poetry also can be used to teach. Writers who have messages to share need not limit themselves to the traditional expository forms, but students often do that, unaware that the possibilities are as wide as their imaginations.

In the example that follows, the writer has used multiple ways of knowing to explore a topic and develop a poem. Because we make discoveries through our senses, through the physical act of being somewhere and seeing, hearing, and feeling what goes on there, the writer began with an experience, a trip to the zoo. There she recorded observations. Later she reflected on them, recording emotions and opinions about the experience and attempting to make sense of them. Finally, she consulted reference materials to help give her needed background and a factual or intellectual perspective to complement the physical and emotional perspectives she had already developed.

By sharing the journal entries below with students, you can show them how a writer might blend these multiple ways of knowing to develop a piece of writing. We encourage students to start all writing this way—with an experience or an observation and a reflection on it, followed by further investigation or research inspired by the reflection. The writer's ownership in the topic will be much greater, and the resulting combination of image, thought, and fact can lead to new insights. This is an especially helpful strategy in getting students away from the "report mode" in content-area writing.

To return to our opening statement in this section, the piece of writing developed through this process does indeed reflect a way of knowing, of discovering a new understanding of the world, as does the process of reading the piece. In the finished poem, which reflects what the writer has learned about her experience, there is an expectation that the reader will learn, too. While evoking an emotion, the poem informs and may even persuade.

Zoo Trip Entry

Five baboons living together in zoo—four stay 15–20 ft. apart from oldest and biggest male, whose appearance is somewhat different because of the shaggy mane of hair on his head and shoulders. Have bright, dark coral-colored skin on upper chest, with coarse brown fur on most of body. Really muscular chests. Ugly but cute face. Eyes seem dull and listless. Attendant throws fresh fruit and vegetables, they catch it easily in their hands; fingers seem long and bony. Sweet potatoes, corn on the cob and apples are clear favorites. Oldest female eats corn like a human would; oldest male does remove husk, but then eats it like a banana, cob and all. Seems to pick out seeds from apple as it eats. Smaller baboons eat further away, against the rocks or in small nooks, but dominant male and female remain in open for best choice of food. Dominant female has piles of food near her, but if others approach—especially the barbary sheep that share the compound—a quick gesture sends them back. (Hicks 1994)

This entry was made during a fifteen- or twenty-minute observation of the baboons at a metropolitan zoo. As you will see momentarily, the writer later selected several phrases from those notes to use in a piece of writing. Other images that found their way into her later poem were not inscribed but were recalled in rereading the entry. This is a valuable function of journaling to share with our students. Even when we do not get everything down, the words we do record help us recreate the memories as we develop pieces of writing from our notes.

In a second entry, the writer tried to capture feelings and thoughts about the experience of observing the animal. While this might have been done in conjunction with the observation itself, recording observations alone tends to consume one's focus. These notes helped the writer explore her point of view. Some of these feelings later found their way into the poem:

Reflection on Zoo Entry

At first I thought they were cute and clever. There was a clear pecking order in the group. The male seemed a bit self-centered, seeming to expect that all the choice items would be his. The smaller ones, possibly all females, although I couldn't be sure, showed him deference. The longer I watched, the less cute it became. There was a mechanistic quality to the way they moved. No real energy. Just another performance. Why did the attendant throw their food? Demeaning. It was a strange show which the performers didn't seem to be enjoying at all. It was curious to see how the baboons looked past the spectators, as if we weren't there. There was no place to hide, no privacy, no way to escape the stares, so they seemed to just ignore us. I began to feel sad and sorry for them. Even pained. I tried to imagine what they would be like in the wild . . . surely not this listless and detached. Might they have a sense of pride? These animals seemed spiritless.

A final entry took the form of a list of facts gleaned from reading and research on baboons:

Research Entry

largest member of the monkey family

smaller than apes

two feet high

fifty pounds

found mostly in rocky hills of Africa

called dog-faced for their long snouts or muzzles

live in troops of 20–100

forage for birds' eggs, lizards, insects, fruits

even raid farms for crops

powerful jaws, sharp teeth

savage fighters; even lions fear to attack them

some types sacred to the ancient Egyptians

some types have startling colors on face and tail—red, blue, yellow, white

The poem, literally and figuratively constructed from the writings above, follows. The title is a play on the phrase "the signifying monkey." Esu, a trickster in African American literary tradition, is the signifying monkey who "displaces and defers meaning through the ongoing play of differences" and embodies the ambiguities of language (Spurlin 1990).

The Dignifying Monkey

Largest of the monkeys
yet smaller than apes,
two feet high if they stand erect,
they carry their name uncertainly—
baboons.
A silly label and yet
far better than their epithet,
Dog-
face.

Clown-like colors,
startling shades—red, blue, yellow, white
on face and rump—
seem a joke
of which they don't approve.

At fifty pounds, they'd make chubby toddlers
but their bodies are sleek,
their muscles are hard
like a body builder's.
No nonsense there.
Their compound suggests
rocky hills of Africa;
but their listless eyes
say otherwise.

Troops of twenty to a hundred
would they form
if given a chance,
but zoo population control
keeps them to a lonely handful.

In the wild
they would forage
for birds' eggs, lizards, insects, fruits—
even raid farms for crops.
Tamely here
they await the keeper's visit,
catch sweet potatoes and apples
in long and bony fingers
with ease, yet disinterest,
like performers
long weary of the show.

Powerful jaws,
sharp teeth,
savage fighters;
even lions fear to attack them.
They guard the troop like soldiers.
But here
only barbary sheep
pay homage to their tempers.
They guard instead
the food that has been tossed them.

Sacred to ancient Egyptians,
curious to Western society,
enduring centuries
of captivity,
they stare into the distance,
avoiding eye contact
and bearing their indignity
with dignity.

What we hope students will discover is that the images and lines for this poem are found in the expressive writing of the author. By expressive, we mean writing that is primarily for one's self, that expresses thoughts, feelings, and ideas. Poetic writing grows out of those expressive roots. Words and phrases have been developed and transplanted into an art form that is meant to be shared with an audience. Too often we have asked students to start at the genre level, to write a poem or story or essay without the benefit of discovering first what it is they have to say. (Poetic writing, by the way, doesn't mean just poetry; all forms of literature fall into this category.) Transactive writing also grows out of those expressive roots but is intended instead to inform or persuade. Had the poet written a letter to the zoo's board of directors or the editor of the community newspaper to protest the conditions that the animals must bear, that writing would have been transactional—designed to get something done.

As students develop their own poems, they should be encouraged to read their work aloud in small groups and to solicit feedback. Readers' or listeners' questions may suggest areas for revision that require additional observation and research. A teacher conference also may be helpful at that point. After the piece has been developed as far as the author can take it, editing and publishing should follow. Students may wish to illustrate their work with art or photographs. Classroom displays, books for themselves or other classes, or even "bulletin-board anthologies" are possible ways to share student work.

Notes

1. For background on a number of learning theories, see *Perspectives on Learning* (Phillips and Solstis 1985).

2. Gilgamesh was a hero of Assyrian and Babylonian mythology and was known in Sumerian and Hittite writings as well. Gilgamesh was the harsh ruler of Erech, the capital of Shinar. To punish him, the gods sent Enkido. Gilgamesh won their battle, and the two became friends. The goddess Ishtar was impressed by Gilgamesh's prowess, but Gilgamesh rudely rejected her love. Ishtar was insulted and had her father, Anu, avenge her honor. Anu created a monstrous bull to attack the city of Erech, but Gilgamesh and Enkido killed it and further insulted Ishtar by throwing the bull's phallus in her face. Ishtar brought about Enkido's death and Gilgamesh's affliction with a leprosy-like disease. Gilgamesh sought help from Utnapishtim, who knew the secret of immortality. He eventually showed Gilgamesh the plant of life at the bottom of the ocean. When Gilgamesh dove for it, though, a serpent ate the plant. Later, the gods took pity on him and allowed Gilgamesh to visit Enkido in the underworld (Barnhart 1954, 1746).

3 Reimagining Ourselves

Possible selves represent individuals' ideas of what they might become, what they would like to become, and what they are afraid of becoming. . . . Possible selves are the cognitive components of hopes, fears, goals, and threats. . . . Possible selves are important, first because they function as incentives for future behavior (i.e., they are selves to be approached or avoided) and second, because they provide an evaluative and interpretive context for the current view of self.

Hazel Markus and Paul Nurius, *Possible Selves*

P*ossible selves* is a psychological term, but it effectively represents what we mean by metaphor as a way of helping us reimagine ourselves. While our focus is on the enabling facet of this notion, possible selves also encompasses the negative or darker side as well. Just as we may reimagine ourselves as competent and successful bed-and-breakfast owners in our retirement years, we can also envision the outcomes we fear—such as becoming lonely hermits or dependent addicts.

Possible selves, then, can be the selves we want to become or despair becoming. They can also include the selves we have been and the selves we escaped being. In his memoir of a troubled boyhood in South Africa, Christopher Hope (1988) describes how he tried to keep in touch with a self he felt he was abandoning when his family moved from a small borough in the Transvaal to the capital of white separatism, Pretoria:

> My horror at the move sent me to the oak tree on the patch of wasteland [where he had previously spent time in contemplation], and I placed in a hollow between two branches a stone. It was one of those roadside stones that washed very white and blue-veined when the rains fell. I put the stone where it would wait in the tree for the moment I chose to return—patient, loyal, faithful, and secret. While the stone remained in the tree something at least would stay the same. (74)

The stone became a symbol of faithfulness and loyalty and represented the self that Hope had been and did not want to lose.

We discover a possible self in virtually every choice we make or act we perform. If a store clerk gives us back too much change, we decide to keep it or give it back according to the strength of a particular self-image—a principled self, one compassionate to the plight of the clerk when the cash is balanced at the end of the day; or a slightly wealthier self, a recipient of unexpected luck that may foreshadow even greater fortunes on this particular day. Throughout life, these selves, realized and unrealized, constitute the parameters of our existence.

In reimagining, we are focusing on a desired possible self and repositioning ourselves in life in order to make that self become a reality. The power of our imagination is so great that we can literally reimagine ourselves. We can set our minds on a goal or an image, and as a well-known politician has said, if we can believe it, we can achieve it. This may seem to be an overstatement on first glance, but we believe there is an enabling quality in well-chosen metaphors. Metaphors are even used in psychotherapy to help patients problem-solve and turn words into actions (Pollio et al. 1977).

Self-disclosure literature is becoming popular; in effect, it provides a historical account of the reimagining process. A powerful narrative of this kind is Sharon Hamilton's *My Name's Not Susie* (1995). In telling the story of her life, she shows how literacy allowed her to reimagine herself. She was able to go from unwanted foster child to college professor.

Hamilton's student Stephanie Rodriguez has also written her story, *Time to Stop Pretending* (1993). Although she eventually was able to reimagine her life outside of an abusive relationship, she shows why many people are unable to do that. The limits of our imaginations can allow invisible chains to strap us down, mentally and emotionally, preventing us from getting out of situations and relationships that keep us miserable. In the preface to her compelling tale about spouse abuse, she tries to explain why battered women often are unable to escape:

> I remember all the people who tried so hard, again and again, to help me out. It's hard to explain why it never worked, but a story told to me by a friend who used to be a train engineer helps a little: One night, on a long stretch of track, he noticed a figure far ahead. On the tracks, he thought. For a long time the distance between the train and the figure appeared to remain the same. He wondered if it wasn't some sort of optical illusion. After a while, however, the train began to gain on the figure, and soon my friend was close enough to see the terrified and exhausted dog, running for all he was worth, looking back over first one shoulder, then the other, at the tremendous monster bearing down on him. He blew the whistle. The dog increased his speed, but was unable to maintain the pace. Finally the train ran him over.
>
> My friend expressed amazement that the dog hadn't simply jumped to the side, out of harm's way. There was, after all, only a small rail on either side of him; nothing at all to keep him on those tracks.
>
> I hate that story. I think I know why the poor dog wasn't able to save himself. He was so involved in the business of staying ahead of

the monster on his tail that he couldn't possibly conceive of another thing. He didn't have time to reason out that a single step in either direction would save him.

It's a lot like that for the battered woman who can see only the monster on her tail. All the people on the sides of the track—the friends, family, and social workers, calling out instructions, trying their damnedest to talk her out of there, are only so much more clamor. They stir up dust, and add to the confusion.

I've run the frantic run for my life. . . . (4–5)

A negative aspect of this ability to reimagine ourselves is reflected in the current debate on whether or not false memories can be implanted through hypnosis. A documentary in The Learning Channel's *Science Frontiers* series (1995) suggests that having "good imagery" (which was defined as the ability to imagine vividly) makes it likely that the memory of an abduction by aliens or of previously unknown sexual abuse is actually false. The more the individual focuses on the supposed incident, the more vivid it becomes, which explains the semblance of reality such pseudomemories take. A psychologist was featured who showed how a patient's comment ("I felt like I was falling") became, with very little probing, an imagined prior life some 250 years before. His contention was that each time this incident was retrieved through hypnosis, it was embellished—not because it was true, but because of the patient's incredible ability to imagine.

Trying It Out

Metaphors for Writers

The metaphors we use for ourselves, and for our lives, can be enabling or disabling. Sometimes they are both. Consider the metaphor that English writer Jean Rhys uses for herself in a conversation with David Plante, who wrote a memoir of his friendship with her:

"You see, I'm a pen. I'm nothing but a pen."
"And do you imagine yourself in someone's hand?"
Tears came to her eyes. "Of course. Of course. It's only then that I know I'm writing well. It's only then that I know my writing is true. Not really true, not as fact. But true as writing. . . . You're picked up like a pen, and when you're used up, you're thrown away, ruthlessly, and someone else is picked up. You can be sure that someone else will be picked up."

When Plante asked if she ever wondered *why* she was picked up, she answered that she didn't know: "'I don't know why,'" she said. "'I don't know, and I wonder if it was right to allow oneself to be picked up. I wonder if it was right to give up so much of my life for writing'" (Plante 1983, 31).

In an article in *English Journal,* James C. McDonald (1992) describes how he asks students to compose metaphors for themselves as writers in order to clarify their attitudes about writing. Students in a remedial course portrayed themselves as turtles, old cars, chemists, and chefs. Many times the metaphors were negative. Students saw themselves as slow, hard to get started, sputtering out and dying, unable to finish the race. Even a student who portrayed himself as an eagle seeking his prey, soaring and majestic, ended up hurt and embarrassed. In the metaphor, he swoops into the lake, grabs his prey, and is stopped in midair. "I then see my mistake as the fisherman on the bank stares in his amazement at what he has caught with the artificial bait" (61). Grammar, spelling, and punctuation problems often stopped this eagle in midflight, he said. He and his fellow classmates saw writing as a risk and feared low grades, red marks, and hurtful comments about their work. Honors students showed more confidence in themselves and used images that focused on control (such as predator, traffic director, business executive), but they feared revealing themselves through writing and inviting criticism or ridicule. McDonald encourages students "to explore the meanings of their own words, to play with unexpected implications and ambiguities in their metaphors" (64) so that they will not see themselves as drowned cats, mockingbirds, or muted alligators but as writers.

Try McDonald's strategy of having students compose metaphors for themselves as writers. Help them extend their metaphors to explore the positive and negative elements that may enable or disable them as writers. After such a discussion, students may be encouraged to develop metaphors for the writers they want to become, or the class may craft such a metaphor together that can help them focus on an image that will be helpful rather than debilitating.

Trying It Out

Using Literature as a Lens for Looking at Our Lives

There are roles that our students try on, for in youth, we are attempting to form a coherent sense of self (Erickson 1988). We are trying to find out who we are, a problem compounded by the many roles we are expected to assume as part of our daily lives. A teenager's identity ricochets from child to student to best friend to rival to older sibling to younger sibling to neighborhood kid to babysitter to . . . well, you get the idea. And that can be all in one day! Add to that the roles we purposefully assume—club president, humanitarian, team member, political activist, flirt—and it's no wonder we sometimes don't recognize ourselves.

When we reach crossroads in our lives, it's not unusual to replay this search for one's identity. When we give up a dominant role, we have to try out other roles to find one that can fill the void. Sometimes, as we try out roles, we are leery of permanent changes. We find a facade that seems to fit our needs and to uphold the image we wish others to see. The "real" us is buried underneath. Sometimes we become so accustomed to the mask we have assumed that we forget we have it on. When someone who "knew us way back when" unexpectedly rips off our mask, we feel exposed and vulnerable.

There are times, then, when people don't act the way we expect them to act. Sometimes it's because they are growing and changing, taking off masks, adopting new roles, but we aren't ready for them to do that. Alana White (1990) creates such a character in *Come Next Spring.* Salina isn't ready for things and people to change. She uses a metaphor to describe the changes in her relationships with her siblings, Mary and Paul: "Other parts of the day did not make sense—the parts where Mary and Paul did not stay in place, and Salina felt let down and sorry. She had put them exactly where they belonged and they had popped back at her, like pieces in a jigsaw puzzle that just won't go, no matter how hard you squeeze them" (40).

Characters in books or stories often provide a safe way to start a discussion or journal-writing activity on our changing roles or on the masks we wear. Cohen's study (1993) of adults who found reading to be helpful in dealing with life's difficulties found that recognition of one's self in literature is therapeutic. It evolves into ways of feeling and ways of knowing. Therapeutic reading is intentional, relational, and transporting, Cohen found. Nearly any story can be used for a general exploration of roles and masks people assume. Later, students may wish to explore in writing their own masks or those behind which they have seen others hide. Another possibility is to imagine what it would feel like to wear the mask of a character or person they know—or how others would feel wearing *their* masks. Are there people who are what they seem, who really have no masks? Is this an ideal toward which we should work? Or is it an impossibility?

Helping students find themselves in the books they read is one of the most important things we can do as teachers. There are several excellent resources for helping us do that (see next paragraph). We need to bring these resources into the classroom for students to consult as well. We also need to assemble thematic text sets of novels and nonfiction works on a variety of issues through which teens need to work.

If you are not familiar with the NCTE booklist series, you have a treat in store. *Your Reading* (Christensen 1983; Nilsen 1991; Webb 1993; Samuels and Beers 1996) is an annotated bibliography of books for middle schoolers. *Books for You* (Abrahamson and Carter 1988; Wurth 1992; Christenbury 1995) is a review of books for senior high students. There is also a collection of *High Interest–Easy Reading* books for junior and senior high students (McBride 1990; Phelan 1996) and an *Adventuring with Books* series (Jensen and Roser 1993; Sutton 1997) for pre-K through grade 6. These booklists are arranged thematically and have enough of a plot summary to help you and your students select fiction and nonfiction books to use in your classroom. Categories include problems that teenagers deal with (growing up, family relationships, love and romance, ethnic relationships, death and dying, and so on) and popular genres (adventure, science fiction, mystery, historical fiction, poetry, plays, etc.). Each volume covers a span of several years.

Two books that will give you a good background in what has become known as young adult literature are *Literature for Today's Young Adults* (Nilsen and Donelson 1993) and *Reaching Adolescents: The Young Adult Book and the School* (Reed 1994). Both provide recommendations by theme and genre, often with brief summaries and interpretations as well as teaching and learning suggestions. Along with the NCTE series, these will help you help your students find themselves in books that are written for them. (As good as these references are, of course, there is no substitute for immersing yourself in the adolescent literature they describe.)

Trying It Out

Guided Imagery

Imagination is one of our greatest human gifts. We can be on a crowded city street on a hot, airless day and yet close our eyes and transport ourselves to a remote mountain meadow—at least for a few seconds. We depend on our senses, or rather our memories of sensual experiences, to suspend the physical sensations of the moment and help us recall the feelings that correspond with the feeling of thick grass beneath our feet and a cool breeze blowing through our hair. This is easier to do if we are not on that hot, crowded street, of course, but rather in a comfortable chair in a darkened room with our feet up and our "guard" down. Relaxation techniques can actually help us visit that mountain meadow in our memories or in our imaginations.

Guided imagery is a prewriting strategy that uses a similar approach. It is being used very successfully with writers of all ages to prepare them to write in journals or writers' notebooks. In current vernacular, it's as close to virtual reality as you can get without electronics. You may want to try it with your students; it's even better if you can get someone else to lead the session, though, because then you get to be a participant!

In many of these experiences, writers are led to see things metaphorically, or to revisit past experiences in order to make sense of them. In the sample guided imagery script below, writers are invited to reimagine their lives by changing a choice that they once made or that was made for them. Before using this strategy, be sure to consider the nature of your particular group of students. This exercise is not intended to upset them or to dredge up feelings that would be better explored with a trained mental health worker. While we have never had negative experiences with guided imagery, it can evoke an emotional response, and some teachers therefore express concerns about using it.

In using this or any guided imagery experience, remember to set the mood. You will probably want to turn off the lights and pull the shades, have everyone spread out, and use a soft, soothing or melodic voice when reading the passage. You're not trying to hypnotize students or put them to sleep, of course, but a relaxed atmosphere can help them focus. Speak slowly. Pause frequently. Above all, provide ample time for writing afterward.

> Sit back and close your eyes. Take a deep breath. Take another. . . . Relax the muscles in your face. Let your chin drop toward your chest. . . . Feel the rhythm of your breathing . . . in . . . out . . . in . . . out . . . slower . . . and slower. . . . Let your shoulders relax . . . and let the tension melt out through your fingertips. Your body begins to sag as each set of muscles relaxes. . . . Your legs are feeling very heavy so you let them go. Nothing can hold you down now. You are completely relaxed. You are lighter than air. You feel yourself floating . . . floating. The ceiling opens for you and the blue sky above beckons. You feel yourself going higher and higher, until you reach an altitude that feels comfortable to you. . . . You level off and enjoy the sensation of being carried along on the wind. It is a gentle breeze. The sun warms your back. Feel the warmth. Feel the tingling in your hair as the wind blows through it. You hear nothing but the wind. Quiet. It is so quiet up here. You look down and see that you are far from where you started. The landscape has changed. You are not sure where you are heading, but it seems familiar to you anyway. The flat ground gives way to rolling hills . . . as you continue to float along, the hills give way to mountains. Ahead you see a small meadow tucked between two peaks. The grasses and wildflowers are waving ever so lightly, pushed back by the breeze. You dip your head slightly and are gently carried down to the ground. . . . The thick grass supports you like a cushion. You sink back into it and

gaze at the clouds above. . . . The sun becomes warmer and you realize you are thirsty. You hear the sound of water in the distance. There is a small stream. It sparkles in the sun as it runs quickly over the rocks in its bed. You walk toward the water, stepping high through the grass and flowers, creating a shush-shush-shush sound as you make your way to the brook. When you get there, you kneel down and feel the cool, damp earth on your knees. You cup your hands and dip them into the clear, cool water. Some of the water runs through your fingers. You drink until your thirst is quenched. . . . Your head feels very clear now. Looking around, you see a path . . . then another. One is a path you have traveled before. It is more than bare earth parting the grasses and saplings. It reflects a choice you made . . . or a choice that was made for you. You can see it clearly. Where does it lead? . . . The other path is not so clear. It turns quickly and is covered with brush. This is the path that you did not take or could not take. You look back at the path you have already traveled. You remember when you traveled it, and where, and why. . . . You remember the people who traveled it with you. You know that path, for good or bad. . . . Now look again at the other path. This is the path that might have been. You stand there a moment, trying to see past the turn, but you cannot. The only way to know what might lie ahead is to walk down the path, or to climb a tall tree to see what experiences await. Take a moment to decide what you will do. You may return to the known path or to the meadow if you like, but can you resist the unknown path? If you decide to try the path, begin to walk down it. . . . Go as far as you care to or dare to. Watch carefully and remember what you do, what you see, what you feel, what you hear. [Extended pause.] Now it is time to leave this place. The winds carry you up and back much more quickly this time, so quickly that you find you have brought back those sensations and experiences with you. When you are ready, return to this room, to your chair, to this time. . . . And now it is time to open your eyes and to write. (Hicks 1995)

This is not an assignment to collect but rather an opportunity for students to write expressively. Some will not take the option of writing about the choice that might have been but will focus instead on the experiences of the imagery—their relaxation, the sensation of flying, or the meadow. And that is fine. Writers must have many opportunities to write without being assigned a topic or a finished product. It is from these beginnings that drafts can later be fashioned, if the writer desires. Having many beginnings is important so that there is a real choice for students when they are asked to develop a finished piece. Many teachers have students keep journals or writers' notebooks in which such writing can be stored—privately.

Voluntary sharing by a few students after such an experience may give writers other ideas for writing. A model of a piece of poetic writing that you have developed from your own expressive entry is an excellent way to help students see the possibilities in their responses to the guided imagery, as long as they don't feel they must mimic your efforts. If you're getting "clone" writing (drafts that mirror your sample), sharing several ideas for pieces you think you might want to develop from that one entry is often helpful.

You probably have noted the similarity between this guided experience and the Robert Frost poem "The Road Not Taken," which describes a traveler standing at a fork in the road and choosing the one that seemed less used (in Aloian 1965, 91). While it would be tempting to use Frost's poem as a model, we caution against that, at least initially. First, students need to see their teachers writing what they write, trying what they try; a professional model can be so intimidating that it thwarts students rather than assists them. Second, the poem does not have the specificity that may be apparent in students' visions of the paths they did not take. We want to encourage that specificity rather than the generality that might ensue after reading Frost's poem. While his vision of diverging paths is the one that has inspired the guided experience, he does not walk down the path, after all. He's left that to us, and that is what we must leave to our students as well.

For other examples of guided imagery, see Chapter 11 of Zemelman and Daniels's *Community of Writers* (1988) and pages 201–6 of Lucy Calkins's *Living Between the Lines* (1991). The Calkins book has an especially effective passage that helps students understand what it might be like to be homeless. Zemelman and Daniels also provide a framework for developing your own guided imagery experiences.

Trying It Out

By Any Other Name

If the title of this activity brings to mind the balcony scene from *Romeo and Juliet*, you've already made a metaphorical connection. You recognize the reference to Juliet's musings on Romeo Montague, sworn enemy of her family simply because of the name he bears, as she implores, "O, be some other name! What's in a name? That which we call a rose by any other word would smell as sweet" (2.2.42–44).

By Shakespeare's time, England had set the fashion for present Western customs in choosing a name. Very likely, we were named because our parents liked the sound of our name, perhaps having skimmed through baby-name pamphlets to select the perfect one. Perhaps we were named after a relative, as a way of honoring that person. If this is the case, we are lucky if we do not consider our name too old-fashioned. Then again, parents who give modern names might not be appreciated, either, as demonstrated in this conversation between teenagers in the film *The Lost Boys* (Warner Brothers 1988):

> What's your name?
>
> Star.
>
> Oh, your folks, too, huh?
>
> What do you mean?
>
> Ex-hippies. I came this close to being called Moonbeam or Moonchild or something like that.

(Fischer, Jeremias, and Boam 1987)

**Activity 1:
Name Stories**

The first story we encounter in life may be our name-story. Students may want to share the stories behind their names and to develop a piece of personal writing that records the story for the family archives. The following questions may help students gather information.

- Who chose your name or influenced your naming? Why? How?
- Traditions sometimes influence name choices. In past centuries, it was typical in some cultures to name the first two boys after their paternal and maternal grandfathers and the first two girls after their paternal and maternal grandmothers. Some names are conferred in religious ceremonies, or a sacred name may be added to a child's "secular" name. Religious tradition may also dictate that we are not named after living relatives. Was there a tradition involved in your naming?
- Some names are based on metaphors, incidents, characteristics, or associations. What did the person(s) who named you have in mind when your name was chosen?
- Is there a family story about your surname? Where did it come from? What does it mean?
- Develop a story, anecdote, poem, or other piece of writing in which you share your name story.

Before the Middle Ages, there was no need for last names. People were given one-of-a-kind monikers. It was only as towns expanded and the population increased that names needed a further description—"Guy, John's son" would become Guy Johnson, or "Hans the Miller" would become Hans Miller, or "Freda-who-lives-under-the-hill" would become Freda Underhill. People became known by their parentage, occupation, or location—if they were fortunate. Some surnames do not have so genial a tradition, such as Emma Spoilale or Muchman Wetbed, which developed from nicknames, according to Leslie Dunkling's *Guinness Book of Names* (1991).

Where are the metaphorical connections to our names? Names originally meant something. Many other cultures make up names unique to the individual, based on characteristics of the person or desired characteristics. Chinese tradition gives to children personal names combining meaningful words that exist in the language, like *de* (virtuous), *chaing* (strong), and *dà* (big). Someone named Dà Chaing has a name that means "big and strong" in the Chinese language as it is currently used. Ju Ao is a masculine name that means "proud chrysanthemum." With someone named Ashley in America, however, we do not usually think of "ash wood or clearing," which is what the name meant in Old English. If we still spoke Old English, we'd also know that Alwin means "elf friend," Balston means "bold stone," and Orrick, "spear powerful" (Dunkling 1991, 65, 82).

Activity 2: Reimagining through Re-Naming

Our names are integral to our identities. They help shape how we see ourselves and how others see us. It's hard to be proud of being named Willoughby Edgar Thompson II, though, when all the kids call you "WET-2" or "Too Wet" for short. Remember the old Barbie™ "Queen of the Prom" Game? No one wanted to get stuck with Poindexter. You're probably familiar with studies that have shown that teachers give higher grades to students with "normal" names and lower grades to students with odd or old-fashioned ones. Children with names like Clyde and Wilhelmina may have had a strike against them, the researchers concluded. (Recent studies indicate that teachers no longer fall into that trap!)

Whether we love them or hate them, our names are not given without reason. The act of putting a label to our thoughts requires processes that eliminate alternatives and select the final product, which may not remain final after all, in the case of nicknames. Even though one of the author's daughters was named Acacia, after a tree, she has always been called Casey. If you and your students' town, school, or birthplaces don't have nicknames, your students may want to do some brainstorming. What geographical features, characteristics of people, cultural events, or industry come to mind? Towns can get nicknames that stick. Detroit, named after a French fort, was nicknamed the Motor City for the automobile industry (shortened further to Motown) and is known at times as Murder One for its homicide rate.

Parents may use a form of free association to name their offspring, reflecting on incidents at birth or even conception. Margaux Hemingway, granddaughter of writer Ernest Hemingway, was named after a bottle of wine her parents consumed on their honeymoon. One author's niece, Hannah Lee, was named for the

Hawaiian town Hanalei, a popular honeymoon spot. Friends named their son Wade Pu'u'o for the vent on the Kailua volcano, also in Hawaii. This same couple named their daughter Junica Nivalis, *nivalis* being the species name of the weasel Junica's father was studying while working on his Ph.D. Another parent named his son Jontue after the scent the father was wearing when the baby was born. (What if Dad had been wearing Old Spice?) Rock star Frank Zappa named his daughter Moon and his son Dweezil. (We can't help wondering what inspired the boy's name.) Whatever one's satisfaction level toward a given name, one could be reminded that "your name is what you make of it."

Although names do have meanings, some of the meanings have roots in unfamiliar languages; the original metaphorical associations are lost. Now that students have researched the meanings of their names, you might ask them to forget for a moment the names they were given and to take new ones based on the meanings in Figures 3.1–3.4. They may choose one or more meanings that help

Figure 3.1.
Meanings of Male Names

one born at night	storyteller	a musician
drummer	cowherd, cowboy	fire and wood
bright, noble	singer	an apprentice
poet	royalty	peaceful ruler
white hawk	brightest in family	fair-haired
happy friend	the littlest one	free
Thor's stone	prince	dark-haired
unafraid, warrior	an artist	arrow, promise
wanderer, stranger	eagle	dragon
guide	protects the land and forest	January child
intellectual	this one will be rich	enjoy cleanness
blessed	he loves the city	God is salvation
handsome, upright	shaggy, hairy	clever, first
he is a leader	facing East	studious, diligent
spear	courageous	straight tree
ruler	exalted, a prince	forever hope
powerful in battle	castle defender	unbribable
king of the earth	enforces peace	stronger than iron

Figure 3.2.
Meanings of Female Names

limit	the sea	white, fair
devoted to Krishna	precious jewel	evening star
rainbow	to be wondered at	the sun
chant	like a kitten	music, song
moon woman	memory	she is trustworthy
the ensnarer	wise	true beauty
dazzling, glorious	strange	obedient child
ruling battlemaid	elegant, beauty	truth
helper	morning rose	my fortune is good
refuge	pretty	born at night
a worker	delicate, smart	moonlight
pure	summit	love
queenly	hesitation	virtue, order
famous	dusky, dark	light of my life
from the seashore	good-looking	contented
happy	cheerful	strong
healing	perfection	tranquillity
life	white wave	merciful

them reimagine themselves as they'd like to be seen. After selecting the meanings (Figures 3.1 and 3.2), they may match them to the original names and origins (Figures 3.3 and 3.4; information is from Asante 1991; Chen 1996; Fujioka 1996; Guralnik 1970; Hook 1983; Mead Johnson 1989; Omar 1996; Sharma 1996; and Turner 1991). Ask students to share whether the sound of their new names met their expectations. Do any of those names convey the designated meaning to us? They did to someone, long, long ago.

Figure 3.3.
Meanings and Origins of
Male Names

one born at night	*Mugeta/African*	protects land/forest	*Karume/African*
drummer	*Tab/Spanish Arabic*	this one will be rich	*Kiambu/African*
bright, noble	*Albert/Germanic*	he loves the city	*Dedan/African*
poet	*Teague/Celtic*	shaggy, hairy	*Esau/biblical*
white hawk	*Gavin/Scottish*	facing East	*Mian Tong/Chinese*
happy friend	*Edwin/Old English*	courageous	*Tracey/Anglo-Saxon*
Thor's stone	*Thurston/Scandinavian*	exalted, a prince	*Zebulun/biblical*
unafraid, warrior	*Harold/Teutonic*	castle defender	*Carnell/English*
wanderer, stranger	*Peregrine/Latin*	enforces peace	*Casimir/Slavic*
guide	*Wyatt/Old French*	a musician	*Kenyatta/African*
intellectual	*Hugo/Teutonic*	fire and wood	*Huo Mu/Chinese*
blessed	*Benedict/Latin*	an apprentice	*Prentice/Latin*
handsome, upright	*Jin/Chinese*	peaceful ruler	*Frederic/German*
he is a leader	*Abeid/African*	fair-haired	*Gannon/Gaelic Irish*
spear	*Gerald/Old High German*	free	*Frank/French*
ruler	*Xerxes/Persian*	dark-haired	*Colbert/French*
powerful in battle	*Caelan/Gaelic Irish*	arrow, promise	*Chiko/Japanese*
king of the earth	*Bhupender/Hindi*	dragon	*Drakon/Greek*
storyteller	*Jojo/African*	January child	*Jarek/Polish*
cowherd, cowboy	*Calvert/English*	enjoy cleanness	*Joeben/Japanese*
singer	*Cantrell/Latin*	God is salvation	*Elisha/Hebrew*
royalty	*Ting/Chinese*	clever, first	*Kenichi/Japanese*
brightest in family	*Kuldeep/Hindi*	studious, diligent	*Tsutom/Japanese*
the littlest one	*Chotu/Hindi*	straight tree	*Naoka/Japanese*
prince	*Kumar/Hindi*	forever hope	*Hisashi/Japanese*
an artist	*Oding/African*	unbribable	*Lian/Chinese*
eagle	*Ying/Chinese*	stronger than iron	*Trahem/Celtic*

Figure 3.4.
Meanings and Origins of
Female Names

limit	*Seema/Hindi*	pretty	*Mei Kui/Chinese*
devoted to Krishna	*Meera/Hindi*	delicate, smart	*Hsiuo/Chinese*
rainbow	*Hong/Japanese*	summit	*Marisa/biblical*
chant	*Yin/Japanese*	hesitation	*Kali/Hawaiian*
moon woman	*Yue Er/Chinese*	dusky, dark	*Kerry/Irish*
the ensnarer	*Becky/Hebrew*	good-looking	*Kiley/Irish*
dazzling, glorious	*Blenda/Old High German*	cheerful	*Hilary/Latin*
ruling battlemaid	*Bertilde/Teutonic*	perfection	*Kamille/Arabic*
helper	*Alexis/Greek*	white wave	*Jennifer/Old Welsh*
refuge	*Avice/Latin*	white, fair	*Gwyn/Celtic*
a worker	*Amelia/Teutonic*	evening star	*Hesper/Greek*
pure	*Agnes/Greek*	the sun	*Kalinda/Sanscrit*
queenly	*Darice/Persian*	music, song	*Melody/Greek*
famous	*Cleo/Greek*	she is trustworthy	*Amina/E. African*
from the seashore	*Delora/Latin*	true beauty	*Mayumi/Japanese*
happy	*Aida/Italian*	obedient child	*Junko/Japanese*
healing	*Althea/Greek*	truth	*Mari/Japanese*
life	*Ashia/E. African*	my fortune is good	*Bahati/E. African*
the sea	*Kai/Hawaiian*	born at night	*Chausika/E. African*
precious jewel	*Cara/Vietnamese*	moonlight	*Chandi/Hindi*
to be wondered at	*Miranda/Latin*	love	*Ai/Chinese*
like a kitten	*Sanura/Swahili*	virtue, order	*Lun/Chinese*
memory	*Una/Hopi*	light of my life	*Nurhayati/Arabic*
wise	*Velda/Teutonic*	contented	*Radhiah/Arabic*
strange	*Miranda/Latin*	strong	*Azizah/Arabic*
elegant, beauty	*Masami/Japanese*	tranquillity	*Sakinah/Arabic*
morning rose	*Hsiao/Chinese*	merciful	*Rahimah/Arabic*

Activity 3:
Naming Traditions

In the book *Knots on a Counting Rope,* an Indian boy and his grandfather relive the boy's birth and naming. Their conversation is represented as alternating verses, as the boy prompts his grandfather, who retells the story. At first, it seemed the baby would die. Then the grandfather carried the baby outside, where two great blue horses galloped up to him and stopped, looking at the baby. When the infant raised his arms to the horses, Grandfather saw it as a sign that the great blue horses had given him the strength to live. As with many retold family tales, the child joins in to help his grandfather:

> And you named me
> Boy-Strength-of-Blue-Horses.
>
> > It is a strong name.
>
> Did I need a strong name,
> Grandfather?
>
> > All children need a strong name
> > to help them grow strong.
>
> (Martin and Archambault 1987, 9–13)

Native Americans traditionally do not name babies at birth. Names come to represent characteristics of or incidents that happen to the person. Names change with the person. Two movie titles with Native American names come immediately to mind, *The Man Who Loved Cat Dancing* (MGM 1973) and *Dances with Wolves* (TIG Productions, Inc. 1990). "Cat Dancing" was the name of a Native American woman whom we can imagine as agile and graceful; "Dances with Wolves" was what John Dunbar (played by Kevin Costner) was doing when the Sioux named him. "A name meant a number of different things and was changed all the time. A boy might be called 'Boy' for five or six years, then be called 'Fleeing Feet of the Prairie' after he shot his first animal. A girl who learned to weave when she was very young might be called 'Nimble Fingers' for a period of time" (Wolfson 1986, 5). In *Dances with Wolves,* Stands-with-a-Fist relates how she was given her name after she became angry and hit an older woman who had been tormenting her. No one called her insulting names after she stood up for herself.

Sometimes, however, meanings are misconstrued in moving between language systems and cultures. "'Stinking-saddle blanket,' the name of a Kiowa chief, is an accurate enough translation of the original but gives a misleading impression. We think only of an unpleasant smell and assume the name is insulting. His own tribesmen knew that the name referred honorably to his being on the warpath so often that he had no time to change his saddle blanket" (Wolfson 1986, 71).

There is a lesson for us in this naming tradition. People do not remain in stasis. As we move through life, our styles and tastes change. We evolve and grow. The nickname we were called as a toddler may not fit us as a young adult. Students may enjoy trying to rename themselves by singling out a characteristic or incident in their lives or by finding a name that fits them now, such as "Skateboarder," "One-Who-Tells-Puns," or "Keyboard Player." In reimagining themselves, they may also want to give themselves a "future" nickname reflecting where they'd like to be in a few years.

**Activity 4:
Name That Pun**

Part of the fun of being a lover of language is in playing games with words. Students may enjoy making name puns, in the tradition of making the name fit the person. The following puns are based on appearance or on professional or personality traits: Anne Teak (for an old woman or dealer in antiques), Eric Nidd (for a spider-lover or arachnid-phile), Howie Smells (for a perfume salesman), and Anita Break (for a student with writer's block).

Trying It Out

**Revisiting
the Self**

Journal writing is not the solitary experience it may seem to be. It is a communicative act, involving not only the immediate conversation of introspection but also communications among the different selves we are at different times. When we express deeply felt emotions, whether happy or painful, we are speaking to a future self who, as a reader, will be in a different mood and have a broader perspective on events that may be affecting us intensely today. That is, as writers today and readers tomorrow, we are our own historians, developing the tapestry that emerges from separate events.

Mallon (1984), in his book about diaries, shares some of his own journal entries, which, over the years, were written for the audience of his own future self. When he looks back, he can compare his experiences and mental states at different times, making contact once again with the person he used to be. Just before Christmas in 1973, for example, he was in a dark mood and compared himself to a "computer which eats the cards and spews forth no print-out," accomplishing "[n]o product. No process" (xi). Less than a month later, however, he was ecstatically watching the snow as "each filament of bare branch is frosted . . . splendid lattices stretching under the lamps. . . . No, a thousand years would not be enough to watch this" (xii).

In rereading these passages, Mallon is glad he wrote both down. He looks back upon himself as another person, seeing "someone who, while he may not have achieved every dream, got what he was so bitter about missing" (xiii). Even in two short passages, a narrative begins to unfold, with a plot and main character.

In a similar vein, one of the present authors, a sporadic journal keeper, found a passage written in the darkness before the dawn of New Year's Day after a flight from Indiana to her sister's home in Coos Bay, Oregon:

> I have passed over the land, back and forth, so many times now that it seems natural to think of cities lying 35,000 feet below, sparkling lights at the bottom of the long darkness like stars fallen in a well, or the branching curves of mountains carved in snow, so cold and empty I feel I should fall into them.
>
> And yes, I am here again, in this house, and in a night that has awakened me, thrown me out of an empty bed, for I know the night with its windy rain at this hour only too well.
>
> Step by step we follow a strange path. If any have passed before us, it has been so long ago that no sign of their lives remain now. The wind has carried away their scent, and the restless growth of the earth has covered their footsteps and whatever else they might have left behind. They are long gone, and the path is ours only, so new to us and the earth that we see what no one else has seen. The wind is what is alive. It draws around us, speaking in a low voice, pushing us backward and forward but never still, changing us as it does everything. We will never be done changing or traveling as long as the wind whips us and howls in our ears. Those who are safe in their beds may sleep, but we cannot stop moving while we are out here, listening for a lull, then climbing onwards, mountain after mountain in the hard snow, our footsteps swallowed behind us in the shifting snow so that, even if our presence on this earth were known to others, we would never be found. (Pugh 1985)

That is the somber, philosophical mood of the habitual insomniac, reflecting on the cosmic scene and mortality. But during the day, it seems, she passed her time waiting in checkout lines by reading the headlines of supermarket tabloids. Here is a list of headlines, remembered or invented, she wrote down in her next entry:

> Boy, 2, Turns into a Woman Overnight
>
> Scientists Bringing Dead Corpses Back to Life
>
> Woman, Age 133, Keeps Alive and Well on Cactus Wine
>
> Dead Babies Smuggle Heroin into U.S.
>
> Forty-pound Tabby Eats Only Vegetables and Beer
>
> Two-headed Man Dies at Age 23
>
> Giant Crocodile Kills 47 Bathers
>
> Woman Gives Birth to 50-Pound Baby
>
> Look Years Younger with Orange Juice
>
> Lose 15 Pounds with Green Peppers

(Pugh 1986)

Like Mallon's juxtaposition, these two passages provide a framework for a story to be re-created from the past, a story that otherwise would no doubt be lost in the jungles of memory. Feelings that might have seemed trivial, exaggerated, or maudlin when they occurred, and even embarrass us when we write about them, are like objects that pass from being common items to valuable antiques because they represent all that we have of an earlier time.

You may wish to read aloud such material—from these excerpts, from Mallon's book, or from your own journals—and ask students to think about the metaphors the writers use. Why, for example, does Mallon compare himself to a computer that eats cards but produces no printout? ("Eating cards" may indeed be a metaphor with no grounding for your students, or even for you, so you will have to refresh your knowledge of computing in the early 1960s and 1970s when stacks of punched cards were fed into large, data-crunching machines.) What about his description of the snow on the branches in January, a quite different metaphor from the one he used a few weeks earlier?

In the Pugh passage above, how does the writer weave together many different images of winter weather into a complex metaphor for the human experience? The wind, especially, is central, suggesting that on that coastal December night it might literally have been whipping through the trees and around the eaves of the house. What about the list of amazing headlines? Are these also metaphorical in some way? What fears, hopes, and fascinations of modern life do they reveal? How would they compare to a similar collection of headlines gathered today?

Ask students to imagine themselves in five, ten, or fifteen years, picking up a diary or letter written by themselves today. What experiences and feelings do they now think are most important to explain their present to their future selves? Students may be interested in trying to keep a diary over a period of time—one week to a semester or grading period. Or they may wish to write a letter to their future selves to be opened at the specified time. This can be done by sealing an envelope with the date on it and even having the teacher arrange to mail these letters to them at the time. Other arrangements might be to have friends or relatives keep the envelope until the specified time, or to hide it away oneself. What is important is for the writer to make a strong, imaginative effort to convey his or her immediate feelings to a distant but surely empathetic reader—one's own self, matured and seasoned with time.

II Multiple Perspectives: Metaphors and New Outlooks

The metaphor is invested with the extraordinary power of invoking multiple perspectives. By shifting focus from the central to the peripheral limits of language, metaphors can jockey around established categories and rule-governing procedures to allow new saliencies to arise. By dislodging us from fixed conceptual schemes, metaphors are primed for helping us place our impressions into newly fashioned units of meaning.

Paul G. Muscari, "The Metaphor in Science and in the Science Classroom"

4 Experiencing Other Lives

[I]f you walk the footsteps of a stranger
You'll learn things you never knew you never knew.

Alan Menken and Stephen Schwartz, "Colors of the Wind"

Perspective in representational art is lines drawn on paper to give us depth perception. In language it is much the same. We use words as lines from which we draw meaning. The art of our imagery can be clear and sharp or abstract and fanciful. Metaphor is a means by which we derive depth of meaning in our communication and writing. When we view and assess another's work of art—just as we make judgments on another's writing—we bring our own experience and viewpoint to whatever we encounter.

We can meet different points of view and try them on, but we can also orient ourselves from different points of reference. Through metaphors, we confront references such as time, mythology, religion, change, fashion, and superstition. The goal is to go beyond the opinions of self and others to subtler and more profound places with imagery so deeply embedded in our personal and cultural consciousness as to be taken for granted. The aim is not just to experience other lives, but to reexperience aspects of our own lives, so familiar that we have become inured to them. We no longer see what is below the surface of the language in our lives until we cast our net in that direction and hold our catch into the light for scrutiny.

With our language explorations, we continually add ways of knowing our world. Other cultures give us fresh outlooks and a means of gaining understanding. We take an unfamiliar image and relate it to what we know. We challenge ourselves by trying to make meaning out of the unknown until we can relate it to the known. Questions, curiosity, our arguments, and the power of our reasoning are the tools that can help in understanding language and the rich ideas other cultures offer in their traditions and imagery. By moving one step, we can change our perspective.

Trying It Out

Persona Writing

Consciously projecting oneself into perspectives and experiences quite different from one's own enhances both empathy and critical thinking. Empathy is the essential base of ethical and moral development. Critical thinking involves the ability to understand complex issues from multiple viewpoints and to realize that, as Richard Paul (1985) has argued, knowledge in any domain develops through reasoning within different and even conflicting frames of reference. Empathy and critical thinking are also pillars of cross-cultural understanding and tolerance. Reading literature and writing expressively are excellent means of developing these qualities.

One way of transcending ordinary experience through literature is *persona writing,* or writing from the perspective of a character chosen to illustrate a viewpoint or experience quite different from one's own. Projection is the tendency to interpret the behavior of others in terms of one's own personality, to project one's own thoughts and feelings onto the actions (or thoughts and feelings) of another. We often seek connections in others, relating in terms of "it takes one to know one." Persona writing can help students discover the metaphorical relationships they have with others.

The more students can move into the minds of characters with whom they are not initially inclined to feel sympathy, the more they are likely to develop the "depth perception" of human issues and relationships that is characteristic of those we consider wise. Students can take characters beyond the narrative of the story as written and collaboratively construct the futures of a number of interacting characters, taking stories beyond the confines of one fiction into fictions of their own. As with themes of imitation and reflection, students experience the enlightenment of stepping out of their customary identities and seeing themselves from the perspective of someone who may not know them well or even view them favorably.

Activity 1: Persona in Practice

- Students can choose characters from novels or stories who seem very different from themselves and then write from the perspective of that character as a way of exploring an alternative or conflicting viewpoint. Their writing can take the form of a narrative, a dramatic monologue, a mock journal entry, or a letter.

- A variation of persona writing could entail selecting a character that is the least sympathetic to oneself and using that character to look at oneself through new eyes. Students can also trade personas to change perspective more than once.

Activity 2: Assuming a Persona from Literature

J. Boreen (1975) wrote "Salmon Swims Up the River," the retelling of a legend told by the Indians of Northwest America. It is a metaphor-laden short story in which Old Man gives a life lesson to Young Man. In preparing to read or listen to this story, students may be asked to consider the greatest thing they have ever received from another person and the greatest thing they have ever given. How much of life would they say is giving, and how much is receiving? Do some people give more while others receive more?

Salmon Swims Up the River

Young Man walked along the grey gravel beach, looking down at the wet rocks on which he trod. Each one was duller and less interesting than the last. They seemed to hinder his steps, but he didn't care.

He was under the power of the twin demons: sadness and anger. They had linked their arms around his shoulders and were holding his head down so that all he could see was the grey gravel at his feet. As he walked, the ocean monotonously washed the small rocks back and forth, unheard by Young Man, but covering all other sound.

Old Man was sitting on a log higher on the beach where he kept his boat this time of year. He was watching the sea moving, the birds diving for fish, a chipmunk looking for tasty bits among the drift. He saw Young Man trudging along the beach. He saw the twin demons with their arms around Young Man's shoulders.

He wasn't surprised. He saw this often among the people. He knew what he should do. He threw a stick at Young Man, knowing his call would not be heard.

Young Man jumped as the stick landed at his feet. He looked around through the eyes of the anger demon. When he saw Old Man, the anger demon subsided to its original sullen position, and Young Man went to Old Man and sat at his side. He knew and respected Old Man. He knew he would receive help here. Perhaps this was where he had been going.

Old Man didn't say anything. He just smiled his greeting at Young Man and looked out at the sea. An otter was swimming in the surf. He had been following Young Man as he trudged along the beach. Young Man now saw him for the first time. The twin demons flinched.

Further out to sea, the gulls were feeding on herring. When Young Man saw this, the twin demons loosened their grip. When Young Man looked up and saw a pair of eagles soaring overhead, the twin demons looked at each other, shrugged, released Young Man from their hold and went away to find someone else to carry them around for awhile.

Young Man looked at Old Man and smiled sheepishly. Old Man was looking at him with his smile. Young Man looked to the sea and said, "All day yesterday I lay in the mud under my friend's car helping him fix it. This afternoon he went to town to go to a dance. I wanted to go, and he knew it. But he didn't offer to take me. He went without saying anything."

Old Man shrugged and smiled. "Life is like that sometimes," he said. Young Man knew that he would say that. He always did. But Young Man didn't mind. It was Old Man's way.

They sat in silence for awhile, then Old Man began his story:

* * *

Salmon was swimming about in the sea, going from one feast to the next, visiting with all his friends, enjoying life. He had been doing this for so long that he thought that was all there was to do. Then one day, after a particularly big feast and fine time visiting, he found himself at the mouth of a river. He tasted the fresh water and it seemed to beckon him to swim upstream.

For the first time in his life Salmon sensed that there was more to life than swimming for the joy of it, feasting until he was gorged, and visiting until he had nothing more to say. He decided to swim up the stream and find out what was up there that called him so mysteriously. He hadn't gone far before he saw some people on the bank.

These people were thin and tired-looking and they called out to him. Salmon swam closer so he could hear what they said. An old man waded into the water up to his knees and said to Salmon, "Salmon, my people are hungry. They have had a very hard winter, eating mostly roots and mussels. But I had a dream last night that you were coming and would feed the people."

Salmon felt very sad, seeing these people. He said to the old man, "I would like to help you but I have nothing to give. I catch my food in my mouth and swallow it right away."

The old man didn't seem disappointed at this. He said, "Yes, I know this. But in my dream you came and gave us one of your sides to eat."

Salmon was very frightened when he heard this and swam back to the middle of the river. He looked back and the old man was standing in the water, with his people shivering on the bank. Salmon felt very sad, but he was afraid to give the people one of his sides.

Then he felt something touch him, and looked down and saw a crayfish on the bottom of the river. Crayfish said, "Why are you shaking, Salmon? Are you cold?"

"No," said Salmon. "I am afraid. The people are hungry and want to eat one of my sides."

Crayfish looked very serious and said, "Well, Salmon, you look like you have been eating well and are strong. You can give them one of your sides to eat. You will still have your other side."

Salmon thought about this and decided to do as Crayfish suggested. He swam back to the old man and said, "I am sad to see your people hungry and have decided to give you one of my sides. But you must put me back in the water after you have eaten."

The old man and his people were very happy and did as Salmon asked. When they put him back in the water, Salmon found he couldn't swim quite as fast, but he was happy to see the people full. He left them and swam up the river seeking that which seemed to call him even stronger now.

Soon he came upon a very ragged-looking bear standing in the water. Salmon asked Bear what he was doing in the river and why he looked so ragged. "I am very hungry and tired," Bear said. "I have had nothing but grubs to eat all winter. I am looking for food."

Salmon felt very sad when he heard this, but again he was afraid and swam away from Bear. As he looked back at Bear he felt something touch him. He looked up to see a water ouzel standing on a half-submerged rock in front of him. Ouzel said, "Salmon, one of your sides is missing and you are shaking. Are you sick?"

"No," said Salmon. "I am not sick. I gave my side to the hungry people and I am afraid Bear wants my other side because he is hungry."

Water Ouzel looked very concerned and said, "Well, Salmon, if you are strong and healthy, why don't you give Bear your other side? You will still have your backbone and tail."

Salmon thought about this and decided to do as Ouzel suggested. He swam back to Bear and said, "I have decided to give you my other side, but you must not take more than that." Bear was very happy and did as Salmon said. Salmon found that he could swim fairly well, being evenly balanced now, and felt good to see Bear's coat looking so much better.

Now the call to swim upstream was even stronger and Salmon swam on. He knew that the thing which called him was not far away. But soon he came to a very ruffled heron standing in the river. "Why do you stand in the river looking so bedraggled?" Salmon asked Heron.

"I am looking for something to eat, Salmon," said Heron. "All winter I have had nothing but periwinkles and I am very hungry."

Salmon again became afraid and swam away from Heron. As he looked back he was sad to see Heron so hungry and he felt something touch him. "Salmon," Frog said. "You are shaking and so thin. Are you hungry?"

"No," said Salmon. "I am not hungry. I have given one of my sides to the hungry people and the other side to Bear because he was hungry. Now the heron is hungry, and I am afraid."

Frog looked long at Salmon and finally said, "Well, Salmon, if you are strong and not hungry, why don't you give Heron your stomach?"

Salmon thought about this and decided to do as Frog suggested. He swam back to Heron and said, "I have decided to give you my stomach, but you must leave me my backbone so I can still swim upstream."

Heron was very happy and did as Salmon said. Salmon felt good to see Heron's feathers fill out and found that with his stomach gone he could swim better in the river that was becoming more shallow.

The call of the river was very strong now, and Salmon swam with all his might to find out what it was that beckoned. Soon he came to the source of the river. It was a very still, springfed pool surrounded by huge cedar trees. In the middle of the pool, a very thin otter floated on his back, looking sadly at the sky.

Salmon swam up to the otter and said, "You look so thin and sad, Otter. You must be very hungry."

"Yes," said Otter still looking up at the sky. "I am starving and waiting to die."

Salmon was not afraid this time. He said, "Otter, I am Salmon, and I seem to have been called to this very spot, for there is nowhere else to go. I am sad to see you so hungry. Therefore, you may eat me and live."

Otter turned his head and looked deep into Salmon's eyes, and Salmon was forever.

* * *

As Old Man finished his story, his voice had quavered, not from age, but from the depth of his feelings. The two men sat on the log for a long time, looking out at the sea.

Young Man let the story run through his mind as he savored the warm feeling in his heart and felt the tightness in his throat.

At last he felt he could speak. He turned to Old Man and said, "Thank you for the story. I must go and try to be more like Salmon."

Old Man turned from the sea, and looked deep into Young Man's eyes. He said, "My son, we are all Otter and Salmon. Giving and receiving are the tides of man. As you walk the beach, you will watch the movement of the sea and know its meaning. Go in joy and thankfulness, and know that the sea and the tides are eternal." (34–39)

One theme of the story is that throughout one's life, one must both give and receive. The important thing is to have the proper attitude toward both. Students may wish to discuss what they consider to be the proper attitude toward giving: When should a person give something up for the sake of someone else? What about receiving? What kind of feelings do you have when you receive something from another person? Do you think that attitudes toward giving and receiving differ across cultures?

Students may try assuming the persona of either Old Man or Young Man. What is that persona's response to the story? Or they may wish to imagine another character listening to the story, perhaps Old Woman and Young Woman. How would either of these characters respond to the story? What accounts for differences projected upon these persons or others that students might imagine?

Trying It Out

Bionic You

Bionics is a branch of engineering devoted to designing machines that imitate the senses of animals. By projecting themselves imaginatively and then scientifically into the extraordinary abilities of other species, people have come up with such inventions as airplanes, radar, and cameras. Even when they don't result in new inventions, such projections can open new worlds of understanding.

In their small book *The View from the Oak*, Judith and Herbert Kohl (1977) explore ways in which imagination can guide us into the experience of other creatures. In so doing, we can gain a deep appreciation of the diversity of life on the earth, understand the intricacies of ecological interdependence, and gain new perspectives on the human experience.

The title of the book alludes to the different ways the same ancient oak tree can be experienced by different animals, including owls, foxes, and people. The owl lives in the upper branches, which serve as habitat and observation tower. The fox lives in the root system, which provides both den and escape corridors. And people—well, it depends on who they are and the value they place upon particular trees.

To imagine the life of another species, the authors suggest focusing on three aspects of experiences all living creatures must deal with: space, time, and response. To acquire these new perspectives, of course, we must suspend our own.

The Kohls' book provides glimpses into the sensory apparatus of other animals, often described metaphorically, so that, for example, the owl's fixed eyes with powerful magnifying lenses are "like telescopes mounted on the swivel stand of its head, which can turn 180 degrees in either direction" (106). Other animal perceptual powers require greater stretches of imagination. For instance, rattlesnakes sense through organs that can detect minute shifts in temperature. One would have to imagine using a thermometer rather than sight, hearing, or smell as a major way of distinguishing the nature of the environment.

Since tempo differs so greatly across the experiences of different species, the Kohls suggest imagining a time microscope that alters our experience with time in the same way the regular versions of these instruments alter our experiences with space. Just as a regular microscope allows us to see what normally is too small for our vision to detect, a time microscope would allow us to observe changes normally too quick for our perception, such as the separate movements of a hummingbird's wings, all the steps in a bee's dance, or the full muscular display of a cheetah's run. Each moment would provide a lifetime of details.

The time telescope, on the other hand, would allow us to see what otherwise is too slow for our senses, such as the growth of a tree or the evolution of a star. It would be as though we possessed a new sense, a sort of bionic built-in time-lapse photography apparatus. Now each lifetime would be merely a moment. These imaginary instruments allow us to put our own experience with time in a new perspective so that we can see how ponderously slow we are from the point of view of an insect and how ephemeral from the perspective of a mountain. From these speculations, we can reflect on how important our ways of organizing time—our calendars and our clocks—are to maintain coherence and sanity. Indeed, time sense is an essential aspect of being human.

The Kohls compare a moment in the life of a snail, with its slow tempo, with one in the life of a spider, which has a fast tempo. What is perceptible to the snail is not to the spider, and vice versa. Both have limitations that make them vulnerable to danger in the larger environment. Both can provide the kind of insight into our human experience that is the material of fables. The snail is too slow to pick up the vibrations of the wing of the bird swooping down to eat it. The spider is so responsive that it will scurry into danger at the movement of a single strand of its web.

The following suggestions for imaginative experiences can lead to stories, essays, or other literary experiments or can simply expand awareness of the meaning of life on this planet (or on other planets, if one wishes).

**Activity 1:
Natural
Imagination**

Students may be invited to select any bird and imagine experiencing its life for any time span, from an hour to a year or a lifetime. A bird is a good species to begin with because most birds can fly and many traverse the earth, and yet they may also perceive reality from an extremely ground-level perspective. Students should do some background research to find out about their birds and how they live.

Questions to consider: How would this bird's experience in space be different from ours? How does time or the seasons of life pass for this bird? What does it respond to most vividly in the environment, and how?

A variation would be to widen the scope. Other kinds of animals can be explored in the same way. It might be especially interesting to pick creatures we don't often think about or even have little sympathy for, such as insects. Students may "enjoy" imagining the mindset of a maggot. Or they might be challenged to relate to a cicada nymph that remains underground sucking juice from tree roots for seventeen years before emerging and metamorphosing into an adult. Or they might write from the perspective of an extinct animal, such as a dinosaur, or perhaps one whose existence over-lapped with human life, such as the dodo bird. Another interesting perspective to explore would be that of an animal in danger of becoming extinct today.

Activity 2: Bionic Adolescents

Another possibility students may wish to try in their journals is to imagine being a human with new sensory apparatuses adapted from other species—a bionic person. Their new personas could have sensory hairs, photoelectric cells in places other than their eyes, radar, the biological clock of another species, or the bioluminescence of a firefly. Groups may brainstorm how to use their imaginations and their knowledge of science together.

You might also share with your students selected passages from David Lindsay's *Voyage to Arcturus* (1963), in which the writer imagines beings on another planet who have both sensory organs and experiences different from ours.

Trying It Out

People as Metaphor

In exploring a broader definition of metaphor, comparisons don't have to be limited to one noun compared to other nouns, or nouns to abstract ideas. A person, including his or her occupation, political orientation, religion, philosophy, or any other characteristic that defines who one is, can be thought of metaphorically. By regarding the differences, similarities, or equality between persons, one can perceive how one person can become a metaphor for another. When a toddler throws his first baseball, a grandparent may exclaim that the child is destined to become another Babe Ruth. Knowing the two people compared in the metaphor, one better understands the meta-phor. If one does not grasp the comparison, one can come to know its meaning by searching the lives of the people until one makes the metaphorical connection.

How do writers use "people as metaphor" to make their points? Columnist Mike Leonard (1994) wrote a piece about advertising firms taking a stand against political mudslinging in the November elections ads. An Indianapolis advertising firm was so disgusted by this practice that they issued a disclaimer stating that their firm did not do any negative campaign advertisements. Leonard writes, "The Young & Laramore message, also delivered across the news wire services Wednesday, raised the specter of an unnamed Darth Vader moving across the political landscape and harnessing the power of advertising for the dark side" (C4).

The George Lucas character Darth Vader, from the *Star Wars* trilogy, also intrigued the late mythologist Joseph Campbell. In his book *The Power of Myth* (with Bill Moyers, 1988), Campbell comments that "Darth Vader has not developed his own humanity. He's a robot. He's a bureaucrat, living not in terms of himself but in terms of an imposed system. This is the threat to our lives that we all face today. Is the system going to flatten you out and deny your humanity, or are you going to be able to make use of the system to the attainment of human purposes?" (144). Campbell likened many characters from *Star Wars* to others from hero-quest literature. He uses "people as metaphor" to aid in his own interpretation of the trilogy. Campbell compares Ben Kenobi to a Japanese swordmaster, an old man as adviser. He also suggests a link between Darth Vader and Mephistopheles in Goethe's *Faust*. And Luke Skywalker is similar to legendary dragonslayers Siegfried from Germanic mythology and St. George.

Finding familiarity among others helps us to relate, to make our point. Comparing two people, whether intended as explanation or argument, may double the chance that our meaning will be understood.

Writer Greil Marcus (1993) draws out an extended "people as metaphor" comparison between President Bill Clinton and Elvis Presley. In his article "The Elvis Test" in the *San Francisco Examiner's Image* magazine, Marcus collected many Clinton-as-Presley connections that others have noticed.

> "The statehouse doors open," Perry thought, "and here's Bill—in a white rhinestone jumpsuit! . . . I imagined him stepping to the microphone, that trademark Elvis curl playing around his lips, hinting at once an arrogant faith in his own power and a secret available to all who believed.
>
> . . . The metaphor of Clinton as Elvis is powerful because of a sense that we may be able to catch what we want from this man, what we hope for and what we most fear, if we think of him as Elvis Presley rather than merely as himself. But which Presley? Elvis contained multitudes, he contradicted himself every time he opened his mouth or took a step. (8–9)

Marcus noted that even Bill Clinton's rival George Bush made Clinton-as-Presley comparisons. "'He's been spotted more places than Elvis Presley. . . . I guess you'd say his plan is really Elvis economics,' the president continued: 'America will be checking into the Heartbreak Hotel'" (11).

Activity 1: Crafting Metaphors

To help generate metaphors, students could start with a file of names of different public figures: athletes, world leaders, musicians, authors, and the like. Then they might pick two or more and make comparisons with a variety of professions. For example, if a plumber, painter, paleontologist, or politician (choose one) were being compared to boxer George Foreman, what would the metaphor be? Does the plumber k-o clogged drains? Does the painter have a no-holds-barred style? Perhaps the paleontologist maneuvers within the bounds of the digging site the way a boxer would circle an opponent within the ring. The politician may use hard-hitting words.

Individually or in small groups, students can develop a paragraph or two extending the metaphor. Students can critically evaluate each others' writing for understanding of the nuances of their imagery.

Activity 2: Metaphor Challenge

To delve more deeply in search of a metaphorical-person counterpart, students may be assigned a famous or infamous person or choose their own, either real or fictional. In order to draw out the metaphor, research may be required if the students are not familiar with their assigned individuals. Each student researches his or her person, noting qualities and background. Then, in pairs, students discuss which autobiographical information, characteristics, or other connections might be used to develop a comparison.

There are many powerful figures from mythology and literature reworked in fiction or used to evoke poetic imagery. For example, Narcissus has become a metaphor for vanity, Midas for greed, Hercules for strength, Lady Macbeth for manipulation, Venus for love. Some figures are gender specific: Machiavelli or Svengali are seen as male only; but Medusa, female. Some entail aspects of psychology: madness is embodied in Lewis Carroll's Hatter from *Alice in Wonderland;* a Napoleon complex refers to France's emperor Napoleon Bonaparte, whose thirst for power was said to be a way of compensating for his short stature.

If students have not yet encountered certain personages from literature, this activity can be a means of introduction to some classic literary figures. To further hone the evaluative, comparative skills, try a grab-bag approach. Students or teacher (or both) can generate a list of interesting people and put each name on a slip of paper. Each student draws a name and then teams up with another to see how creative he or she can get with the comparison in this metaphor challenge.

This activity could include historical or contemporary figures, even symbolic figures such as Uncle Sam or the Statue of Liberty. Given the famous poem by Emma Lazarus inscribed on the pedestal of the Statue of Liberty, could a student find a metaphorical-person counterpart in which to flesh out a comparison? Perhaps Mother Theresa comes to mind:

> Give me your tired, your poor,
> Your huddled masses, yearning to breathe free,
> The wretched refuse of your teeming shore,
> Send these, the homeless tempest-tossed to me:
> I lift my lamp beside the golden door.

> (153)

For practice, discuss an example before students begin. How might Lech Walesa be compared to Joan of Arc? Walesa became a leader somewhat against his will in Poland, a country that is 90 percent Catholic. Joan of Arc stirred up political turmoil, historically against her will, and has become a Catholic saint. Possible questions for further discussion: What was the relationship between the church and the individual's rise to power or celebrity? How did each lead the people? What effect did each have on those in power at the time?

Activity 3: Thinking Dialogically about Cultural Metaphors

The idea of a deity incarnate is found in many different religions and in mythology. The Greek god Zeus often took animal form to pursue his amorous affairs and to avoid detection. The idea of people and animals as gods incarnate is an old one. For some, this notion is reality; for others, it is a representation of reality. Use of such a metaphor can be a bridge between myth and reality, but when taken as reality there can be conflict, as highlighted in the following incidents.

In the fall of 1994, pneumonic plague in India spread quickly over hundreds of miles in less than two weeks. Confirmed plague cases numbered in the hundreds. Even though in this modern era, most are aware that plague is spread by rodents, some people in India, according to their religious traditions, protect and feed rats. People started dying of pneumonic plague, spread by rats. Fearful of a growing epidemic, the health officials and others were at odds with the traditional beliefs of the people:

> In Hindu mythology, the elephant-headed god Ganesh is accompanied by a rat whenever he travels. No Hindu worship is complete without an offering to Ganesh and his small companion. . . . The deadly epidemic in this nation of 900 million people has raised concern about rats, which like cows are deified in India. "This nonsense has to stop," said Kolomesh Chandra Dev, a retired government official who has started a neighborhood campaign to kill

rats in New Delhi. "The time has come for people to realize it is either us or the rat." [An opposing view was expressed by a devout Hindu.] "I do trap a rat when I see one in my kitchen, but I can never kill it," Amita Roy, a resident of the Vasant Kunj section of New Delhi said Thursday. "It is a sin to kill the companion of our God." (Associated Press 1994b, A1)

The conflict of freedom of expression, whether in speech or in action, can be debated. In America, Christian Scientists believe illnesses are errors in human consciousness to be dispelled through faith and prayer. Yet when parents do not seek medical intervention for their deathly ill children, it brings the state into conflict with religious practice. Should parents be allowed to follow their religious beliefs, even if those beliefs might mean the death of a child? Should rats be pampered and protected in India, even though they may be carriers of plague? Letting go of the notion of a right or wrong answer, students can take on the different viewpoints of people unlike themselves to achieve understanding, if not consensus. Being able to represent both sides in an argument sharpens reasoning skills.

Another recent event in the news is intriguing because it contains multiple metaphors: it combines art as visual metaphor, people as metaphor, and people-as-animals metaphor. It also presents a conflict—an artist's right to express himself versus the rights of animals. French authorities shut down an artist's show in which spiders, snakes, scorpions, and toads were to eat each other in a metaphorical statement on humankind's dog-eat-dog world. The animal rights activists who protested the exhibition also used a visual metaphor, wearing colorful butterfly masks, to get their point across. The article may help spark discussion about persona and metaphor:

> It may be the law of the jungle, but that doesn't make it art, said French authorities who shut down an avant-garde show of spiders, snakes, scorpions and toads devouring each other.
>
> Chinese artist Huang Yon Ping put the caged creatures on display at the Georges Pompidou Center, where they were to eat each other in a statement on humankind's dog-eat-dog world.
>
> The city's veterinary services and police banned the work on Tuesday, citing laws forbidding cruelty to animals and unauthorized animal shows. The Chinese artist's creation now features photos of the animals.
>
> The ban was a victory for the National Society for the Defense of Animals, which had taken the center to court.
>
> The exhibition, "Hors Limites, l'art et la vie, 1952–1994" (Beyond Limits, art and life), opened Tuesday at the Pompidou Center, a showcase for contemporary art.

Dozens of animal rights crusaders protested outside the center wearing white ponchos, their faces covered by colorful butterfly masks.

The center stood behind its aesthetic choices.

"Rumors have exaggerated the violence of the work, which is supposed to appear as a metaphor of humanity," curator Jean de Loisy was quoted as telling the *Figaro* newspaper. (Associated Press 1994a, A7)

Live reptiles, arachnids, and amphibians are representative of the "dog-eat-dog" animal metaphor, which is further representative because it is used to describe human behavior. The protesters embody animals, donning insect personas to express themselves. Mimicry as a theme in performance art is evident in the work and in the protest. The title of the exhibition tweaks us with its multiple perspectives. Many layers of metaphor can be peeled off and examined in the article as well as in the issue it raises.

Keep in mind the people-as-animals and animals-as-people metaphor from the above article while reading the piece below. The writer projects her idea of self into dogs; they embody her identity as she chooses a puppy from an animal shelter:

I would only consider a King, a loyal Robert or a stalwart Max. No Duchess, or Mitzi or inferior Fifi would be coming home with me. A male dog was more desirable, less capricious than the females, less expensive when fixing control over future generations of animal overpopulation. But King was a tyrant who growled his litter mates out of the way, and Robert had far too great an interest in my leg than I considered proper for a first encounter. Max was an enormous glutton who raided the others' food supplies. It was the gentle female, second smallest of her siblings, who let the others scramble out ahead of her and had to be coaxed from the pen. She then trotted straight for the newspapers set out on the cement floor and did the admirable, the acceptable, that which was expected of her. Did I really long for in a pet a gender-related aggressor, or one more like myself, a compromiser, a potential high-achiever, perhaps a wry observer of the human condition? And so Neelix came home with me; "Neelix" is what happens when you let your children name the puppy. (Davis 1995)

The metaphors as well as some of the thought-provoking issues raised in the excerpts above are worth discussing. Contrast ideas from two articles. In the art exhibit, the animals-as-people metaphor both represents reality and is a physical reality to those who experienced it. In the other, the animals-as-people metaphor is the writer's device. It is a connection we read; we experience the author giving dogs human qualities as a metaphor for self. Is the pen mightier than the sword? Would witnessing the devouring of live creatures be a more powerful experience than reading about it? Would every witness experience the metaphor that the artist or writer intended?

As a further activity, the class can collect and compile examples of people as metaphor from media sources.

Change

The times of drastic change are times of passions. We can never be fit and ready for that which is wholly new. We have to adjust ourselves and every radical adjustment is a crisis in self-esteem: we undergo a test; we have to prove ourselves. A population subjected to drastic change is, thus, a population of misfits, and misfits live and breathe in an atmosphere of passion.

Bruce Lee, *Tao of Jeet Kune Do*

The Greek philosopher Heraclitus, the French statesman Disraeli, the Scottish poet Robert Burns, and many others have echoed the paradox that change—what Edmund Burke called the most powerful law of nature—is the only constant in the universe. And certainly change is the most salient feature of experience. Whatever we touch, we change. We change a book by reading it, change a story by telling it, and change a problem by solving it. Whenever we make something new out of what is at hand, compare and find the likeness of one thing in another, look at phenomena from different perspectives, or use language to say something new, we are experiencing change and drawing meaning from it. Change is a kind of energy by which our minds grow.

We use our experiences to help us define and measure the changes in our lives, from the passage of time to the rites of passage. Metaphors not only express transitions imaginatively but also lead us to insight about our changes. We may retreat from changes like a turtle into its shell. We may open windows when the doors are closed. We may explore new situations as if releasing a grip on a swinging rope above a river.

The power of metaphor to lead us to insight is a truth known best, perhaps, by the writer and the scientist. Consider the following quotations, the first by the author of *A Gift So Rare* and the second by the director of Bell Laboratories' Quantum Electronics Research:

> The world within a world, where lives repeat
> Their own small cycles, infinite, complete . . .
>
> (Marshall 1969, 17)

> The atoms become like a moth, seeking out the region of higher laser intensity.
>
> (Stephen Chu 1986 in Simpson 1988, 138)

By looking at the world around us, we can see metaphors for understanding the nature of life. That understanding is embodied in the changes that make up life in the physical world. Conceptualizing the vastness of time is possible when we see rock formations that began eons ago. Appreciating time's transitory qualities is possible when we see a blossom fade in the three o'clock summer sun. We can see the interconnectedness of the web of life in this line from nineteenth-century poet Francis Thompson: "One could not pluck a flower without troubling a star" (in Eiseley 1957, 63).

Change through growth is one of the fundamental natural metaphors of life. In comparing human stages to those of the biological world, William Bridges (1980) notes that both involve periodic accelerations and transformations: "Things go slowly for a time and nothing seems to change—until suddenly the eggshell cracks, the branch blossoms, the tadpole's tail shrinks away, the leaf falls, the bird molts, the hibernation begins" (5).

The story of Krakatau, the Indonesian island that disappears and reappears periodically, provides us with another metaphor for growth and the aging process. Through volcanic action, Krakatau undergoes a transformation. Its rapid disappearance and slow reappearance is a regeneration image. As Krakatau "grows" over fifty to a hundred years, it progresses from "Baby Krakatau" (another organic image) to "adult" size. Thus, Krakatau provides us with a second avenue for understanding tangible, physical change, in addition to the intangible change involved in aging.

When human beings inadvertently or intentionally affect the balance of nature, unnatural change may result. Decades of abuse of our air, water, and land because of industrial practices and unchecked consumption have resulted in nightmarish pollution problems. Ecological activism on behalf of the earth has been a hallmark of the late twentieth century. The power of metaphor to focus attention on the pressing concerns of our planet is demonstrated in Rachel Carson's *Silent Spring* (1962). She assails the indiscriminate use of pesticides and fertilizers: "As crude a weapon as a cave man's club, the chemical barrage has been hurled against the fabric of life" (368). Our clumsy machinations with the balance of the natural world is expressed in another metaphor by Erwin Chargaff (1969), professor of biological chemistry at Columbia University, who complains that "we manipulate nature as if we were stuffing an Alsatian goose. We create new forms of energy; we make new elements; we kill crops; we wash brains. I can hear them in the dark sharpening their lasers" (in Simpson 1988, 138). Our manipulations often have disastrous results, as Jacques Cousteau asserted to the 1971 House Committee on Science and Astronautics when he called the sea "the universal sewer" (in Simpson 1988, 138).

Natural and Unnatural Patterns for Understanding Change

Activity 1: Natural Frameworks for Transition

Our lives have many stages. Periods of transition are what connect one stage to the next. We often describe these changes in terms of the changes we see in the world around us.

Using metaphors from nature extends our thinking from ourselves to our connection with the earth. Students may wish to consider the life experiences they have had that remind them of these metaphorical stages, perhaps choosing one to expand on in their journals.

Water Imagery

A fork in a river

A change in course or speed of a stream—rushing or stagnating

A watershed

Tide: ebb, flow

Wave action: lap, roll, crash, pound, churn

Weather Imagery

A storm: from raindrop to rainbow; precipitation cycle

Blizzard

Eye of a storm

High pressure fronts, lows

Jet stream, changes in direction, zephyr, breeze, hurricane

Seasonal Imagery

Seasons, especially the change from one to another

Sunrise, sunset

The drying of a wet-weather spring

Fallow period: barren surface with replenishing, life-giving nutrients below ground

Leaf-fall

Plant growth: rooting, budding, blooming, seeking sun, setting fruit, ripening, dispersing seeds

Activity 2: Metaphors for Understanding Unnatural Change

Small groups may be interested in selecting an environmental issue that affects the community or the world. Since the earth is vast and has no physical borders, a concern in another hemisphere could have a local effect. People in the United States have worried about the spread of the Mediterranean fruit fly, the killer bee, and the zebra mussel—problems that originated elsewhere. It has been said that the motion of a butterfly's wings can change the weather in another part of the world.

Natural connections are inherent in the way we think of our environment. Metaphors such as *web of life, food chain,* and *circle of life* express this thought. We cannot sever the actions of humans from the effect on the earth. It is the disruption of the natural rhythms of the earth that can cause unnatural change.

Wendell Berry, poet and environmental activist, "suggested purging our vocabularies of words that reflect black-and-white, dualistic thinking: words like 'spiritual' and 'physical' that suggest our spirits are separate from our bodies. Even the word 'environment,' he said, implies a false division between us and the air, water, soil, plants and animals around us" (in Aprile 1994a, H01).

Students can try devising metaphors to illustrate the nature or severity of the problem they chose. After discussing their metaphors and seeking responses from their peers, they can select one to develop into a convincing poster, video, editorial, or other persuasive message. Your local cable television has a public access channel that could be used to publicize students' work and air their environmental messages.

Trying It Out

Changing Your Mind about Superstitions

Are you superstitious about walking under a ladder? having a black cat cross your path? getting a room on the thirteenth floor of a hotel? If you are, then you are engaging in a ritualistic behavior that has no basis in fact, according to dictionary definitions. You would also be sharing that behavior with people through the centuries, who probably passed their superstitious traditions to you.

How did superstitions start? They may have begun through the linking of circumstances to explain events that were beyond people's control or understanding. Life was seen as a series of good and bad luck—fate controlled our lives.

When people changed their behavior from their set patterns, they invited bad luck; when they *didn't* change their behavior, they also invited bad luck. Perhaps that's where the saying "damned if you do, damned if you don't" has its roots. Change is associated with a number of interesting superstitions (Opie and Tatem 1989). Changing the name of a boat, for example, spelled doom—probably because people were always looking for explanations of tragedies and because they could point to boats whose names had been changed and which later sank. On the other hand, it was okay to change the boat's crew. In fact, it was recommended to do so once a year, for luck. To stay with the same fishing companions invited a dry year.

Changing one's chair during a streak of bad luck at cards is another superstitious behavior. Changing one's doors was thought to be a way of averting misfortune of a more general nature. Perhaps that explains the side-by-side doors one often sees in pictures of older homes. People actually blocked an existing door and opened another nearby.

Changing the way a door is hung was once thought to keep out ghosts. So was changing the route home from a funeral. If you went home the same way you came, the ghost was likely to follow you back there. In Sussex, England, it is still customary for a friend of the family to rearrange the furniture in the bedroom of the deceased. This practice is based on the superstitious belief that with the room changed, the ghost wouldn't recognize his old home and would therefore leave the family in peace.

Change has also been associated with weddings. People were not to go home from a wedding the same way they came, a saying that sometimes crops up today. It's likely that you've also heard that it's bad luck to see one's future mate on the day of the wedding before the ceremony. That one may have started when a prospective bride or groom changed her or his mind about getting married, based on a pre-ceremony encounter. Even changing one's name at marriage had its own rhyme:

To change the name and not the letter
Is to marry for worse and not for better.

In other words, Miss Smith would not have wanted to marry any man whose last name began with an *S*, if she were superstitious. That suggests interesting possibilities for the future, now that it is becoming more common for women to retain their surnames at marriage. Will the superstition be completely obliterated or will it be reversed, making it unlucky to change one's name, period?

Activity 1: Oral History Project

Your students may find it both educational and fun to collect superstitions that family (especially older members) and neighbors remember hearing. Folk wisdom containing superstition was passed down in the oral tradition. Consulting almanacs and books on customs and folklore will also help students frame questions that will jog memories. For example, they might ask people if they recall rhymes that would help to remember superstitions, such as

> Red sky at morning, sailors take warning.
> Red sky at night, sailors delight.

or

> See a pin and pick it up,
> All the day you'll have good luck.
> See a pin and let it lay,
> You'll have bad luck all that day.

Your local library will have handbooks on conducting oral history projects. The Foxfire book series provides an excellent model of how high school students have collected mountain folklore and published it for what has become an international audience. If students decide to tape and transcribe their interviews, it is helpful to make notes during the interview anyway, as machines have a way of malfunctioning at critical moments.

To publish their findings, the students might compile a book of superstitions that are familiar to your community, perhaps even researching the origins of these beliefs to include in their explanations. Copies of the books should be placed in the school and community libraries, as well as with the local historical society.

Activity 2: Measuring Superstitiousness

How superstitious are we? What superstitions, if any, have we ever allowed to change our normal routines? A class sharing-session on superstitions we follow may set the stage for the survey project described below. Will your students have heard of crossing one's fingers behind one's back when telling a fib? Do they wear the same dirty shirt for every game they compete in, or throw salt over their shoulders when they accidentally spill the shaker? Are there any superstitious behaviors that they have outgrown? What led them to give up those superstitions?

This discussion may lead to interest in pursuing a survey of peers, family, neighbors, or heroes and leaders of our society. (The hunt for celebrity addresses can be a learning experience in itself. Students will learn to associate names with positions such as secretary of state, city comptroller, or attorney general. Don't overlook the possibility of contacting people over the Internet.) The class may want to ask such questions as

- What superstitions do you recall being told?
- What kinds of superstitions, if any, did you follow as a child?

- Have you ever given up believing in a superstition? Why?

- What superstitious behaviors do you follow now? (For example, do you have a lucky piece of clothing that you wear on important days? Do you feel uncomfortable getting a room that has a "13" in the number? Do you read your horoscope regularly?)

- Do you think people of this generation are

    —more superstitious than people used to be?

    —about as superstitious as they used to be?

    —less superstitious than they used to be?

- How would you rate your superstitiousness today?

    5   I am extremely superstitious.

    4   I am somewhat superstitious.

    3   I occasionally follow superstitions.

    2   I almost never engage in superstitious behavior.

    1   I am not at all superstitious.

Students may develop graphs and charts to summarize the findings from their superstition survey. Individuals or groups may write articles about the survey results and submit them, along with their charts, to the school or community newspaper for possible publication. Quotes from the responses from the celebrities are certain to capture readers' attention.

**Activity 3:
Convincing
Others:
Changing
Attitudes**

Which of the behaviors found in student surveys or in class discussions of superstitions were most unusual? most sensible? most harmful? most harmless? Why?

Students may be inspired to choose a superstition to debunk, perhaps even for the school science fair, if local guidelines permit. Challenge students to devise an experiment or demonstration to prove that a particular ritual is neither causing something to happen nor preventing something else from happening. For example, examining the results of baseball games may show that refraining from showering doesn't control the number of hits a player gets. Students should try to use scientific data to frame an argument that will convince others (or a particular person) to stop engaging in a certain superstitious behavior.

Others may be interested in researching the use of superstition as a psychological tool. Possible research questions include "In what ways can this power be used advantageously?" and "In what ways can it be used as a weapon?" (Students could consider opposing ends of the spectrum, from good luck charms to "voodoo.")

Activity 4: Beyond the Rabbit's Foot: Superstitions in Other Cultures

In ancient Egypt, cats were deified and honored, and to kill one meant a death penalty. Yet in Puritan America, cats were associated with witchcraft and could lead to persecution and death for the owner.

Bats have a bad reputation for some who link them to night-time terrors and vampires. Yet in China, bats are symbols of good fortune, known to consume great quantities of mosquitoes. What makes a thing a blessing to some and a bane to others is largely a matter of perception. Fears, likes, and dislikes can be the result of training or tradition.

The class may brainstorm as many American good luck and bad luck symbols as they can and then compare them with luck symbols from other countries. For example, birthday candles in Germany bear special symbols of good fortune representing wishes for the coming year. Commonly featured are four-leaf clovers, chimney sweeps, ladybugs, mushrooms, and pigs with lucky pennies in their mouths. Many of the good luck and bad luck symbols that we associate with superstition were imported from other cultures, so it is not surprising that some may seem familiar. Upon closer examination, one can discover the reason behind the symbol. Farmers, for example, consider ladybugs lucky because they rid crops of harmful insects.

After gathering symbols from other cultures, students may be encouraged to devise interesting metaphors by mixing symbols from other countries. In Asia, if a gecko barks while a baby is born, that is a sign that the house will be blessed. In tropical climates, lizards scurrying along the floor and walls may be the norm, but in the Midwest we may not consider ourselves fortunate to have barking geckos in our homes at any time. One might write "No gecko barked at my birth" as an introduction in a journal entry reflecting a bad day. Students can play with our culture's symbols for a change in meaning, such as "At the end of my rainbow was a pot of brussels sprouts." They may then use these ideas to lead to an extended metaphor.

Activity 5: Acting Out Superstitions

To ward off bad luck or to invoke good fortune, Americans knock on wood. People from England touch wood. In some regions and countries, the act of spitting seals a vow or brings good luck. American moms kiss boo-boos to make them feel better (no more sanitary than spitting for luck!). Students can look for how we act out our superstitions in making cultural comparisons. What do the actions mean? How do our beliefs reflect on society?

In their journals, students may wish to consider whether superstition will be wiped out as the educational level of a country's population increases. Can a person be both educated and superstitious at the same time?

Fashion Icons

The raccoon coat in the 1920s . . . the poodle skirt in the 1950s . . . bell-bottom jeans in the 1960s . . . what do all of these items of clothing have in common? We could call them tidal waves in the sea of fashion, fads that became fashion icons and symbols of a changing society. Each has become representative of a time period and evokes mental images of the youth of those decades. We can picture a college student waving a pennant while wearing his raccoon coat and a hat with a turned-up brim. The bobby-soxer of the 1950s wears a white blouse with her poodle skirt, a scarf at the neck or around a ponytail, and saddle shoes (and probably some shoe polish in her purse to keep them gleaming white). The '60s teen has a tie-dyed shirt and soft, faded blue jeans with a threadbare spot or two (all from natural causes—no acid-prewashing or shredding by manufacturers in those days). The hem is pulled out so the billowing bell-bottoms can fringe and drag the ground. There's probably a peace sign drawn on one leg with a blue fountain pen or white paint.

All of these images are tangible reminders that fashions change. In previous decades, we wanted a deep, "healthy" tan. But because of current medical and scientific knowledge about the connection between skin cancer and ozone depletion (which allows more of the sun's dangerous rays to reach the earth), tans will not likely enjoy the fashion renaissance that faded jeans have. Similarly, because of ecological and animal rights concerns, raccoon coats may never come back again (although they did experience a brief revival in the 1950s, when children or grandchildren of their original owners were attending college). There are other fashions that are being recycled, however. Miniskirts from the '60s showed up again in the '90s. The first time around, they caused comment (if not commotion): "Never in the history of fashion has so little material been raised so high to reveal so much that needs to be covered so badly" (Cecil Beaton 1969 in Simpson 1988, 269). In their resurrected version there has been little of the fury that accompanied the introduction of the mini. Perhaps that's because adults between the ages of thirty and fifty have already "been there, done that." Whereas there was a flurry of hemming in the '60s to update wardrobes, the '90s reaction has been relatively ho-hum.

Each of the activities below might culminate in a discussion of the ways we use these icons as metaphors for times past or for types of people.

Activity 1: Recycled Fashions

Long skirts and white tennis shoes, pegged jeans and white socks reappeared during the late '80s and early '90s, looking very "'50s-ish." Students can use costume books, encyclopedia articles on fashion, and the memories of older adults that they interview to locate other examples of fashion encores.

Activity 2: Borrowed Fashions

The Nehru jacket was a high-fashion item borrowed from India. Silken clothing came from China. Beaded dreadlocks originated in Jamaica. Using the resources such as those listed in Activity 1, students can find fashions in this country that were borrowed from other cultures.

Activity 3: Icons for a New Age

The high-collared dress with puffed sleeves and parasol accessory evokes the Gibson-girl look of the turn of the century. Women wearing long faux pearls over calf-length dresses and topping off their ensembles with skull-hugging hats evokes the flapper era of the 1920s. Hip-huggers, bare midriffs, bandannas, and macrame belts evoke the early 1970s. A certain "look" can be a bookmark in history. Ask your students to write descriptions of a current fashion look that pinpoints this era, such as the Prep Look (from attire popular at college preparatory schools), the Punk Look, or the Grunge Look.

What fashions of the last ten or so years do your students predict will become icons of our time? A brainstorming list has been started below.

leather jackets	sweatsuits
"The Pump" (or other athletic shoes)	windsuits
hand-decorated sweatshirts	designer diapers
baggy pants belted below the waist	oversized shirts

Activity 4: Slaves to Fashion?

What is the metaphor implied in the term *slave to fashion?* The following comments, most made by people prominent in the fashion world, imply that we lack individuality and perhaps even common sense when it comes to our appearances. Students may choose one of the following (taken from Simpson 1988 unless otherwise noted) to respond to in their journals. A small-group or whole-class discussion can follow writing time so that students can share their ideas with others.

[Rich . . . clients] all wanted the same kind of different thing.

Billy Baldwin, interior designer (266)

It was just a whimsical idea that escalated when so many crazy ladies took it up.

> Rudi Gernreich on his topless bathing suit design (267)

The soul of this man is his clothes.

> William Shakespeare, *All's Well That Ends Well* (2.5.48)

Some women won't buy anything unless they can pay a lot [for it].

> Helena Rubinstein (269)

Fashion is a social agreement . . . the result of a consensus of a large group of people.

> Stella Blum (269)

Activity 5: Fashion Irony

The following are examples of ironic twists in the fashion world:

In a day of perma-press technology, the wrinkled or "relaxed" look was in.

The lowly tennis shoe, once an inexpensive and simply designed sport shoe or alternative for school shoes in warm weather, has become a symbol of wealth and status. It has also become the object of muggings and, sadly, murders.

Youth had its own look until the Baby Boomers grew up; now everyone dresses alike.

Invite students to add examples of their own.

Activity 6: Transformation

Levi Strauss's 1870 design using blue denim to produce durable work pants has been one of the fashion world's greatest success stories. With a little informal interviewing, the class may be able to devise a timeline of blue jean style changes (bib overall, cuffs, tight, pleated, designer, relaxed fit, etc.). What hypotheses can they offer to explain not only the many transformations that jeans have undergone but also the fluctuation in status that jeans have had over the years?

Time

I should command here—I was born to rule,
But do I rule? I don't. Why? I don't know.
I shall some day. Not yet. I bide my time.
I once was Some One—and the Was Will Be.
The Present as we speak becomes the Past,
The Past repeats itself, and so is Future!
This sounds involved. It's not. It's right enough.

    W. S. Gilbert and Arthur Sullivan, *Princess Ida*

The concept of time is a prime example of how we attempt to make abstractions tangible through metaphorical ways of knowing. Even though we commonly do speak of present, past, and future, some scientists have decided that these are not meaningful terms when it comes to exploring the nature of time. Physicist Paul Davies has written a book for lay readers called *About Time: Einstein's Unfinished Revolution* (1995) in which he discusses the implications of Einstein's theory of relativity. Time is not a mathematical measurement, he says, but rather is organic and elastic. It can be warped by rapid motion or gravitation, and it has a beginning and an end. He challenges us to prepare for conceptual change, noting that many implications of Einstein's theory are "counterintuitive . . . [to] our commonsense notions of reality" (15): time travel, time dilation (there is more than one "now"), black holes as gateways to the end of time, cosmic time, intrinsic time, spacetime, temporal flux, and backwards time. *About Time* is full of metaphors, literary allusions, and thoughtful consideration of topics that have heretofore been more at home in the realm of science fiction than of science fact. For example, "[s]ince Einstein, physicists have generally rejected the notion that events 'happen,' as opposed to merely *exist* in the four-dimensional spacetime continuum" (253).

Is time an abstract construct, as Newtonian physics suggests, or an organic reality, as Einstein theorized? In our daily lives, we have treated it as both. We classify the word *time* as an abstract noun and then we personify it in our speech and in our poetry. We speak of time as a human invention and then we blame our "circadian rhythms—those neural timekeepers in the brain that regulate everything from waking times to hormone levels" when we can't stay awake during an afternoon meeting (Markels 1995, E6).

In *The Magic Mountain*, Thomas Mann (1924) describes our keen awareness of time and our constant attempt to make it tangible:

"Time has no divisions to mark its passage, there is never a thunderstorm or blare of trumpets to announce the beginning of a new month or year. Even when a new century begins it is only we mortals who ring bells and fire off pistols" (in Bartlett 1980, 755). It's not surprising, then, that we also sound noon whistles or sirens. And we have come to depend upon other physical markers to measure the passage of time, such as clocks, calendars, appointment books, radio news updates at the top and bottom of the hour (how can time have a top or a bottom?), and even tombstones.

Our fascination with time as a subject for study and contemplation has been fueled by the dawning of a new millennium. Ordinarily, one minute or one hour or one day isn't much different from any other, but the ten seconds before midnight on December 31 are an exception to that. The New Year's Eves that usher in new decades achieve even more attention. December 31, 1999, will surely feature the "Watch Party" of the century! (But while this date, often referred to as the end of the twentieth century, will be a memorable date indeed, mathematicians remind us that the actual turning of the century—and the millennium—will be the next year. January 1, 2001, is the first day of the twenty-first century.)

There is something about the turning of a century that invites introspection. Compare the following two passages (you'll note that Naisbitt and Aburdene mistakenly call 2000 the millennium):

> It may indeed be something more than a coincidence that placed this decade at the close of a century, and *fin de siecle* may have been at once a swan song and a death-bed repentance. (Holbrook Jackson 1913 in Stevenson 1958, 43)

> We stand at the dawn of a new era. Before us is the most important decade in the history of civilization, a period of stunning technological innovation, unprecedented economic opportunity, surprising political reform, and great cultural rebirth. It will be a decade like none that has come before because it will culminate in the millennium, the year 2000. (Naisbitt and Aburdene 1990, 11)

Even though the two quotations were written at "opposite ends" of the century, they demonstrate the dichotomy or at least ambivalent feelings humans have about the changing times. On the one hand, there is a kind of magic and excitement about the century change; on the other, there is fear and dread. As Naisbitt and Aburdene note:

> For centuries that monumental, symbolic date has stood for the future and what we shall make of it. . . .
> Already we have fallen under its dominion. The year 2000 is operating like a powerful magnet on humanity, reaching down into the 1990s and intensifying the decade. It is amplifying emotions, accelerating change, heightening awareness, and compelling us to reexamine ourselves, our values, and our institutions. (11)

In this chapter we will look at time through literary and socioeconomic frameworks. While time may be money in the business world, it is many other things in the arts. Time, and our awareness of how precious a commodity it is, has been sung by the poets since, well, time immemorial. Since 1558, there have been no fewer than 227 songs featuring "time" in the title (Lax and Smith 1984). There are hundreds of poems, short stories, and movies and countless books that play on our bittersweet feelings about fleeting time.

With so many possibilities to choose from, there are sure to be some words about time that speak to each of us. We can say, as Louise Leighton did, that "time is a fox on quick, velvet feet" (in Bartlett 1980, 270); or that "time is our sculptor" (Sir Francis Meynell in Bartlett 1980, 328); "Time is the rider that breaks youth" (George Herbert in Bartlett 1980, 883); "Time is the fire in which we burn" (Delmore Schwartz in Stevenson 1958, 43); or as P. G. Wodehouse did, "Time [is] like an Ever-rolling Stream" (in Stevenson 1958, 2002).

Trying It Out

Metaphors for Time in Literature

Activity 1: Time Sifting

Have students assist in compiling a literary file or resource center on the theme of time. Items to gather could include quotations, poems, stories, and passages from novels that use metaphors for time. Consult *Bartlett's Familiar Quotations, Granger's Index to Poetry, Short Story Index* (edited by Fidell), and novel indexes such as NCTE's *Books for You.* (You may want to use descriptors besides "time," such as "hour," "era," and so on.) Nonprint resources may be found by consulting film and video guides. You and your students will enjoy sifting through your time files until you find a nugget of interest to use in future writing. To expand this file into an interdisciplinary one, consult such nonfiction resources as Davies's *About Time* or Stephen Hawking's *Brief History of Time* (1988).

An example of an item that might find a place in the file is Oliver Wendell Holmes's poem (1895) "Our Banker," written in 1874. The first stanza shows clearly the banking metaphor that Holmes has developed to describe time:

> Old Time, in whose bank we deposit our notes,
> Is a miser who always wants guineas for groats;
> He keeps all his customers still in arrears
> By lending them minutes and charging them years.
>   (135)

The class may be asked to consider to what Holmes is comparing time (a banker). That suggests other questions: What is Time's bank? Who are Time's customers? What are our notes? Why is Time miserly? Students may be asked to decide whether they need to know what guineas and groats are to understand the metaphor; what do they think they are? Which is larger? Other questions to ponder include the following: In what way does Time lend us minutes? In what way does Time charge us in years? Do we pay, for example, for moments of happiness with years of drudgery? Why or why not?

The class may find it fun to locate a copy of the entire poem and develop individual or collaborative rewrites of Holmes's "Our Banker" using modern money imagery. They could first brainstorm modern banking references, such as money machines, C.D.s (certificates of deposit), checking accounts, or traveler's checks. It might be interesting and helpful for them to get feedback from some bankers before completing the final draft. They could then send their updated version to literary and financial publications for possible use in an upcoming issue. They must be sure, of course, to include a line that shows where the idea for the poem originated. Some authors do this by saying something like "With apologies to Oliver Wendell Holmes" or "After O. W. Holmes's 'The Banker.'"

Activity 2:
A Time for Time

If students do not keep daily journals, one way to initiate journal writing is through a "quote of the day" format. At the beginning of class, write one or more "time" quotations on the board or on an overhead projector transparency. A selection of time metaphors follows. Other quotes may be gleaned from the file suggested in Activity 1.

Allow five minutes for students to freewrite on the topic. Ask volunteers to share their entries, or conduct a general discussion about the quotation. What does the metaphor reveal or conceal about the concept of time?

By losing present time, we lose all time.

Old Proverb

[Time is] just like a river
Flowing out to the sea.

Cliff Friend and Charlie Tobias, "Time Waits for No One" (1944)

It is only in appearance that time is a river. It is rather a vast landscape and it is the eye of the beholder that moves.

Thornton Wilder, *The Eighth Day* (1967; in Simpson 1988, 245)

Time rushes toward us with its hospital tray of infinitely varied narcotics, even while it is preparing us for its inevitably fatal operation.

Tennessee Williams, *The Rose Tattoo* (1951; in Simpson 1988, 245)

Time . . . is not a great healer. It is an indifferent and perfunctory one. Sometimes it does not heal at all. And sometimes when it seems to, no healing has been necessary.

Ivy Compton-Burnett, *Darkness and Day* (1951; in Simpson 1988, 224)

Our attitudes toward time are very different. I hoard it and spend it like a miser; she rides the rhythms of the day like a surfer. She lets things happen when the time is right for them to happen.

Karen McCarthy Brown, *Mama Lola: A Vodou Priestess in Brooklyn*
(1991, 136)

Activity 3:
Other Metaphors
for Time

What do other writers of poems, songs, and stories say about time? Invite students to read, view, or listen to several pieces from the classroom resource center (or literary file) and then choose one they particularly like. In their journals, they might write about the piece, focusing on one or more of the following questions:

- What do you like/dislike about the author's description of time?

- What is the metaphor the author uses for time? Is this an experience that you can identify with? Why or why not?

- What common features do you see between time and the object or event that time is being compared to? What dissimilarities do you see?

- What are the connotations of the metaphor? What makes the connotation positive or negative?

- Is this a good metaphor for time? Why or why not?

- Prepare to read and explain your passage in an informal sharing session. (If the class is interested, this session could be the basis of a program for a nursing home or community group.)

- Develop your own metaphor for time. Use poetry, story, drama, art, or video to represent and share your metaphor with the class or with another appropriate audience.

Trying It Out

Century Watch

Locate copies of George Orwell's *1984* and H. G. Wells's *Time Machine* (or find film versions of them)[1] as well as copies of John Naisbitt's *Megatrends* (1982) and *Megatrends 2000* (with Patricia Aburdene, 1990) and any other resources you may be aware of that show how people have envisioned the future. Ask small groups of students to preview each and share their impressions with the class as an introduction to study of the fast-approaching future and the quickly receding past.

**Activity 1:
Analyzing the Past**

Seeing time in chunks of years, decades and centuries lets us isolate sociopolitical trends. We then give these chunks of time such labels as the Roaring Twenties, the Depression Years, the War Years, the Egocentric Eighties, and so on. Depending on your political views, you might label the 1960s as turbulent and drug-infested or as the "Age of Aquarius." A popular song of the time epitomized the idealism of the decade of the flower children:

> When the moon is in the seventh house
> And Jupiter aligns with Mars,
> Then peace will guide the planets,
> And love will steer the stars;
> This is the dawning of the age of Aquarius,
> The age of Aquarius,
> Aquarius . . .
>
> (Howe 1966 in Beck 1968, 914)

When we look at centuries in the same way we look at decades, we come up with such epithets as the Age of Enlightenment, the Dark Ages, and the Industrial Revolution. Small groups may be asked to discuss and share their answers to the following:

- What label would you give the 1990s? Why?
- What label would you give the twentieth century? Explain. (Some possibilities include the Atomic Age, the Age of Technology, the Computer Age, the Clash Between Democracy and Totalitarianism.)
- What label do you think or hope the twenty-first century will earn? Explain.

**Activity 2:
Do Centuries Turn
(or Do They Just
Roll Over)?**

What kind of images do "turning" and "rolling" evoke? Ask students to interpret and evaluate Oliver Wendell Holmes's metaphor for the waning—a metaphor in itself—of a century: "The century shrivels like a scroll" (in Stevenson 1958, 205). Challenge them to devise another description for the ending of a century that depends on a different visual metaphor, perhaps a more modern one.

**Activity 3:
Only the
Beginning or
the Beginning of
the End?**

Some people live their entire lives without seeing the century turn. Perhaps that is one reason that the dawning of the century excites our imaginations: it retains a sense of mystery. It can also make us a bit fearful to face the uncertain future. Some people forecast gloom and doom, saying "things can only get worse."

The following comments by eighteenth- and nineteenth-century writers (taken from Stevenson 1958) show this dichotomy between optimism and pessimism:

What age was not dull? When was not the majority wicked?
or what progress was ever made by society?

> Ralph Waldo Emerson (85)

The golden age never was the present age.

> Benjamin Franklin (43)

For each age is a dream that is dying,
Or one that is coming to birth.

> Arthur O'Shaughnessy (43)

Oftentimes the past evokes a sense of nostalgia:

The world that I was born into bore little resemblance to the world
we live in today. It was so close to the nineteenth century that I have
always felt a kinship with that era, which was then very slowly
beginning to disappear. I remember these: horse-drawn carriages,
button shoes, corsets and feathered hats for women, maypoles in the
schoolyards in springtime, quiet orderly schoolrooms, five-cent soda
pop and snack foods, mule-drawn wagons and plows, quilting bees,
spelling bees, magic lanterns, kinetoscopes, and silent movies. Mark
Twain died when I was two, but as a youth I was very much aware
of the unseen yet living presences of Buffalo Bill Cody, Thomas
Edison, Teddy Roosevelt, President Woodrow Wilson, Henry Ford,
Kaiser Wilhelm of Germany, Mrs. George Armstrong Custer, and real
cowboys and Indians, including Hollow-Horn Bear, the Sioux chief
whose face appeared on a postage stamp after his death. (D. Brown
1993, 9)

Invite students to write their own reflection on the passing
twentieth century. Brainstorming questions for the class to consider
follow:

- How can you summarize the last century? What might be representative of this era? What trends, household conveniences, games, and people who make a difference have you seen come and go?

- How many of the people and things from Dee Brown's piece (above) do you recognize? Who or what are the modern equivalents of each?

- Whom might we interview to have a more inclusive view of this century?

- What feelings do you have about seeing a new century dawn? Are you optimistic or pessimistic? Why?

Activity 4: What's to Come in 2001?

Predicting the future is big business. Writers like John Naisbitt of
Megatrends fame make money on their educated guesses. In 1982,
Naisbitt foretold these changes in the United States:

1. a shift from an industrial to an information society
2. increased technology accompanied by increased human contact
3. a shift to a global economy from a national one
4. a shift from short-term to long-term planning in business
5. a shift to decentralization of power
6. a shift from institutional help to self-reliance
7. a shift from representative to participatory democracy
8. replacement of hierarchies with networks
9. a population shift from the North to the South
10. a shift toward multiple lifestyle options

Look at Naisbitt and Patricia Aburdene's book, *Megatrends 2000.* Which of these trends does Naisbitt still support? What new ones are added? The lists of trends for the 1990s below may be of some help in drawing your conclusions:

1. global economic boom with the end of the Cold War
2. renaissance in the arts, with arts replacing sports as the dominant leisure activity (in 1988, we spent $3.7 billion on arts, $2.8 billion on sports)
3. emergence of free-market socialism in Third World and communist countries
4. consumer-driven global lifestyles (Japan, which is only 1 percent Christian, celebrates Christmas) and an accompanying cultural backlash (to preserve traditional national lifestyles)
5. privatization of welfare state (led by Margaret Thatcher's successful defeat of socialism and return to individual ownership in Great Britain)
6. the rise of the Pacific Rim through the information technology boom
7. increased numbers of women in leadership
8. the Age of Biology, with genetic engineering making great advances for agriculture and the environment and with medical technology and ethics receiving continued attention
9. religious revival worldwide
10. the "Triumph of the Individual" with people being more responsible and independent, especially through technology (13)

Activity 5: Poll Time

The class may be interested in examining projections by other analysts, such as Judith Waldrop, the research editor of *American Demographics.* She has identified twenty-one trends for the twenty-first century. How many do the students think will come true? What evidence do they see around them that these trends are or are not accurate interpretations of American life? Which is their favorite prediction (the one they most hope will happen)? What would students least like to see happen? Why?

1. Everyone will belong in a minority group.
2. The word "family" will have to be redefined.
3. Parents will no longer dream of better lives for their children.
4. Full-time homemakers will nearly disappear.
5. Bosses and corporations will bend over backwards to retain good workers.
6. Most people will work in small service businesses rather than in large companies.
7. Job specialization and competition will increase.
8. Careers will have many sidetracks.
9. The retirement population will explode.
10. Life will become more leisurely because of a "crack" in the work ethic (an interesting metaphor).
11. Staying healthy will become a priority because of severe health care shortages.
12. People will live longer than they want to, making the right to die an increasingly important issue.
13. "Cooking" will mean pushing the right buttons.
14. People will read computer printouts more than they'll read books.
15. People will customize their own newspapers from computer data bases.
16. Consumers will have it all: smart TVs that will record our favorite programs when we miss them; charge cards and medical cards that will keep track of our expenses; and pill bottles that will beep when it's time to take our medicine.
17. All the environmentalists' dreams will come true.
18. Nostalgia for small-town life will be prevalent.
19. Big cities will be in trouble.
20. Women, Blacks, and Hispanics/Latinos will have more political clout.
21. "Expecting the unexpected" will be the winning business strategy. (25)

Students may research and write about one or more of Naisbitt and Aburdene's or Waldrop's predictions. They should explain not only what they think will happen, but why. They could also imagine what might happen if the prediction comes true; what would be the effect on life as we know it? Such imaginings can also lead to fictional pieces.

Before developing final drafts, students might exchange predictions with a partner. On a separate sheet, each could write about additional repercussions that the partner's prediction might have in order to help the writer expand his or her vision of the potential effects.

Activity 6: Time Capsule

At this point, your students will probably be ready to develop a few predictions of their own. These might be compiled in a class book of predictions and placed in a time capsule, along with copies of Waldrop's article and Naisbitt's books. Students might choose other print and video materials that show what people of the present think life will be like in the future.

The next task will be to decide on an appropriate receptacle to serve as a time capsule. Students should consider whether it should be waterproof or reinforced. They must also arrange for the capsule to be stored for the number of years they choose. Students may decide to ask a class member, teacher, library, or museum to house the time capsule; the opening could become part of an alumni reunion in the future. Placing a notice about the capsule in a public record might ensure that it is eventually remembered, although someone is sure to suggest the strategy that Doc used in *Back to the Future, Part III* (Universal Studios 1990): he paid to have a telegram delivered to Marty many years in the future. Students might explore having their chosen date for the opening placed in the memory of a computer, with a command to print out a reminder in 2020.

Trying It Out

Does Anybody Really Know What Time It Is?

Does anybody really know what time it is?
Does anybody really care—about time?

(Robert William Lamm in Sharma and Gargan 1988)

Does anyone know what time it is? It depends. If you use the Gregorian calendar, then you are measuring time from the date of the birth of Christ. At the time this book was being written, that was 1,997 years ago. The Chinese call a similar chunk of time the Year of the Ox. Muslims refer to our 1997 as A.H. 1418, because they count time from the date that Muhammad migrated from Mecca to Medina.[2] The Jewish calendar calculates the year based on their determination of the creation of the earth, making 1997 equivalent to A.M. 5757/5758.[3] Other cultures, especially ancient ones, used their own reference points. So in a sense, nobody knows what the correct time is; it all depends on one's perspective.

On the other hand, we could argue that the divisions of time are scientifically based. Day and night follow the rotation of the earth; years correspond with the revolution of the earth around the sun. Furthermore, through carbon dating of archaeological artifacts, we are becoming increasingly more precise in our ability to determine the beginning of humankind—and, therefore, of "time." (We could also debate whether time truly existed in the natural world before people started keeping track of it. Yet, consider growth rings on trees or strata on rock formations.)

Whether or not the beginning of time is ever pinpointed is probably moot in regard to our system of time-keeping. It would be confusing to make adjustments in the way we calculate the year. The last major overhaul of the Western calendar was in 1582, when the Julian calendar was corrected to eliminate ten extra days caused by inaccuracies in calculating the solar year. Delays by Protestant countries in adopting the new Gregorian calendar (named after Pope Gregory XIII) further complicated matters. It still causes problems for genealogists who try to determine correct dates of birth and death. (Fortunately, an earlier calendar adjustment, made by Julius Caesar, was so long ago that making 45 B.C. into a year of 445 days did not have much effect on record-keeping today!)

Activity 1: How Universal Is Time?

Students can search for information on the time-keeping systems of other cultures, both modern and ancient, in order to determine whether the advance of civilization has made our system of time-keeping a universal one. Other systems might be compared with the concept of Greenwich mean time.

Interesting facts to note about other systems include the number and names of months, including the meanings of those names, and the features of the natural world evident in those time systems.

Activity 2: Time for Comparison

The class should determine a useful way to compare and contrast the data gathered in Activity 1. Key questions to focus on might include "In which cultural groups did time have the most significance? The least? Why?"

Trying It Out

Time to Read

Locate, read, and discuss stories or books in which time is central to the story. Suggested works are described below:

Bellamy, Edward. 1968. *Looking Backward, 2000–1887.* New York: Lancer Books.

This utopian romance was first published in 1888. Its interest is primarily the vision of the future of a nineteenth-century writer.

Bethancourt, T. Ernesto. 1978. *Tune in Yesterday.* New York: Holiday House.

Two teenage jazz fans travel back to the 1940s. Written by musician Tom Pasley under a pseudonym.

Bierce, Ambrose. 1891. "An Occurrence at Owl Creek Bridge." In *Tales of Soldiers and Civilians.* San Francisco: E. L. G. Steele.

Present, past, and imagined present shift in this story where a man is about to be hanged.

Blair, Cynthia. 1987. *Freedom to Dream.* New York: Fawcett Juniper Books.

History-hating Katy can't fathom the fuss over the upcoming bicentennial anniversary of the United States Constitution—until she is sent back to 1787.

Delaney, Sarah L., and A. Elizabeth Delaney with Amy Hill Hearth. 1993. *Having Our Say: The Delaney Sisters' First 100 Years.* New York: Kodansha International.

The life stories of living history embodied in the reminiscences and unpretentious wisdom of two centenarians.

Eagar, Frances. 1976. *Time Tangle.* Nashville, Tenn.: Thomas Nelson.

A girl meets a boy who seems to be out of sync with the present century. She suspects that he is a ghost from the 1500s trapped in a time tangle and seeks to help him.

Hilton, James. 1933. *The Lost Horizon.* New York: William Morrow.

Accidentally discovered by modern travelers, an ancient utopian community exists without sickness or aging. Time stands still for the inhabitants, but only while they remain within their long-lost mountain retreat. This book was adapted for a 1937 Frank Capra film released by Columbia Pictures with the same title. Columbia tried again in 1972 with a not-so-well-received musical version of *The Lost Horizon.* The Lerner and Lowe play *Brigadoon* (1947) may have been inspired by Hilton's work as well. The MGM musical *Brigadoon* (1947) has modern-day travelers discovering unchanged residents of the Scottish Highlands who age only one day every hundred years.

Lee, Robert C. 1982. *Timequake.* Philadelphia: Westminster Press.

An earthquake during a camping trip causes two cousins to shift to the year 2027. The boys find the future a blend of technology and primitive tribes. They attempt to adapt while they seek a way to return to their own time.

L'Engle, Madeleine. 1962. *A Wrinkle in Time.* New York: Farrar, Straus and Giroux.

> The Newbery Award-winning fantasy classic of a misfit teenage girl's encounter with the tesseract, a wrinkle in time, the last known work of her missing physicist father. Her quest to find her father becomes a rescue mission when her brother is trapped on a planet where individuality is not allowed.

Pascal, Francine. 1977. *Hangin' Out with Cici.* New York: Viking.

> A girl suddenly finds herself in an unfamiliar time and place, only to discover that her new friend, Cici, actually is her own mother, as a teenager. Her return puts a new perspective on the mother-daughter relationship.

Peck, Richard. 1989. *Voices after Midnight.* New York: Delacorte Press.

> The supernatural story of two siblings who begin to move in and out of the present to the previous century after their family rents a New York townhouse.

Schotter, Roni. 1981. *A Matter of Time.* New York: Learning Corp. of America.

> A girl learns to understand and appreciate her mother and the people around her when she comes to terms with her mother's terminal illness.

Stannard, Russell. 1990. *The Time and Space of Uncle Albert.* New York: Henry Holt.

> A science fiction work based on Albert Einstein's thought experiments. A girl journeys into space for a science project through the relativity experiments of her eccentric uncle.

Wells, H. G. [1895] 1990. *The Time Machine.* Adapted by Les Martin. New York: Random House.

> This science fiction classic has an inventor leaving nineteenth-century England to seek his future, hoping that man has become more at peace with himself and others. His time travels take him both into the past and into a less-than-perfect future.

Yolen, Jane. 1988. *The Devil's Arithmetic.* New York: Viking.

> Hannah resents stories of her Jewish heritage until one night during a Passover Seder dinner, she opens a door to the Poland of the past and discovers the horrors of a concentration camp. She comes to realize the importance of one's cultural history. Recommended for middle-school age and up.

Notes   1. The film version of *1984*, released in 1956, is available through British and Pathe Film Distributors. *The Time Machine* (1960) is an MGM film. Information about these and other books made into films is available in *Filmed Books and Plays* by A. G. S. Enser (1987).

2. A.H. stands for *anno Hegirae*, meaning "in the year of the Hegira" (Muhammad's migration from Mecca to Medina). The conversion from the Gregorian to the Islamic calendar year can be made by subtracting 622 from the current Gregorian year and multiplying that figure by 1.031. For example, 1997 - 622 = 1375; 1375 x 1.031 = 1417.625.

3. A.M. means *anno mundi*, referring to the creation of the world. Because the Jewish new year is in the fall, each Gregorian year straddles parts of two Jewish years.

7 Exploring Cultures through Traditions

The metaphor is the mask of God through which eternity is to be experienced.

Joseph Campbell with Bill Moyers, *The Power of Myth*

From birth to burial, we are surrounded by ritual. The customs incorporated in the way we eat, live, play, and die often have mythological roots. Symbolism in religious ceremonies is especially rich in metaphor and is repeated across cultures. For example, the Christian custom of saying grace before a meal is akin to the Native American hunter or African tribesman paying homage to the animal that was slain in order to sustain the life of the people.

Rituals evolve with time. Within Greek and Roman myths dating back more than two thousand years could be the basis of some of the festivals and rites that are still practiced in the West. Eastern sun worship goes even farther back in prehistory. Modern religions have borrowed from these pagan roots. Did you ever wonder why a new ship is christened by breaking a bottle of champagne against its prow? In Rome, it was the duty of a priest to make an offering of wine to either the god for whom the ship was named or to the sea god (Tuleja 1987). By analyzing American culture and ceremonies, one discovers other modern examples of rituals with mythological roots. Today, when we christen a ship, we do so without thinking of an offering to a Roman sea god. We have kept the metaphor, that is, the act of pouring alcohol into the sea for good luck. We have replaced the myth, the story, but the metaphor remains. As another example, Christianity changed the meaning of the Celtic new year's celebration of Samhain on the first of November. Previously, human and animal sacrifices were made to the Lord of the Dead and the sun. People dressed up and went around at night to scare away evil spirits of the dead. Christianity changed the focus, and November 1 became the day on which deceased saints were honored.

Because we live in a society where church and state are separate, dual ceremonies have evolved accordingly. Marriage, for example, could first be solemnized by a religious ceremony in a church or temple and later celebrated with a party, possibly with presents, dance, food, and drink. Or the ceremony may be performed in a courtroom, bypassing the religious rites, yet complete with its own rules of etiquette, form, function, and response, depending on the orientation of the celebrants. When we participate in such a ceremony, we are living the metaphor within the ritual, whatever its original purpose and pageantry.

Customs and traditions continue to develop. Greeting card companies have promoted new occasions for celebrations, such as Secretaries Day and Grandparents Day. Mother's Day and Thanksgiving were started by letter-writing campaigns appealing to the president to designate these as special days.

Prevalent in American culture is a heightened social sensitivity to others' beliefs and traditions. Schools reflect this and are often the first indicators of change. Christmas break has become winter recess. Classroom Easter parties are now spring celebrations. We try to honor the perspectives of religious or ethnic minorities. Because for many Native Americans the idea of harmony between pilgrims and Indians is a myth, Thanksgiving may be a day of mourning rather than celebration. In recognition of this perspective, the Walter Hays School in Palo Alto, California, does not have the standard Thanksgiving celebration in its kindergarten. No pilgrims or Indians sit down to share a fall harvest meal. Instead, Indigenous Peoples Day is celebrated. Students wear cloaks of their own design and wreaths of autumn leaves atop their heads. They help in the preparation and serving of a variety of ethnic foods, as diverse and representative as the students themselves.

In the activities in this chapter, students may explore the metaphors in our traditions, rituals, and proverbs. In the process they will learn much about the diverse cultures which we celebrate as part of our American heritage.

Trying It Out

Mind Your Myth

By exploring the countless holidays and school and societal functions with which we mark our calendars, we can discover echoes far back into history, still resounding and evolving in our modern era.

Activity 1: Living Metaphors

Select a ceremony or tradition to write about and list the details unique to that event. Here are some possibilities to examine:

birth	inauguration	funeral
baptism	groundbreaking	family reunion
wedding	sharing a meal	housewarming
baby shower	anniversary	bar mitzvah
prom	bat mitzvah	class reunion

graduation	divorce	date
going steady	court procedures	confirmation
communion	wedding shower	introductions

For example, what are modern birthday rituals? What can we say about the elements that make up birthday celebrations and our roles in them? Ask your students if they have ever wondered why we might encounter a game of pin-the-tail-on-the-donkey, cake and ice cream, lighted candles on a cake, black balloons and arm bands, or a banner proclaiming "Over the Hill." Has anyone experienced birthday spankings or a pinch to grow on? Have students find the metaphors we live and why we enact them. Discussing one together (below) should help them see how they might explore other rituals on their own or in small groups:

Birthday Rituals

- Consider the age of the person. A five-year-old's birthday will be different from a sweet sixteen's or a forty-year-old's.

- Consider how ceremonies involve the participation of others. Keep in mind three perspectives: community, family, individual. The community can be any larger group of which the family is a subset, for example, the religious community or the school community. What if the celebration were in honor of Dr. Martin Luther King Jr.? If the birthday is a fellow student's or co-worker's, perhaps it doesn't affect the community at large, but what is the expected response to such an event? We might simply wish the person a happy birthday or perhaps send a card. If this were a child's birthday at an elementary school, such activities as making and presenting a paper crown, singing a birthday song, and sharing cupcakes with the class could be listed.

  What celebrations take place within the sphere of family and friends? What is shared and what is the expected function of each celebrant? Celebrants might give wrapped gifts and cards and share a special cake, ice cream, song, party, or a champagne toast.

  What is expected of the individual? This will depend on whether you are the birthday person, a guest, or a family member celebrating a relative's birthday. The birthday celebrant, for example, is often expected to make a wish and to blow out a certain number of candles on a special cake. (If you were writing about a wedding, on the other hand, an individual's roles might include guest, mother of the bride, groomsman, ring bearer, or bride—and would vary according to the rituals each enacts and represents.)

- Once a general descriptive narrative is written, list and analyze the individual items:

  Birthday crown: Celebrating the individual's birth, we honor him or her as king or queen for the day (or at least for a brief moment). The living metaphor is that celebrants become subjects, elevating the birthday person to the highest honor, the monarch. Even in America, where the president is our highest government official, the crowned birthday celebrant hearkens back to our link with the European monarchy where the crowning of a monarch has its mythological roots.

Presenting gifts: Honoring a birth with gifts had been clearly established in biblical times, evidenced by the three wise men presenting gifts to the baby Jesus, so we can surmise it predates this time, most likely having a Roman influence.

Birthday song: Singing "Happy Birthday to You" has become an American tradition, established in the last century by sisters Mildred and Patty Smith Hill, who wrote the song in 1893.

At first, the assignment may seem ordinary to the students. They are writing details of traditions and ceremonies practiced in a familiar way in their own society and home. By examining something so seemingly common, we may lose the perspective that this is special to our culture. It is not until one's own experience with the event is compared with that of others, and the common elements and individual details are analyzed, discussed, and discovered, that the uniqueness of the event manifests itself. What are the similarities and differences in each? How do we live the ritual? What does each represent? Students should keep these questions in mind when writing about their chosen perspectives.

Activity 2: Across America, across the Calendar

Peel back the layers of metaphor to discover the underlying myth in a present-day tradition, custom, or ceremony. Students can help start a list, perhaps by a brainstorming session of holidays, starting with New Year's Day on January 1. Go through the calendar, month by month, and select special events from which to dig out buried metaphors (whether we live them out consciously or unconsciously). A detailed calendar will help. Many rites in the traditional holidays with religious associations, such as Christmas and Hanukkah, include pre-Christian or pagan myths imported by immigrants to this country. For instance, the seventeenth-century German tradition of the decorated Christmas tree, introduced to this country in the nineteenth century, recalls the time when trees were used in worship by Druids (a Celtic religious order of priests in ancient Britain, Ireland, and France). Within all holiday celebrations are symbolic aspects used to enact or live the metaphorical associations. Find them and write the rituals, discovering the meaning behind our actions and symbols.

Suggested Resources

Bulfinch, Thomas. [1913] 1979. *Bulfinch's Mythology.* Reprint, New York: Crown Publishers.

Bulfinch's compendium of mythology contains historical and literary information on classic stories. His complete nineteenth-century texts (*The Age of Fable, The Age of Chivalry,* and *The Legends of Charlemagne)* are included.

Cohen, Hennig, and Tristram Potter Coffin. 1987. *The Folklore of American Holidays.* Detroit: Gale Research Company Press.

This compilation details the origins and stories behind some common and not-so-common celebrations and features superstitions, proverbs, songs, dances, and games and their association with American customs.

Cohen, Hennig, and Tristram Potter Coffin. 1991. *America Celebrates! A Patchwork of Weird and Wonderful Holiday Lore.* Detroit: Visible Ink Press.

From native origin to roots across the globe, Cohen and Coffin reveal the purpose and pageantry contained in countless American celebrations.

Cosman, Madeleine Pelner. 1976. *Fabulous Feasts: Medieval Cookery and Ceremony.* New York: George Braziller, Inc.

From menus to manners and the medicinal uses of food, Cosman presents a well-researched book about medieval food lore and history.

Cosman, Madeleine Pelner. 1981. *Medieval Holidays and Festivals: A Calendar of Celebrations.* New York: Charles Scribner's Sons.

The book takes the reader through the meaning behind the main calendar events in a medieval year, starting with January's Twelfth Night celebrations. Historical details enrich the many activity descriptions.

Cosman, Madeleine Pelner. 1984. *The Medieval Baker's Daughter: A Bilingual Adventure in Medieval Life with Costumes, Banners, Music, Food, and a Mystery Play.* Tenafly, N.J.: Bard Hall Press.

Cosman has bridged cultures and time to create a guide for students and teachers. The split Spanish/English text tells the story of a young girl and her life in the fifteenth century. A glossary, information on period clothing, recipes, and songs will help to recreate a medieval marketplace or feast like the one detailed in the book.

Eley, Mary M. 1996. *Chase's Calendar of Annual Events.* Chicago: Contemporary Books.

Each yearly edition of this information-packed calendar lets the reader know what is happening and where it takes place. Check for lesser-known holidays such as Arbor Day, or ones that may be unfamiliar, such as Waitangi Day in New Zealand.

Frazer, James G. [1894] 1981. *The Golden Bough: The Roots of Religion and Folklore.* Reprint, New York: Gramercy.

Frazer takes a comparative view of the rituals in mythology, primitive customs, and folklore. He uses the rites of other cultures to gain insight into his own.

Henisch, Bridget Ann. 1976. *Fast and Feast: Food in Medieval Society.* University Park: Pennsylvania State University Press.

This book tells us how a medieval kitchen functioned, from tools to table preparation. Modern differences in etiquette dictate that dipping one's fingers in shared sauces is no longer encouraged, yet some threads of commonality exist across time. For example, even children of centuries ago made mudpies to share with friends at play.

Martin, Judith. 1982. *Miss Manners' Guide to Excruciatingly Correct Behavior.* New York: Atheneum.

Judith Martin, as Miss Manners, presents a compilation from her syndicated etiquette advice column. Her comments on American social customs encompass many cultural rituals: birth, marriage, death, and much in between, such as gift exchanging, etiquette in the workplace, and correct behavior at the White House.

Martin, Judith. 1984. *Miss Manners' Guide to Rearing Perfect Children.* New York: Penguin Books.

Essays on American social customs are mixed with excerpts from Judith Martin's internationally syndicated etiquette advice column as she takes family members from birth to leaving the nest. Her topics are directed to parents and children and include living with one's family, visiting relatives, and living with college roommates.

Root, Waverly, and Richard de Rochemont. 1976. *Eating in America: A History.* New York: William Morrow.

American mealtime traditions are explored as well as the detailed history of what we eat and why certain foods are included in the American diet.

Santino, Jack. 1994. *All Around the Year: Holidays and Celebrations in American Life.* Urbana: University of Illinois Press.

From the annual Rattlesnake Round-up in Sweetwater, Texas, to the Green Corn Dance purification rites by Florida Seminoles, both old and new traditions are examined. This compilation is enhanced by Santino's entertaining commentary on the American experience.

Tuleja, Tad. 1987. *Curious Customs: The Stories behind 296 Popular American Rituals.* New York: Harmony Books.

This text details the hows and whys of American social customs. Behaviors that are linked to religion, superstition, and region are examined.

Activity 3: Evolving Rituals

The centuries have taught us that even if the original purpose of a ritual celebration is cloaked, that purpose still remains. Pagan spirituality is intertwined in the roots of modern religion. "Holidays" still come from "holy days," even if we blend the word.

What other modern rituals are evolving? We set aside special days for what is important to us. Holidays wax or wane in popularity. Armistice Day, which commemorated the end of World War I, was changed to Veteran's Day, which honors veterans of all wars. Holidays exist on paper on many calendars. It is only when we incorporate them into our actions that they hold meaning for us. Students might examine:

> **Martin Luther King Day** (January 19): How are schools and the community honoring the slain leader of the civil rights movement? What do we enact? What is the metaphorical goal or purpose behind some of our actions (speeches, programs, essays on peace, or poster contests promoting tolerance, understanding, and harmony among different religious denominations)?

> **Earth Day** (April 22): Earth Day had its twenty-fifth anniversary in 1995. It promotes ecology themes and awareness of our natural resources. The emphasis is on recycling and the cleaning and preserving of our environment. How do we enact these beliefs? By planting trees? cleaning up litter in parks and on playgrounds?

> **Kwanzaa** (December 26–January 1): *Kwanzaa* means "first fruits" in Swahili and is an African American holiday invented by a professor in 1966. Having gained in popularity in the last ten years across America, the celebration of Kwanzaa in schools, communities, and homes is fairly recent. The emphasis is on ties to the family, to the community, and to the African past. It is enacted by lighting candles, singing, dancing, and storytelling (Cohen and Coffin 1991).

Kwanzaa is a good example of how new traditions take root and grow. The old can be borrowed from, altered, and expanded upon. Our rituals are in constant change, just like the language we use to express our ideas.

Activity 4: Regional Rituals

Tightening the view to popular American culture, we can make further connections to mythology-turned-metaphor. There are regional and school-related rituals we take part in, perhaps without even being aware of it. New Orleans has its Mardi Gras, San Francisco its Chinese New Year celebration. Ask students to investigate the local celebrations or gatherings that have been ritualized in their community. What metaphors live in the meanings behind the celebrations?

Students may also wish to consider national rituals. What does a beauty pageant mean? to the contestants? to the students themselves? What is represented in a display of costumes and talent and the wearing of a banner or crown? How have we tried to shift the focus to brains as well as beauty? Have we succeeded?

College towns with a subgroup of fraternities and sororities engage in ritualistic behavior with pledges, rush week, singing, skits, dancing on lawns, and decorating trees with toilet paper. What do these behaviors mean? Ask students to consider how their opinions may differ from those of the people who participate in the rituals.

Michigan has a celebration of cherry blossoms; Western towns have frontier days; in Tennessee there is even a pilgrimage to Graceland by Elvis Presley fans on August 16, the anniversary of his death. How are these events ritualized? What metaphorical connections can students make? Here's one metaphorical explanation: "Asked if he was an Elvis fan, Wooton replied: 'Elvis doesn't have fans. They're more like worshipers. He has an unusual god-like status. That's part of the package when you're one of the chosen few, one of the immortals'" (Cohen and Coffin 1991, 250). Students may choose one of these or other cultural happenings and hunt for the hidden metaphors.

Activity 5: Sports

Since the Olympics of ancient Greece, athletics and athletes have been celebrated and honored. Students can see what ritualistic parallels they can find in the traditions and treatment of sporting events. For example, what can they say about the homecoming game parade and pageantry with a king and queen after a sporting event? Is this akin to a medieval joust, with favors being awarded to champions, followed by feast, drink, and dance? What occurs in your area?

Sports-associated traditions have other, newer ritual associations, such as a tailgate party before a game. Sports have their season and region: water and surfing events on America's coasts, annual races across bridges, rodeos in the West, and tractor-pulls in the heartland. We have walkathons and marathons showing we're ready to "go the distance" for personal and charitable goals. Such activities become annual events. Repetition becomes a tradition in itself. The Kentucky Derby, well past its hundredth anniversary, is on the first Saturday in May in Louisville every year. Although it's a mixed metaphor, the Derby is called the first "leg" of the coveted Triple Crown of American thoroughbred racing; the other "legs" are the Preakness in Baltimore and the Belmont Stakes in Elmont, New York. The Indianapolis 500 race is a Memorial Day tradition, thanks to the media. Santino (1994) finds a gruesome parallel between what happens on and off the track in *All Around the Year: Holidays and Celebrations in American Life:*

[I]t is ironic that more deaths occur due to automobile crashes during Memorial Day weekend than at any other comparable period of the year. Coincidentally, the Indianapolis 500 auto race is held on Memorial Day. While this particular race is going on, every year thousands of Americans are killed on the highways. On holiday weekends, especially Memorial Day weekend, we keep count. So we can see in the Indianapolis 500 a kind of symbolic exaggeration of our mechanized society and the kind of death it brings. (121)

Fall means football and tailgate parties, pep rallies and Monday nights around the television. It also means "my team is better than your team" talk, often accompanied by friendly wagers and football pools. Betting on the Super Bowl is representative of American capitalism, according to Santino, who credits the media with the origin of Super Sunday as a national holiday: "The Super Bowl's relationship to American capitalism is basic to its success and to our understanding of it as an event that tells us something about ourselves. . . . Commercial television time is more costly then than at any other time of the year. Money is of course won in victory, but success on the field also translates into increased salaries the following season. The Super Bowl crystallizes American capitalism" (53–54).

Spring has evolved for some into what begins the rite of baseball training—at least this year. Is the effect of the baseball strike of 1994–95 on "America's favorite pastime" a sort of de-evolution? What would happen if the strike were not settled and the controversy lasted years? Would baseball evolve or be replaced?

Students may choose to investigate a sporting event and its link to a season or region. What ritualistic behavior have fans borrowed, such as painting faces or dying hair, to show a bond with a certain team? What can be said about the players and the promotion of the game or its effect on American society? How are these events like holidays?

Activity 6: Across History

Is there a social evolution in our ceremonies and customs? Valentine's Day celebrations were quite different in the medieval time of their origin. Lovers literally "wore their hearts on their sleeves." A red heart sewn to the sleeve meant that the person was devoting herself to St. Valentine or to one of the gods associated with love. People played games in pairs in order to promote romance among the couples. Many games had to do with divining the identity of a future mate. Hemp seed was sprinkled over the shoulder into a bowl of water. The pattern would supposedly foretell the future spouse as the hopeful lover chanted:

Hemp seed I sow,
Hemp seed will grow.

Let him who loves me
Come and mow.

(Cosman 1981, 39)

This is a tradition that, if it were not already obsolete, would be illegal in the United States. A particular type of hemp seed, of course, produces the marijuana plant. But even fifty years ago, hemp was better known as a plant used in making rope. Its quick growth (often several feet in as many weeks) may explain the mowing reference. And given its woody stalk, one would *really* have to love someone to tackle mowing a patch of hemp!

Divination represented an important medieval idea, that everything in the universe was interrelated. It was believed that human destiny could be revealed in the patterns of the trees, plants, stars, and stones of the natural world. Foods for the Valentine table were apples (from association with Eve and the Garden of Eden), figs, and pomegranates. Any fruit with abundant seeds was thought to be a fertility symbol. Today, people send Valentine rhymes on cards, and perhaps a form of a divination game is played with candy conversation hearts.

Students may work with a partner to view a modern custom or holiday from different perspectives of time, describing how the event changed with the generations. For example, "courting" once meant sitting on a porch or in a parlor under the watchful eye of a married chaperone. Now in most American cultural groups, girls can initiate contact by telephone, live in coed dormitories, and no longer need their father's permission when their hands are asked for in marriage—if their "hands" are even asked for. Communities in which old courting customs are still practiced are considered old-fashioned.

Ask students to consider what has remained the same or changed since their grandparents' time or their parents' time. What is the cause or reason behind the change? Customs in communication might be especially interesting to examine. The class can compare the tradition of correspondence by letter writing to currently evolving "netiquette" (etiquette on the electronic network).

**Activity 7:
Across the Globe**

Another class project is exploring and comparing how other cultures celebrate similar traditions. What are their symbols, and how does the significance relate metaphorically to the ritual? Other cultures use different symbols to enact their traditions, such as the breaking of a piñata in Hispanic cultures. Japanese custom forgoes individual children's birthdays and instead celebrates once a year a separate Girls Festival and Boys Festival. What do celebrations and traditions say about the society that holds them? How do they compare with our own? What is the cultural significance?

Some calendars list holidays from other lands, illuminating the metaphor *shrinking globe.* That is, as we grow in understanding our worldly neighbors, other cultures do not seem so mysterious. Once we learn about others' customs and traditions and comprehend them, differences seem to disappear, and their ways become incorporated with our own. Trans-Can Greetings (based in Hong Kong, British Columbia, and Canada) publishes a calendar with a multicultural focus. With its multinational origins and French Monet illustrations, it certainly illustrates the shrinking globe concept. Inside, it does so even more obviously: January 26 is Waitangi Day in New Zealand; February 2 is Groundhog Day in America; March 12 is Commonwealth Day in the United Kingdom; and June 5 is Foundation Day in Australia and Wales and a bank and public holiday in the Republic of Ireland. With curiosity and a few reference books, students can discover the meanings of the metaphors represented in these rituals and others across the globe.

Trying It Out

My Metaphor, My Self

Every religion is true one way or another. It is true when understood metaphorically. But when it gets stuck to its own metaphors, interpreting them as facts, then you are in trouble. A metaphor is an image that suggests something else. For instance, if I say to a person, "You are a nut," I'm not suggesting that I think the person is literally a nut. "Nut" is a metaphor. The reference of the metaphor in religious traditions is to something transcendent that is not literally any thing. If you think that the metaphor is itself the reference, it would be like going to a restaurant, asking for the menu, seeing beefsteak written there, and starting to eat the menu. (Campbell with Moyers 1988, 56)

An important realization is that the rituals we perform are in themselves metaphors for something else, representations of reality. Defending his collaboration with Joseph Campbell on the study of mythology against those who believe "'all these Greek gods and stuff' are irrelevant to the human condition today," Bill Moyers writes:

[T]he remnants of all that "stuff" line the walls of our interior system of belief, like shards of broken pottery in an archeological site. But as we are organic beings, there is energy in all that "stuff." Rituals evoke it. Consider the position of judges in our society, which Campbell saw in mythological, not sociological, terms. If this position were just a role, the judge could wear a grey suit to court instead of the magisterial black robe. For the law to hold authority beyond mere coercion, the power of the judge must be ritualized, mythologized. (xiv)

In looking for modern examples of mythology-turned-metaphor, students can come to understand and appreciate the historical and cultural significance of our rituals and the metaphors that link them.

Transformational Metaphors

A transformational metaphor is one in which the self stands for another or for a group in ceremonies. To understand the transformational metaphor, think of the synecdoche, where a part stands for a whole. For example, *the Gray* represents all of the Southern army in the Civil War, and *the Blue* stands for the Northern forces. Other examples are *town and gown* to distinguish between the residents of a city and the people in the university located within it; *three-piece-suit* for men; *skirt* for women.

All cultures have transformational metaphors, which are often associated with holidays. A person is chosen to represent another person or force (such as one occurring in nature) for a specific purpose. For example, the first day of May is associated with fertility rites to force the Earth into spring. A Queen of the May is chosen. "She may be the prettiest or youngest or tallest or most honored guest. No matter how she is chosen, the queen must represent a particular quality in the superlative" (Cosman 1981, 52). The queen presides over a maypole dance or games. Traditionally, dancing and athletic contests were supposed to awaken the earth after the winter dormancy—hence the winter-as-sleep metaphor.

Many pagan or sun-worshiping ceremonies were blended with Christian themes, and new rituals were created. The ancient Druidic bonfires of Scotland (known in the central Highlands as the Beltane fires) were once used to sacrifice a human victim. In later centuries, and in other European countries, the human sacrifice was transformed into a straw or wicker man and burned. May Day and summer solstice ceremonies (midsummer) were enacted in order to ensure a goodly supply of sunshine for bountiful crops.

The Catholic community links the ancient May Day rites with the Virgin Mary. A young girl (virgin honoring Virgin) places a wreath of fresh flowers on a statue of Mary in the church. Symbolically, Mary is crowned as Queen of Heaven. A maypole dance may be performed along with songs honoring Mary.

A transformational metaphor common to many cultures is the idea of scapegoat, a person taking on the sin and suffering of the people:

> [I]n New Britain and Peru, the devils are or were driven out at the beginning of the rainy season. When a tribe has taken to agriculture,

the time for the general expulsion of devils is naturally made to agree with one of the great epochs of the agricultural year, as sowing or harvest. . . . Some of the agricultural communities of India and the Hindoo Koosh . . . hold their general clearance of demons at harvest, others at sowing time. But whatever season of the year it is held, the general expulsion of devils commonly marks the beginning of the new year. For, before entering on a new year, people are anxious to rid themselves of the troubles in the past; hence the fact that amongst so many people—Iroquois, Tonquinese, Siamese, Tibetans, etc.—the beginning of the new year is inaugurated with a solemn and public banishment of evil spirits. (Frazer 1981, 203)

Activity 1: Cultural Transformations

In the Swedish tradition of Saint Lucia day, the oldest daughter of each household dresses up as the Saint Lucia girl. She wears a white dress with a red sash and an evergreen wreath on her head with glowing candles to symbolize the coming of brighter days. She wakes her family before daylight, bringing them coffee and sweet buns.

The oldest daughter has become a transformational metaphor, which we defined earlier as occurring when the individual stands for a group or for someone else, often in association with a holiday. She symbolizes Saint Lucia. Looking closely at the symbols within the tradition, one can find other metaphors. Greenery symbolizes the coming of spring. The candles light the way on the winter solstice, the darkest day of the year.

Certain symbols are played over and over again in mythology and have similar meanings from across cultures. Symbols communicate the metaphor to us. This symbolic language speaks to us, sometimes with a jarring shout, sometimes with the delicacy of a whisper, enhancing the ritual and the meaning we have presented in our rite or in other contexts. Pick a festival, tradition, or ceremony and analyze aspects of metaphors. Unmask the myths behind these transformational metaphors. Discover the meaning with the categories in Table 7.1 as a guide. The table has been filled in with an examination of the symbols and metaphors in the Saint Lucia ritual as an example.

In medieval times and even earlier, it was believed there were four elements (air, fire, earth, water) out of which everything was composed. Think of how many rituals use water for a ceremonial death and rebirth. The four elements went along with the seasons, colors, parts of the body, and constellations of the zodiac. People took for granted their connectedness to the earth. Repetition of pattern was looked for and became symbolic when a connection was made. Symbols serve as a reminder of that connection.

Students may be invited to look for the patterns in symbols and to consider the form, shape, and color they take. All have mean-

Table 7.1.
Symbols in Rituals

Four Elements (Air, Fire, Earth, Water)	The candle flame represents bringing light into the darkness of the longest night.
Physical Properties (Shape, Color, Number, Sound)	Shape—The wreath is a circle, which has no beginning and no end. It represents the cycle of the seasons. Spring will follow winter.
	Color—The green of the wreath represents nature. The "evergreen" trees remain so even in winter as if the promise of spring to follow is embodied in the plant. Life will continue. The white in the dress stands for bright light, the white of winter, and the brightest color to contrast with the darkness of the shortest day of the year. The red in the sash could evoke the yule season or the red of holly berries.
	Number or age—The eldest daughter performs the rite. She becomes the embodiment of Saint Lucia (whose name means "light").
Temporality (Season, Time, Date)	Celebration in Sweden takes place on December 13, the feast day of Saint Lucia. Originally, the rite took place on the winter solstice.
Action	Breakfast is served in bed by the Saint Lucia girl, who carries the food on a tray to her parents and family members.
Physical Objects (Props, Clothing, Food)	Lit candles are worn on a wreath on the head. The girl wears a white dress with a red sash. The breakfast consists of sweet rolls and coffee.

ing. Number can be important, whether in age or number of the participants or number of days. Bris, a ritual circumcision in the Jewish faith, is performed exactly eight days after birth. In looking for patterns, students should be alerted to the fact that time sequence may be important.

Seasons are bound to the turning of the earth and the earth's position in relation to the sun. The calendar is solar in origin. The position of the sun told people when to plant and when to harvest. Agricultural rituals often took on symbolic clockwise movement, which is the direction of the sun's path. Movement also could signal a change or transition from one stage of life to the next, such as the graduation procession. Action can take the form of mimicry, dance, the spoken word, song, or the ceremonial lighting of a candle. Alert students to look for stylized movements in rituals.

Often, special clothing is required. When a person takes on the role of another, a mask or costume helps define the identity and disguise the individual. Uniforms remove the individual and replace the person with representative powers, whether soldier or cheerleader. We all recognize hats associated with different professions. The firefighter is distinguished from the police officer, the jester is distinguished from the king. The hat alone can be a symbol with a specific meaning to convey.

Physical objects help to convey the ritual. The scroll is still placed in the hand of graduates, even though the actual stiff diploma (suitable for framing) may be mailed later. The gavel in the judge's hand is just as important as the turtle-shell shaker in the hand of the medicine man. The shepherd's crook in the hand of a bishop is the same physical metaphor as the candy cane in the hand of Santa Claus, whose origin can be traced to a Turkish bishop known as Saint Nicholas.

Students may also search for other physical symbols in ceremonies—the candles, incense, oil, ashes, jewelry, and other tools that we use to build our rituals. The parts are bound to the whole and aid the representation. (Presentation is part of the word *representation*—to present again).

Students may also seek out other people as transformational metaphors from traditions and ceremonies: trick-or-treaters on Halloween, May Queen, prom queen, TV or movie action heroes, star athletes, and so on. They can use Table 7.1 to record the symbolic connections and their meanings. Challenge them to research and reason out the metaphors behind the transformations.

Activity 2: Personal Transformations

Students may enjoy making metaphors for themselves. Questions to get them thinking include:

- What would you be chosen as? What would you represent?
- How are you a metaphor for the coming of a season? an event?
- To what are you devoted? Borrow or invent the symbols associated with you and tell why you chose them.

Atlanta artist Miriam Karp's use of personal symbols in her art has been described as presenting "dreamy maplike sequences in which she mixes symbols from the Anasazi culture of the American Southwest with symbols from the atomic age. (You may recall that atomic testing took place in the deserts of that region.) The point, [Karp] said, is to show how 'signs and symbols travel between one culture and another, how the experience of place is a layering of perception, history, reverie and loss'" (Heilenman 1995, I4).

What complex meanings can your students develop using symbols they create or select? Their symbols can be taken from any aspect of their experience. What holds meaning for us is part of our uniqueness.

Activity 3: Rites of Passage

Students will have strong opinions as to what makes an American an adult, whether it's becoming eighteen, earning the right to vote, or reaching the legal drinking age for the state. In prior generations, we would have added "eligibility for the draft" to our list. Although young men still must register at eighteen, the fact that there is not currently a draft lottery may mean that today's teens will not view that as a rite of passage. What do other cultures do to show that adulthood has been attained? How does this compare with what happens in America?

Trying It Out

The Archeology of Proverbs

Proverbs are another way of capturing the traditions that define our cultures. Proverbs, ancient sayings, even fortune cookies espouse the beliefs of the country from which these words of wisdom originated. By analyzing proverbs, one can discover a country's doctrine, morals, and way of life. Sayings not only reflect values and conventions but also give a cultural perspective. Consider the Japanese proverb "While on a journey one need feel no shame," meaning "A man away from his town may do what he likes with impunity. A traveler can do anything" (Okada 1963, 150). The suggestion is that someone on a business trip, perhaps, may act in ways that the individual would not in his or her hometown (and get away with it). This proverb, however, implies not just acknowledgment that such behavior occurs, but also acceptance of it—"one need feel no shame."

Each country has unique imagery that may not ring familiar in our culture's metaphors. For example, the Japanese phrase "greens sprinkled with salt" is a metaphor for a disappointed and dejected person (Okada 1963, 19). This may not be the image that comes to mind when we think of dejection and disappointment. In the same way, metaphors from proverbs that we hold familiar may also sound strange outside our culture. Think of how expressions like "She got his goat" or "He's pulling your leg" sound to someone unfamiliar with the meaning behind those particular idiomatic images.

Very often, concepts within the metaphors of proverbs overlap and have similar meanings in different cultures:

Eastern Proverb	Western Proverb
A nail that sticks out is hammered.	The squeaky wheel gets the grease.
What is not said is flowers.	Silence is golden.

The metaphor within a proverb need not be equivalent to one of our familiar expressions for us to appreciate the imagery. We need only to be able to compare or relate to something we know. This is how metaphors evolve. Consider this proverb from the Jabo tribe of Liberia: "He is a pretty pebble; water will not carry him away" (Herzog 1936, 236). Can students relate to the meaning that a favored person is not punished for his wrongdoing? Have they known a student who has the favor of the teacher, so that even if she goofs off, she is excused, whereas another in the same situation might be held accountable? (This proverb brings to mind a certain Indiana basketball coach whose chair-throwing, cursing, and assorted infractions are often overlooked as long as he brings his team closer to the championship.) If students can think of a way to personalize an unfamiliar proverb, then they can understand the metaphor and perhaps glean some knowledge of the culture. Another Jabo proverb is "A man is a pumpkin; he has no unripe parts" (233). The thriftiness of the African tribe is revealed in this maxim. They make use of all the parts of a pumpkin: its hollowed shell can become a lantern or a container to hold water; its meat and seeds can be eaten. Nothing is wasted. So a person should be, utilizing all aspects of the self. Would these people be proponents of recycling? Values taken from a culture's proverbs can be applied to their societal mores.

From a list of proverbs from assorted countries, ask the class to try to decipher the underlying meanings. They should try to identify the metaphor, relate or compare the proverb to something that is familiar to them, and see what they might be able to say about the culture based on the proverb. As an example, we offer this analysis of the Japanese proverb "A rosy face in the morning; white bones in the evening":

1. Identify metaphor: Life exists in a fresh, rosy face in the morning; death strikes—a skeleton in the evening. What had life in the beginning of the day now has ended. Life is ephemeral.

2. Relate to familiar concept: "Here today, gone tomorrow."

3. Inferences about the culture: The culture is aware of the uncertainty of life; the proverb reminds us not to take anything for granted.

Now try these:

1. There is no medicine for a fool. (Japanese; Okada 1963, 29)

2. The fruit must have a stem before it grows. (Jabo; Herzog 1936, 31)

3. If two persons are of the same mind, their sharpness can divide metal. (Chinese; Smith [1914] 1965, 43)

4. If fire and water can make friends, anybody can live together. (Jamaican; Beckwith 1970, 117)

5. The dog's owner is the one who takes the bone from its mouth. (Jabo; Herzog 1936, 91)

6. Though in rags, he has a heart of brocade. (Japanese; Okada 1963, 32)

7. You cannot put doors to others' mouths. (Japanese; Okada 1963, 61)

8. A stupid man has no eyes in his heart. (Chinese; Smith [1914] 1965, 342)

9. The tree grows up before we tie a cow to it. (Jabo; Herzog 1936, 31)

10. One whose hand is full, has plenty of company. (Jamaican; Beckwith 1970, 118)

Further Activities

- Students might enjoy making a collection of opposite proverbs, such as "Absence makes the heart grow fonder" contrasted with "Out of sight, out of mind."

- Some classes may want to try their hands at writing words of wisdom for fortune cookies. Suggest that they try to express some of their values (or some of their culture's) metaphorically. They can write their best metaphorical statements on slips of paper to exchange with one another.

III Imagining Language

My plea is for a greater recognition of the poet in each one of us—to recognize that figuration is not an escape from reality but constitutes the way we ordinarily understand ourselves and the world in which we live.

Raymond W. Gibbs, *The Poetics of Mind*

8 English as a Metaphor for Multiculturalism

Language is a living thing. It has to grow and respond to its environment in order to survive. Because American culture is ever-changing, always drawing in new themes and threads and ways of looking at the world, our vocabulary never sleeps.

Jim Carnes, "An Uncommon Language"

Language is always an expression of culture and politics as well as a vehicle of communication, and English is in the midst of controversy on both fronts. Politically, the world has a love-hate relationship with English as the dominant language of global communications, a status that has emerged in the wake of its use as a tool of imperialism. In many states in our own country, we have the "English Only" movement, expressing a resistance to the fact of multilingualism among our population. According to the U.S. Census Bureau, over 31 million people in the United States speak a language other than English at home.

We also have dialect battles as English is viewed as a weapon of discrimination by some and as a vehicle for transcending ethnic and class differences by others. These important perspectives have been treated extensively by scholars such as Willinsky (1984) and should not be ignored as the larger context in which all English teaching takes place. In this chapter, however, we are focusing inward upon the resources of the language itself and its possibilities for raising our multicultural awareness and appreciation.

In their extensive treatment of the history and diversity of English, McCrum, Cran, and MacNeil (1986) estimate that English is used by 750 million to a billion people, only half of whom are native speakers. They point out that three-quarters of the world's mail, cables, and telexes are in English, as are more than half the scientific and technical periodicals, and English is the language of 80 percent of the world's information stored in computers. As we near the end of the twentieth century, they describe English as "more widely scattered, more widely spoken and written, than any other language has ever been . . . the first truly global language" (19–20). This image, however, is not so much one of a single language streaming all over the earth as of a stream that starts out as itself but gathers in other sources until it has changed into something as different from its origins as an ocean is from a river.

English also has developed an oceanic vocabulary, which has been estimated in the millions of words but cannot be pinned down for the very reason that it is always expanding and changing. It has borrowed from every language, culture, and subculture with which it has made contact, resulting in the proliferation of terms in any given dictionary as well as in the proliferation of dictionaries themselves. This absorptive quality of English is illustrated in its many variations, both in countries where it is the native language and in the many countries where it has become the language of commerce and international communication. Linguist Donald S. McDonald has pointed out ways in which onomatopoeic aspects of the Aboriginal language have enriched Australian English with words like *digeridoo,* the name of a primitive wind instrument that resonates with its sound, and *tumbarumba,* which "rumbles through the Latin *tonitrus,* the French *tonnerre,* and the German *donner"* (1994). *Walkabout,* a word derived from Aboriginal culture, has been associated with the native word for the marsupial *wallaby,* so that the local phrase "on the wallaby track" is often a synonym for the wandering associated with "dreamtime" or *alcheringa.*

Goodspeed (1981) has charted a kind of American language pie, tracing word origins not only to Latin, Greek, and the Romance and Germanic languages but also to Sanskrit, Hindi, Arabic, Egyptian, Iranian, Celtic, Persian, Turkish, Japanese, and Chinese and the languages of the Africans, Pacific islanders, Malay and Indonesian peoples, and Native Americans. Because of its liberal immigration policy, therefore, English is an immense pastiche of languages and cultures, so that even the most monolingual of us can find in our native tongue links to the rest of the world. And we do not have to have an especially extensive vocabulary to do so; most speakers operate with a few thousand words, perhaps our greatest writers with twenty to twenty-five thousand (Borgmann 1967). But even the small core of words most of us find familiar can take us all over the world and surprise us in other ways as well.

Trying It Out

Multicultural Food Basket

Food itself is a common medium of cultural exchange, and often our introduction to another culture is a visit to an ethnic restaurant. Grocery stores also connect us with other cultures. For example, fruits converge in our produce shelves from many parts of the world, sometimes after complicated journeys. *Apples* and *berries* are linguistically English, but most other fruits have immigrated into our language from elsewhere.

A list of familiar fruits with etymological histories provided is given in Figure 8.1, indicating the multicultural nature of one of our main food groups. Invite students to extend this list with etymologies of other fruits they add to the list themselves. Word histories here are from the *American Heritage Dictionary of the English Language.* Other dictionaries with etymological information can also be consulted.

Figure 8.1.
Fruit Names and Their
Etymological Histories

Fruit	Etymology
Orange	Middle English from Old French, from Arabic, from Persian, from Sanskrit
Cantaloupe	French from Italian, named for the villa Cantalupo, where first grown
Banana	Spanish and Portuguese from a West African name
Apricot	Catalan from Arabic, from Late Greek, from Latin
Pear	Old English from Latin

A spurious story has it that the phrase "e pluribus unum" was originally uttered by a cook who had just invented the salad. Be that as it may, we can justify the salad metaphor for the diversity of American culture just by considering the names of common vegetables in the same way as the fruits above. Among truly "English" vegetables are beans, corn, and garlic. As shown in Figure 8.2, others have come to us from other languages and cultures. Again, students can add the names of other vegetables and their histories to discover some of the implications of the salad, stew, or bouillabaisse metaphors often applied to American culture as being more accurate than the melting pot.

Many, but not all, staples in the American pantry have names originating in English. For example, *salt* is English, though *pepper* comes from Latin, Greek, and ultimately Sanskrit. *Flour* is English, but *butter*, which means "cow cheese," came into our language through German, French, and Latin, from Greek. What does some dictionary investigation reveal about the linguistic and cultural connections of foods we consider basic stock for a kitchen? Again, students can extend the list in Figure 8.3 as they choose, perhaps after some data-gathering in their own cupboards and refrigerators at home, which may disclose some quite different "staples" from this Anglo-Saxon fare.

Figure 8.2.
Vegetable Names
and Their
Etymological
Histories

Vegetable	Etymology
Tomato	Spanish from Nahautl (Central American) *tomatl*
Potato	Spanish from Taino (West Indian) *batata*
Broccoli	Italian, diminutive of *brocco,* "shoot"
Squash	Algonquian/Massachuset (Native American) *askootasquash*
Okra	West African *nkruma*
Spinach	Old French, from Old Spanish, from Arabic *isfanakh*
Pea	Latin, from Greek *pison*
Onion	Old French from Latin *unus* for "one" or "unity"
Cabbage	Old French *caboce* for "head"
Avocado	Spanish, from Nahuatl *ahuacatl* for "testicle"
Yam	Portuguese *inhame,* "edible," possibly from Fulani (North Africa) *nyami,* "to eat"
Rutabaga	Swedish from Old Norse, *rotbagge,* "baggy root"
Carrot	Old French, from Latin, from Greek *karoton*
Turnip	Latin *napus*
Celery	French, from Italian, from Latin, from Greek *selinon*

Figure 8.3.
Food Names and
Their Etymological
Histories

Food	Etymology
Rice	Old French, from Italian, from Latin, from Greek, from East Iranian, from Sanskrit *vrihi*
Wheat	Old English original from the Germanic protolanguage
Oats	Old English original
Milk	Old English original
Egg	Old Norse *egg*
Honey	Old English original
Sugar	Old French, from Old Italian, from Latin, from Arabic, from Persian, from Sukarit, from Sanskrit *sarkara*
Chocolate	Spanish from Aztec *xocaltl,* "bitter water"
Cinnamon	Old French, from Latin, from Greek, from Hebrew *qinnamown*
Clove	French, from Latin *clavas de girofle,* "nail tree"

The English of Geography

Place names are another source of information for following our cultural/linguistic connections, to both Native American origins and the countries from which explorers, conquerors, and immigrants came. For example, any map of the Americas is studded with place names derived from Native American languages, preserving something of the culture and experiences of the people who were here before the Europeans. The chart in Figure 8.4 shows some familiar American place names, their linguistic sources, and their original meanings in their Indian languages.

Figure 8.4.
Place Names and Their Sources and Meanings

Place Name	Language	Original Meaning
Chattanooga	Algonquian	Mountain rising to a point
Kalamazoo	Iroquois	Boiling pot
Roanoke	Algonquian	Shell money
Schenectady	Algonquian	End of trail
Alabama	Algonquian	I clear the thicket
Dakota	Shoshonean	Friendly
Kansas	Siouan	People of the south wind
Oklahoma	Muskogean	Red people
Mexico	Aztec	God of war
Panama	Chibchan	Plenty of fish

Students can start with a map of their own state to find Indian place names and investigate the sources of these names, the individuals they honor, or the metaphors they express. Further investigation can be made into other local or state place names. Often the name of a town or body of water will be eponymous, derived from the name of an individual or family. Other messages may also be embedded, containing clues as to the history or characteristics of the place. In one county of southern Indiana, for example, there are small towns named Gnaw Bone, Bean Blossom, Pike's Peak, Stonehead, Beck's Corner, and Story. Within the state of Indiana, there are at least thirty towns named after foreign countries, including Cuba, Lebanon, Poland, Peru, and Brazil. There is also a sizable French connection in such towns as Versailles, West Lafayette, Terre Haute, Vincennes, and Dubois. A map of any state can be the beginning of a linguistic expedition into the history and metaphorical naming of places by those who lived close to the land.

Metaphorical Travels of Words

Just as travel changes people, it changes words, which go through metaphorical transformations as they cross borders of cultures and times. Metaphors are like offspring: they start out living close to their parents but in time move away to lead their own lives, often getting farther and farther away from home. There are many words whose modern meanings bear no obvious relationships to each other but whose histories reveal a common ancestor. One example is the surprising relationship between the words *cheetah* and *chintz*, both derived from the Sanskrit *citra*, meaning "brightly marked, spotted, variegated." Another set of unlikely kin includes *cave, decoy,* and *jail,* whose common meaning is "enclosure" or "cage." *Decoy* comes from the Dutch *de kooi,* an enclosure for trapping fowl, which in English shed the meaning of "enclosure" and kept the associated meaning of "trap" or "lure." *Kooi* is related to the Latin term meaning "hollow," hence *cave,* which in turn evolved through French into the English *jail.*

Activity 1: Long-Lost Relatives and Adopted Kin

Using an etymological dictionary such as Eric Partridge's *Origins* (1958) or David Crystal's *Cambridge Encyclopedia of the English Language* (1995), students can investigate the origins of the following pairs and sets of words and construct their etymological stories:

orphan, robot
prestige, prestidigitation
roast, roster
turkey, turquoise
bereavement, robber, robe
heavy, havoc, hawk
pickle, pinch, woodpecker
rival, river, arrive
sarcasm, sarcoma, sarcophagus
surge, source, resurrection
tact, taste, tax
tropical, trophy, entropy
shell, shield, scale, scull
shoot, sheet, shut, shout
thigh, thumb, tomb, rifle
share, shear, score, shore, short, shirt, skirt

**Activity 2:
Casual Strangers**

On the other hand, there are words that look related but aren't. For example, *tattoo* meaning a picture stippled upon the skin is unrelated to *tattoo* meaning a military call, though one might seem to be a cross-sensory metaphor for the other. The first comes from Tahitian *tutu*, "a picturing," which refers to the method of injecting color into the skin. The second comes from Dutch *taptoe*, meaning the shutting down of taps or faucets, hence, a piece played in the evening or at the close of something. The latter, moreover, has only an apparent relationship to *taps*, the musical signal for sleep, which derives from Old English *tappen*, "to strike lightly." Following are other apparent relatives who come from entirely different sources:

> turtle (the amphibian) and turtle (in turtledove)
>
> round (shape of a circle) and -round (in surround)
>
> root (of a plant) and root (what a pig does)
>
> orb (in architecture) and orb (a circular object)
>
> lift (raise) and lift (steal)
>
> male (masculine gender) and -male (in female)

What do these investigations into the meanderings of words toward and away from each other tell us about the nature of language? What seems to be common across all languages in terms of the relationships among words, meanings, and cultures?

Trying It Out

Word Stories

Another way to observe the living and changing nature of language is to look at the stories of particular words brought into our repertoire from distant origins in time and space. Following are some of the stories related by Robert Claiborne and the editors of the *American Heritage Dictionaries* (1986) that illustrate how malleable a substance language is for fashioning meaning.

Words That Have Changed in the Course of Travel

Curfew: This story illustrates how a word can change from its original meaning to an associated meaning. According to the *American Heritage Dictionaries'* editors, the original meaning was to cover fires, derived from the Old French *cuevrefeu*, formed from *couvir* and *feu*. A bell was rung at a certain hour signaling time to put out fires, most likely as a preventative measure. Over time, when the original need for the signal was no longer necessary, the idea of a command was retained. Eventually, the notion of a bell or sound was dropped and the contemporary meaning of the word evolved, an order for certain people to go into their residences at a specified hour.

Peculiar: This word derives from the Latin *pecu,* meaning "cattle," generalized to refer to private property. From this meaning came the sense of "belonging to oneself alone," which then assumed the meaning of uniqueness or singularity, which in turn took on the connotation and then the denotation of "unusual" or "odd." Over time, the term has become increasingly disparaging, so that now to call someone "peculiar" is to signal that this person is abnormal and probably suspicious.

Is It Real or Metaphor?

Bed: Most of us think of the beds we sleep in as primary and the beds in which we plant flowers as metaphorical, but according to the history of the word, it is not so clear which, if either, came first. The *American Heritage* editors trace the roots of this word to Indo-European *bdeah-,* meaning "to dig." In prehistoric Common German, the reconstructed ancestor of English, German, and Swedish, the word meant both "a garden plot" and "a sleeping place," suggesting that sleeping places for our European ancestors were at one time dug out of the ground.

Our National Costume

Jeans: Despite their status as an American clothing statement, jeans probably began in Genoa and derive their name from the Middle English *Gene fustian,* a combination of the first part of "Genoa" and the word for "a kind of cloth made from cotton, flax, or wool." In the language process called metonymy, the modifer came to stand for the noun, resulting in *jean* for the cloth and *jeans* for the garments made from it. The editors of the *American Heritage Dictionaries* cite the first appearance of the modern use of the term in a nineteenth-century novel by Robert Smith Surtees, *Handley Cross,* in which he wrote, "Septimus arrived flourishin' his cambric, with his white jeans strapped under his chammy leather opera boots" (30).

Whose Word Is It?

Words that have been derived from people's names, termed *eponyms,* provide personalized glimpses into cultural transformations, though sometimes these origins are in dispute. For example, the term *fudge* with the meaning of "obscure the truth," according to Boycott (1982), was attributed by Benjamin Disraeli's father to "one Captain Fudge, commander of a merchantman (the Black Eagle), who upon his return from a voyage, how ill fraught soever his ship was, always brought home to his owners a good crop of lies; so much that now, aboard ship, the sailors when they hear a great lie told, cry out, 'You fudge it'" (47). However, the *American Heritage Dictionaries* ascribes it to an archaic word *fadge,* related to *fake,* itself listed simply as a word of "obscure origin," although there was a Middle English word *fake* that meant a single loop of a coiled rope. Does anyone see a metaphor here?

Another word with alternative stories is *blanket*, conventionally described as developing from the French word *blanc*, meaning "white," which when coupled with a diminutive ending became the Middle English word for a white woolen material. However, the alternative story is that "the first blankets ever produced in England were spun on the loom of Thomas Blanket, a weaver who set up shop in Bristol" (Boycott 1982, 20).

Many eponymous words are scientific terms, named after proud discoverers of one phenomenon or another. In just one field, energy, we have the terms *ohm, volt, watt, joule, Fahrenheit,* and *Celsius* from the names of scientists. *Amperes* or *amps*, units of electricity, are named for the French scientist Andre Marie Ampere, who provided the basis for the study of electrodynamics (Beeching 1979). The human body has hundreds of parts named for individuals who identified them, and many diseases are named for those who first diagnosed them or perhaps for famous sufferers, such as Lou Gehrig's disease. In a lighter vein, such treats as pralines and marmalade are supposedly named for distinguished gourmets who enjoyed them. The latter is attributed to Mary, Queen of Scots, who is said to have called for the sweet preserve when she was ill, so that it acquired the name *Marie malade* (sick Mary). Another and more likely explanation for the name, however, is that it came into English from the Portuguese *marmelada,* "quince preserves" (Boycott 1982). There is also a real Mary in *Bloody Mary* (Mary Tudor, during whose reign in the sixteenth century three hundred English subjects were put to death) and a real Melba in *peach Melba.* Dame Melba was an imperious Australian opera singer who ordered an unavailable dessert, so the chef improvised a confection of peaches and ice cream and declared it created in her honor. Unsurprisingly, it became her favorite sweet (Beeching 1979).

Activity: Metaphors from People

Many common phrases commemorate individuals who themselves may be forgotten. A *Hobson's choice* is a choice between one thing and nothing, so it is no choice at all. This phrase is attributed to the practice of Thomas Hobson, sixteenth-century English carrier, who hired out horses and would allow his customers the option of either the next horse in line or none at all. A *Pyrrhic victory* is an expression derived from Pyrrhus, a successful general among the ancient Greeks, who was saddened by the deaths that resulted from war and so believed that all battle victories were gained at too high a price (Beeching 1979).

Molotov cocktail may represent distant history to your students and therefore require explanation, but some at least may be familiar with the concept behind *Reaganomics.* Recently the phrase *doing the Macnamara* was coined in reference to Robert Macnamara's apology for his part in the Vietnam War twenty years later (Buckley 1995). Although the authors haven't heard it, we wouldn't be surprised if someone had coined *Quayle-lude* during the late eighties, and we will leave it to the imaginations of others to decide what the concept might be behind that term. Similarly, we are waiting to read about *Newt-onian physics* to refer to a certain politician's zeal for getting rid of excesses in government. Have students bring in similar examples from news media and other sources, or, better yet, think of their own.

Some words may be surprisingly eponymous, such as the following:

Batty: We would think this comes from "bats in your belfry." But according to Boycott, "the word derives from Fitzherbert Batty, an eccentric barrister who lived in Spanish Town, Jamaica. In 1839 he was certified as insane which attracted considerable interest in the London press" (16).

Monkey wrench: "A spanner or wrench with an adjustable jaw set at right angles to the handle, probably the invention of Charles Moncke, a London blacksmith. An alternative origin is that the name derived from an American called Monk, *c.* 1856" (81).

Students can identify other terms or phrases that might have eponymous meanings. Following are some resources for exploring this aspect of our English vocabulary.

References

Books on Eponymous Words

Boycott, Rosie. 1982. *Batty, Bloomers and Boycott: A Little Etymology of Eponymous Words.* London: Hutchinson.

A collection of nearly three hundred words derived from individuals with an account of how each word came to be established in the language. Herself the bearer of a name that has entered the common vocabulary as a term for an effective social weapon, the author documents a process that illustrates how a receptive language can store nuggets of history, politics, discovery, and adventure in its vocabulary.

Dickson, Paul. 1986. *Names: A Collector's Compendium of Rare and Unusual, Bold and Beautiful, Odd and Whimsical Names.* New York: Delacorte Press.

This varied collection treats a number of interesting phenomena related to names and provides some new vocabulary for the subject, including the terms *aptronyms* ("names that fit real good"), *astronomics* (cosmic nomenclature), and *automonyms* (for the cybernetic revolution). Also included are chapters on names of famous animals, stage and pen names, extraterrestrial names, and the naming of storms, streets, teams, and fashions. One treasure in the book is the author's personal collection of odd and amusing names collected from telephone books and other sources over the years. His general collection includes such gems as Phoebe B. Peabody Beebe and Beveridge Moose, while his "complementary" list, which consists of names that form phrases, includes Holland Tunnel, Sally Forth, and the Reverend Adam Baum.

Espy, Willard R. 1978. *O Thou Improper, Thou Uncommon Noun: A Bobtailed, Generally Chronological Listing of Proper Names That Have Become Improper and Uncommonly Common; Together with a Smattering of Proper Names Commonly Used . . . and Certain Other Diversions.* New York: Clarkson N. Potter.

As the subtitle implies, this book takes a different tack in organizing these nouns by date and by subject rather than alphabetically. You'll meet people you never knew existed, such as the Marquis Frangipani, who served under Louis XIV and is credited with inventing frangipani, a pastry filled with cream, sugar, and almonds. Meanwhile, Louis's dishonest steward, the Marquis de Béchamel, was busy creating a cream sauce thickened with flour.

Partridge, Eric. 1950. *Name into Word: A Discursive Dictionary.* New York: Macmillan.

Nearly half a century old, this dictionary by one of the preeminent historians of modern English is an especially valuable storehouse of antique collectibles as well as name-based words that endure. A broad collection that includes words evolved from place, group, brand, and other names as well as those of individuals, the dictionary proper contains some twenty-five hundred entries. Also of interest is an appendix of another fifteen hundred words that Partridge considered "borderliner" and "potential candidates." This book would be a gold mine for experimenting with a created dialect.

Further Resources for Exploring the Metaphorical Roots of the English Language

Ammer, Christine. 1989. *Fighting Words: From War, Rebellion, and Other Combative Capers.* New York: Paragon House.

There are over 750 words and phrases in our vocabulary with military origins, but few are so obvious as words like *bazooka.* For example, did you ever get cold feet and back out of a commitment? Napoleon's retreating troops got them first, literally, leaving snowy Moscow (sometimes with rags on their feet instead of boots). Some of our most common words began in military circles: *campaign, rally, avant-garde, deadline, magazine, pioneer, wardrobe,* and *logistics.* A narrative format makes this book highly readable. Other books by Ammer include *Seeing Red or Tickled Pink: Color Terms in Everyday Language; Have a Nice Day—No Problem! A Dictionary of Clichés;* and *It's Raining Cats and Dogs—and Other Beastly Expressions* (below).

Ammer, Christine. 1989. *It's Raining Cats and Dogs—and Other Beastly Expressions.* New York: Paragon House.

The natural world has inspired much of our speech, as this book will show. Perhaps you recall that Shakespeare mentions the "dogs of war" in *Julius Caesar,* a reference to the common practice of dog fights as entertainment. Dog fighting has inspired several common expressions. The underdog and top dog were the expected loser and winner. The fierceness of these fights led to the use of the term *dogfight* for World War I air battles. If you've heard someone ask for "some of the hair of the dog [that bit me]," they're using a metaphor based on a folk remedy for warding off rabies. You'll enjoy all one thousand of her anecdotes and explanations for the origins of animal expressions.

Ammer, Christine. 1993. *Southpaws and Sunday Punches: And Other Sporting Expressions.* New York: Dutton.

Over five hundred sports-related expressions have made their way into our daily language. *Sunday punch* was first used in boxing, for instance, but has come to mean a powerful blow of any type, whether literal or figurative. It's thought to have ties to the notion that one saved his or her best (clothes, behavior, manners) for church on Sundays. Similarly, if you're *swinging for the fences,* you're going all out—based on a baseball batter's efforts to hit a home run.

Cutler, Charles L. 1994. *O Brave New Words!: Native American Loanwords in Current English.* Norman: University of Oklahoma Press.

There are a thousand North American Indian, Inuit, and Aleut words in the English language. Many of these are names for plants, animals, and places. Cutler organizes them into glossaries with pronunciations, dates of first recorded use, etymologies, and definitions. Over half the book is a detailed historical background of the acquisition of Indian words.

Ison, Isaac, and Anna H. Ison. 1993. *A Whole 'Nother Language: Our Personal Collection of Appalachian Expressions.* Ky.: Isaac and Anna H. Ison.

The Isons have collected over thirteen hundred "Appalachianisms" in an attempt to preserve post-World War II rural culture. Many are familiar, but to reflect pronunciation variations, spelling is nonstandard. For example, *aggin' him on* denotes "egging him on" and "rinse" is *rench.* Others are colorful and sometimes humorous expressions that are pure country: *as sure as the world is square* (in other words, "not"), *back door trots* (diarrhea), and *yaller dog Democrat* (one who would vote for a yellow dog if it were on the Democratic ticket).

Jacobson, John D. 1990. *Toposaurus: A Humorous Treasury of Toponyms.* New York: John Wiley and Sons.

Toponyms are words and phrases derived from place names. Some are metaphorical. Inspired by the gangster heyday in Chicago, we have a *Chicago overcoat* (coffin), a *Chicago piano* (submachine gun), and a *Chicago pineapple* (a small bomb used during Prohibition). A Quonset hut, that sparse metal semicylindrical temporary military shelter first used during World War II, was named after the Quonset Point Naval Air Station in Rhode Island where it was first built.

Jeans, Peter D. 1993. *Ship to Shore: A Dictionary of Everyday Words and Phrases Derived from the Sea*. Santa Barbara: ABC-CLIO.

A number of the nautical expressions in this book are out of use now, but they present a fascinating picture of the culture of the days when sailors walked the streets on shore leave, "poodle faking" to attract the attention of a young lady. Give up? That refers to admiring the dog in order to make points with the owner. Other navy terms have changed meanings over the years. If you were "broke" in the British navy, you were court-martialed and pronounced unfit to serve. Often, you would have been dumped on shore without a cent. Today, being broke has come to mean being fundless.

Major, Clarence, ed. 1994. *Juba to Jive: A Dictionary of African-American Slang*. New York: Penguin Books.

This 548-page book specifies usage (African American slang, Southern slang, drug culture, jazz and blues, prison slang, youth culture), etymology, geographical location, and approximate date of use. For example, a *banter play built on a coke frame* was a Harlem expression from the 1930s and 1940s for an attractive young woman. *Banter* is a variant pronunciation of *bantam*, a type of chicken or "chick." A *coke frame* referred to the similarity between her shape and that of a Coca-Cola bottle.

Urdang, Laurence, Walter W. Hunsinger, and Nancy LaRoche. 1991. *A Fine Kettle of Fish and Other Figurative Phrases*. Detroit: Visible Ink Press.

Origins, connotations, usage, definitions, and illustrative quotations for nearly twenty-five hundred metaphorical expressions are provided in thematic categories. Many are familiar in everyday speech, such as *cut and run* (a sailing term meaning to cut the cable and set sail immediately). A number of phrases are obsolete or at least not widely known, such as *guts for quarters*, which now means you are in serious trouble. Originally it meant someone was about to slice an opponent into quarters with his sword. Other expressions are taken from popular culture, such as *beautiful downtown Burbank*, a catchphrase from the old *Laugh-In* television show.

9 World Literatures in English

Now I've got wings!
I am a bird with wings!
Remain behind with your spears!
Remain behind with your assegais![1]
You satans with degrees!
You holediggers who never sleep!
You elephants who grind everything!

Vusi Bhengu, Goodman Kivan, Nester Luthuli, Gladman 'Mvukuzane' Ngubo, and November Marsata Shabalala, "The Man Who Could Fly"

English is a metaphor for multiculturalism not only in terms of its vocabulary but also—and even more powerfully—in the wide range of world literatures it embraces. As English speakers, we enjoy the extraordinary privilege of being able to open so many books in our own language and immerse ourselves in other cultures and perspectives. The literary dimension of our multicultural language is a treasure that, while it may be ill-gained through a shady past of colonialism and linguistic imperialism, has inestimable value and inexhaustible rewards.

Christopher Clausen (1994), professor of English at Pennsylvania State University, has characterized literature in English as an "international imaginative creation" and "a collective literary achievement that offers extraordinary rewards if explored as a multiethnic, multicultural whole" (A48). Like spoken English, first-rate written English is not the preserve of native speakers. Wonderful stories abound in authentic world Englishes—the English of Ghana, of Malaysia, of India, of Trinidad, of the Philippines, and of many other countries as well as of immigrant and minority groups in the United States. To speak of the language as "our" English is to join voices and pens with people from virtually every part of the world.

World English literature often deals with the most exciting and important themes of our times: people struggling to choose between tradition and new values, people attempting to communicate across various kinds of cultural obstacles and differences, people holding on to their own identities in a shifting world. And because these writers come from all over the world, they inform; they enrich our literature with the story-telling traditions of their own countries and cultures as well as images and metaphors that may bring us closer to lands otherwise considered exotic and far away. The common tongue may also illuminate diverse perspectives on a central theme, as one can see in the following variations on the theme of the Second World War.

Albert Wendt (1986), a Samoan writer of mixed German and Polynesian descent, has a story entitled "The Balloonfish and the Armadillo" in which a man like himself is cleaning out his German father's papers and dealing with painful memories of his own youth. He picks up two small boxes out of which spiders and roaches explode, "dripping insects that hit the floor and fled like the boyhood years I didn't want to trap me" (63). When he burns the materials, they seem to come alive as they curl into ashes, and bits of black shards float into the trees and lake "like shattered pieces of a black mirror" (64). A leather notebook burns in a way that reminds him of flesh and then evokes a horrifying vision of Nazis burning books and corpses. In this remarkable story, the English language is the imaginative medium through which readers gain insight into the confusions of the narrator's own mixed Oceanic and European heritage, his fear of his father, and the possible reasons behind that fear.

Quite a different metaphorical vision transforms a young man's understanding in Jeanne Wakatsuki-Houston and James Houston's partly imagined memoir of the experience of Japanese Americans during and following the Second World War (1974). Wakatsuki-Houston imagines the reminiscences of her brother during a visit to his deceased father's village in Japan. She pictures him lying in bed and, with his hands, finding his father's image in his own features, amazed at the resemblance he'd never noticed before, because he "never thought to compare himself with papa, never dared" (107). In this moment of understanding, he knows that he has metaphorically enacted his father's return to his native land.

A third theme drawn from the Second World War is captured in the English writer Dilys Pegler Winegrad's "Flying Coffin: Memoirs of a Wartime Childhood" (1987), in which he compares the unbelievable presence of German bombers over England with a story, told over a forbidden campfire during a blackout, of a dead child's coffin that floats over the forest and has no bottom. When his story-telling friend screams the corpse's cry, he recalls, "All my dread is focused on a dark emptiness indistinguishable from the hollow night—the flying coffin I am not even sure I believe in" (75). All three voices, in different images in English, tell of alienation and self-recovery of three boys, made necessary by the experience of war.

In yet a different kind of story, "The Gentlemen of the Jungle," Jomo Kenyatta (1959) offers a parable to explain the culture and politics of colonial Africa. This story features an elephant seeking to make good on his friendship with a man during a hailstorm. Because the man has a little hut, the elephant asks to put just his trunk inside, which the man grants, but then the animal pushes his head in and the man out. Settling down comfortably inside, the elephant explains his action by arguing that his skin is the more delicate and so deserves the shelter. After this beginning, it is not hard to predict what happens next and how the parable/metaphor unfolds. The ironic contrast between the story's bantering tone and the relentless invasion of the huge animal and his allies is part of the overall metaphor: the colonists smoothly and wittily rationalized their theft of land every step of the way.

Using Cross-Cultural Stories in the English Classroom

Discussion is at the heart of literature, and the emphasis should be on response. Response-centered discussion emphasizes students' *use* of language: to interpret, to understand, and to communicate. Such discussions should be student-centered, with the teacher talking as little as possible.

To facilitate such discussion, it may be useful to prepare a question/study guide that reinforces basic knowledge of a story—plot structure, characters, themes. This can be used as a visual support to cut down on the amount of explanation a teacher might ordinarily be asked to do. The kinds of questions that are most interesting to pursue in literature are text-based but interpretive, leading to different perspectives on the story.

Students should be encouraged to respond to each other rather than to the teacher. When students ask questions, the teacher should leave it up to their classmates to respond and try to avoid stepping in to settle disagreements or choose among varied interpretations. Students may want to know the teacher's reaction to the story, and it might be shared at the end of the discussion, but not as the "definitive" interpretation. Before joining into literature discussions themselves, teachers should make sure that students are not seeking "right" answers.

Dillon's seven alternatives to teacher-centered questioning (1983), summarized below, provide a useful set of guidelines for facilitating a student-centered discussion. This summary is exemplified with references to a chapter in Polingaysi Qoyawayma's autobiography (1964) recounting her life as a Hopi woman adjusting to the wider world. In this episode, the writer recalls the time in her childhood when white missionaries literally raided Hopi villages for children to send to their schools. Despite her family's efforts to hide her, the small girl follows her friends to the school, where she is dressed in a "mother hubbard" dress and set down in front of a slate.

Her fear gives way to curiosity and then the inner conflict of divided cultural loyalties that she will experience for the rest of her life.

Dillon's Seven Alternatives to Teacher-Centered Questioning

1. Make a declarative statement (not a question) and signal that you want to elaborate on this statement. For example, referring to Polingaysi's experience of growing up in one culture and being educated in another, you might say something like, "Polingaysi was torn between two worlds," and nod to the class. Students will be encouraged to fill in the ensuing pause with discussion of the two worlds, what it means to be torn, etc.

2. Make a reflective statement on something a student has said. For example, if someone has observed that Polingaysi's situation is like that of many young people who must choose between their parents' ways and the larger world, you might say, "From your point of view, then, there is often a conflict between the generations." This observation will invite students to respond from their personal experience.

3. Describe what you think is the student's state of mind. You might say, "You seem to be feeling some of Polingaysi's sadness at the end of the episode." Such a guess at the student's internal response, even if it's wrong, will encourage further disclosure of emotional reactions to a piece.

4. Invite students to elaborate on their own statements or on each others'. For example, you might say, "I'd like to know more about why you sympathized with Polingaysi's parents even though you also agree with what she did."

5. Encourage students to ask questions. This can be a way to start things up again when a discussion has come to a halt. You might need a "jump-start" question, such as, "You need to ask why it was so important to the missionaries to educate the Hopis their way." Even though it is your question, you have handed it over to the students with the expectation that they will frame it in their own words or follow up with further questions of their own.

6. Encourage students to ask questions of one another. When a student has posed a question, let other students answer. This may be more difficult than you think, since teachers are well trained (by students) to provide answers themselves. More generally, develop an atmosphere in which students feel comfortable calling for information or viewpoints whenever they wonder about something. For

example, a student might want to know about Hopi traditions, and other students in the class might have insights to share. Any student request for explanation can initiate discussion in which the teacher remains silent for as long as is practical.

7. Maintain a deliberate silence. To be deliberate, a silence must be three seconds or longer. Often it may be used for dramatic effect, as when a student has given an especially interesting insight. Too often our own talk steps on the heels of what students say, and their best contributions are lost. A deliberate silence can also signal a change in the direction of the discussion or simply provide a chance for anyone to say anything.

Writing in Response to Cross-Cultural Stories

There is a natural connection between literature and writing. Stories elicit stories. Interpretation itself is a creative act. The reader is joining with the author in telling the story, filling in details and insights, going beyond the events described. Expressive and poetic writing are natural responses to literature and, like open discussion, will give students the opportunity to combine linguistic and nonlinguistic knowledge in fashioning their own texts.

We suggest that the kind of writing done in response to stories encourages reader-based rather than text-based content. In responding to literature, students should be more concerned with developing their insights and reasoning or with telling their own stories than with formal and technical aspects of writing, though these might come later in more polished versions of response writing. Journal keeping might encourage informal but thoughtful response and help students focus on their own ideas and meanings rather than on what they view as requirements for a writing task. Writing should be generated rather than elicited.

Students should be invited to extend stories they read. For example, in "Like the Sun," by Indian writer R. K. Narayan (1985), Sakhar, the narrator, decides to spend one day telling only the literal truth. After reading about the consequences for Sakhar at the end of that day, students can make up their own stories to tell what happens in his future life as a result of his one day of telling the truth. One of the immediate consequences is that his wife, who expected a compliment but got criticism instead, is angry at him. But will she eventually benefit from the criticism? Or will she try to get back at him some day? Will people like Polingaysi in *No Turning Back* eventually find a middle ground between the two cultures in which they must live? Such invitations call on students to stretch their reasoning and predictive powers as well as use their imaginations.

Resources for Teaching Multicultural Literature in English

Trying It Out

Following are synopses of seven American stories that represent the experiences of different groups. Employing these or any set of stories that you assemble, use Dillon's seven-step guide to support student discussion and writing. Each story synopsis is followed by an illustration of one of Dillon's suggested strategies for promoting student-centered discussions.

1. Alvarez, Julia. 1984. "Snow." *Northwest Review* 22 (1–2): 21–22.

   This story is told from the perspective of a young girl whose family has fled political repression in the Dominican Republic and are experiencing the first cold winter of their lives in New York. The time is the early 1960s, when there was much fear of nuclear attack on the United States. The girl is sorting through her fears, her imaginings, and the realities in her new and strange environment. Her first vision of snow becomes first a source of fear and then a stunning metaphor.

   Making a deliberate statement on which students can elaborate: "The child in this story has experienced fear in both her old country and her new one."

2. Big Eagle, Duane. 1983. "The Journey." In *Earth Power Coming: Short Fiction in Native American Literature*, edited by Simon J. Ortiz. Tsaile, Ariz.: Navajo Community College Press.

   A fevered boy's train ride to visit a medicine woman becomes a metaphorical journey into his native culture and its magic. As his illness grows strong, he sees in the passing landscape a series of mystical symbols that foretell his fate. This story explores the nature of healing as well as the initiation of a youth into the powers of his own culture.

   Making a reflective statement on what a student has just said: If a student has remarked that the story suggests that "witch" doctors can cure diseases better than "real" doctors, you might respond, "Your experience then is that only medical doctors know how to make people well," inviting all students to share their own and others' experiences with healing and the different people who might have been involved.

3. Coleman, Wanda. 1988. "The Seamstress." In *A War of Eyes and Other Stories*. Santa Rosa, Calif.: Black Sparrow Press.

   This story is told by the daughter of a seamstress in a garment factory in which workers are paid by the piece, driving them to work hard for a low wage. The mother comes home exhausted, but there are four children who need her, and she manages to summon up new energy to do things for them. The child accurately perceives the depth of the woman's love for her children.

Describing what you perceive to be a student's state of mind: If a student says the story is about a child whose mother must work and therefore cannot be at home with her children as much as they would like or need, you could say, "You seem to feel that this situation makes life difficult for such a child," inviting all students to respond emotionally to the characters in the story and their hardships.

4. Wakatsuki-Houston, Jeanne, and James Houston. 1974. "Kake, NeHiroshimaima: April, 1946." In *Farewell to Manzanar.* New York: Bantam.

   In this excerpt from her account of her experiences as a Japanese American during World War II, Wakatsuki-Houston imagines her brother's experience as an American soldier who goes to Japan as part of the occupation after the war. He travels to his father's native village, which is near the city of Hiroshima and therefore affected by the tragedy of the atom bomb. The story is about his feelings as he stays in the house of his father's aunt and thinks about his father as a young man.

   Inviting students to elaborate on their own statements and each others': If a student says that it must have been difficult to be a Japanese American soldier during the Second World War, you might say, "I wonder what others think about being a member of a group that might be associated with the enemy of one's country. Do we have instances of this sort of experience today?"

5. Lee, Audrey. 1971. "Waiting for Her Train." In *What We Must See: Young Black Storytellers,* edited by Orde Coombs. New York: Dodd, Mead and Co.

   This is a character study of a homeless woman living in the Pennsylvania Train Station. She has obviously seen better days but still strives to keep up appearances, acting as if she is perennially waiting for a train. We see how clever she is and what she does to survive, such as pretending to be grocery shopping while snacking on food she has gathered in her cart. Twenty-five years ago, when the story was written, the plight of the homeless was not as visible as it is today. The story invites comparisons between the earlier time and now.

   Encouraging students to ask their own questions by giving them a starter: Prime the question pump by suggesting, "You might try to speculate beyond the story by asking what happens when the homeless woman runs out of supermarkets in which to play her shopping cart trick."

6. Norman, Gurney. 1977. "The Dance." *Yardbird Reader* 1 (1): 115–16.

   Through television, an old Kentucky coal miner is brought into contact with a group of his peers in China. What happens as a result is quite surprising and beautiful to his grandson, who is secretly watching. The story illustrates both cultural contrast, especially in the difference between Eastern and Western attitudes toward old age, and the affinity of people no matter what their cultural differences may be.

Encouraging students to ask questions of each other: Although a student may direct a question to you in the reasonable belief that you are in the best position to answer, such as why it seemed so unusual to see Chinese people on television at the time of the story, relay the question to the class instead: "Does anyone know what was happening between China and the U.S. at the time of this story?"

7. Wong, Jade Snow. 1972. "A Measure of Freedom." In *Asian-American Authors,* edited by Kai-yu Hsu and Helen Palubinskas. Boston: Houghton Mifflin.

In this excerpt from her autobiography, the author describes how she decided to attend a community college in San Francisco without the support of her Chinese-born parents. To pay for her tuition and books, she worked as a servant for an American family. In this episode, she confronts her parents' traditional values concerning female behavior with views she has learned from an American teacher.

Maintaining a deliberate silence: You might pose a general question such as "What do you think is the most important thing going on in this story?" Instead of breaking an ensuing silence by making that question more directive or giving prompts of what *you* think is the most important thing going on, maintain a silence for students to fill. If you must talk, simply repeat the original question.

Trying It Out

Resources for World Literatures in English

The resources described in this section are not intended to be exhaustive but rather suggestive of the richness of literature available with its multitude of cross-cultural and intracultural themes. For every story collection here, the reader can probably find ten more in an hour's browsing in the library or bookstore.

Multicultural Literature

Allen, Paula Gunn, ed. 1989. *Spider Woman's Granddaughters: Traditional Tales and Contemporary Writing by Native American Women.* Boston: Beacon Press.

This collection captures the oral tradition of storytelling as it has passed through generations of Native American women. Woven together are the themes of the unifying force of nature, the endangerment of Native American culture, the powerlessness of the people, and the invisibility of Native women. The voices represented here, therefore, have the poignancy of being both a plea for survival and an expression of faith in the magic of stories. Gunn, a Pueblo-Sioux Indian poet, has selected stories of women warriors to exemplify the persistence of the Native spirit against all odds and hopes. Writers include Allen herself, Louise Erdrich, Leslie Marmon Silko, Linda Hogan, and Vickie Sears as well as nameless storytellers from the Oneida, Okanogan, Cochiti Pueblo, and Laguna Pueblo traditions.

Anaya, Rudolfo A., ed. 1987. *Voces: An Anthology of Nuevo Mexicano Writers*. Albuquerque: El Norte Publications.

This anthology includes both established and new Mexican writers living in the United States and Native American writers whose territories changed nationalities but not cultures. Their mother tongues often are the native languages of the region. They write primarily in English and Spanish, and this compilation of stories and poems mixes the two, sometimes passing gracefully between them in the same piece. Themes include the confusions and insights of living biculturally, the spirit of the land and the peoples who have inhabited it, and the harshness of social and economic marginalization.

Bissoondath, Neil. 1990. *On the Eve of Uncertain Tomorrows*. New York: Clarkson Potter Publishers.

The author of this story collection is a Trinidadian now living in Canada, where he writes deftly about the delicate balancing act of crossing cultures. Finding themselves alone in different ways and by necessity reliant on their own inner resources, his characters reveal themselves through introspection and careful observations of the world around them. Bissoondath carefully draws the reader into the worlds of his characters, who evoke empathy even when they may shock.

Bruchac, Joseph. 1992. *Turtle Meat and Other Stories*. Duluth, Minn.: Holy Cow! Press.

The writer of these stories traces his maternal roots to the Abenaki tribe of the northeastern forests, a heritage he combines with that of European settlers in the Adirondacks region. His stories capture the mystical heritage of the hills and its peoples in contemporary settings, exploring the possibilities for relationships with nature. The stories are illustrated with designs by a descendant of the Kentucky Cherokees, Murv Jacob, self-described as a painter/pipemaker.

Conley, Robert J. 1988. *The Witch of Goingsnake and Other Stories*. Norman: University of Oklahoma Press.

The Cherokee author of these stories speaks for his people by bringing traditional stories from their cultural sources into contemporary language, a movement he leads to promote the creation of new literature by indigenous people. Some stories capture historical moments, while in others layers of time seem to blend together in modern settings. In her forward, Wilma Mankiller, principal chief of the Cherokee Nation, praises the collection for representing the perspective of the Native people themselves rather than outsiders' interpretations of their experiences and culture.

Hiura. 1986. *The Hawk's Well: A Collection of Japanese American Art and Literature.* San Jose, Calif.: Asian American Arts Projects.

> The anthology combines visual art, poetry, and fiction to celebrate contemporary Japanese American artists and introduce their work into the currents of American literature. The predominance of visual and poetic forms suggest an aesthetic of spareness and clarity characteristic of traditional Japanese art.

Hsu, Kai-yu, and Helen Palubinskas, eds. 1972. *Asian-American Authors.* Boston: Houghton Mifflin.

> This is one of the first story collections to acknowledge the major contribution to American literature by immigrant writers and their first-generation American children from China, Japan, and the Philippines. Several of the stories touch on the distances between the older and younger generations created by different cultural loyalties. But perspectives can be entirely different within generations, too, as some stories show, and the constant change of life itself pulls people apart or bonds them together in an infinite variety of ways.

Kanwar, Asha, ed. 1993. *The Unforgetting Heart: An Anthology of Short Stories by African American Women (1859–1993).* San Francisco: Aunt Lute Books.

> Spanning nearly a century and a half, this anthology plays the important role of bringing together the artistic contributions of an often overlooked group of writers, making visible their cumulative impact on contemporary literature and thought. The stories are arranged chronologically to provide a historical perspective. Included in the book are stories by Zora Neale Hurston, Paule Marshall, Nikki Giovanni, Alice Walker, Toni Cade Bambara, Gloria Naylor, and Wanda Coleman.

McKnight, Reginald. 1988. *Moustapha's Eclipse.* Pittsburgh: University of Pittsburgh Press.

> McKnight writes about multiple alienations, including that of the son of a career officer, moving from place to place, that of racism as an African American, and that of culture, as he seeks some connection with his African heritage.

Minnesota Humanities Commission. 1991. *Braided Lives: An Anthology of Multicultural American Writing.* St. Paul: Minnesota Humanities Commission and Minnesota Council of Teachers of English.

> An anthology compiled by teachers for teachers, *Braided Lives* brings together stories and poems of more than forty Asian, African, Hispanic/Latino, and Native American writers to celebrate the literary and cultural diversity of the United States. The selections represent both relatively unknown works and what may be considered the canon of American multicultural literature, including Rudolfo Anaya's *Bless Me Ultima*, N. Scott Momaday's *House Made of Dawn*, Zora Neale Hurston's *Their Eyes Were Watching God*, James Baldwin's "Sonny's Blues," and Maxine Hong Kingston's *China*

Women. The book is organized in cultural groups with an introductory essay on the literary contribution of each.

Poey, Delia, and Virgil Suarez, eds. 1992. *Iguana Dreams: New Latino Fiction.* New York: HarperPerennial.

The "iguana" of the title is a metaphor for the surprising, sometimes elusive, always intriguing lure of literature into places that might otherwise remain undiscovered. This collection represents the cutting edge of contemporary writing in some thirty selections that are drawn from the heritage of the far-flung geography of cultures we designate as Latino.

Reed, Ishmael, Kathryn Trueblood, and Shawn Wong, eds. 1992. *The Before Columbus Foundation Fiction Anthology: Selections from the American Book Awards, 1980–1990.* New York: W. W. Norton.

The American Book Awards has recognized more multiethnic American authors than any other national prize, highlighting such writers as William Kennedy, Louise Erdrich, Leslie Marmon Silko, Paule Marshall, Frank Chin, Sandra Cisneros, Bienvenido Santos, Russell Banks, and Toni Cade Bambara. All of these and other Asian, African American, Hispanic/Latino, European American, and Native American writers are represented in this volume celebrating the whole heritage of the North American continent. Thirty pieces from prize-winning books provide a panoramic view of the sweep of American literature, metaphorized by editor Ishmael Reed as an "ocean."

Santos, Bienvenido N. 1979. *Scent of Apples: A Collection of Stories.* Seattle: University of Washington Press.

Perhaps the best-known Filipino immigrant writer in America, Santos writes with the tragedy of the exile but also with the compassion of the universalist who understands the essential experience of being human. His stories encompass the generations, from the young visitor to New York who finds his immigrant cousin living a life of quiet despair, to the old man in Chicago who eagerly awaits the dance troupe from his home country only to be snubbed by them. The title story is Santos's reminiscence of visiting a Filipino apple farmer in the Midwest and listening to the old man's stories of his youth in the Philippines that pour out when the two are driving on an old country road. Although the farmer's American wife saved his life, there is a poignant hint of another, perhaps more cherished life that he left behind.

Particular Perspectives

Cahill, Susan, ed. 1975. *Women and Fiction: Short Stories by and about Women.* New York: New American Library.

Many of the best-known writers of stories in English, representing the development of feminine consciousness through three-quarters of the twentieth century, are included, ranging from Virginia Woolf and Kate Chopin at the beginning of the century to Grace Paley, Joyce Carol Oates, and Alice Walker, who are writing today. Other writers included are Katherine Mansfield, Gertrude Stein, Flannery O'Connor, and Margaret Drabble.

Cresswell, Rosemary, ed. 1987. *Home and Away: Travel Stories.* Ringwood, Victoria: Penguin Books of Australia.

These stories capture the adventure of travel and the experience of being a stranger that it affords. Presenting the Australian perspective among an international range of settings and characters, the stories illustrate how inexhaustible this theme is. Twenty-four Australian writers are featured, including Elizabeth Jolley, Kate Grenville, and Michael Haig.

Ellison, Emily, and Jane B. Hill, eds. 1987. *Our Mutual Room: Modern Literary Portraits of the Opposite Sex.* Atlanta: Peachtree Publishers.

This collection consists of stories by leading contemporary writers crossing gender perspectives: women writing in the voices of men and men writing from the point of view of women. Among the authors featured are Ann Beattie, Raymond Carver, Michael Dorris, Louise Erdrich, Gloria Naylor, and Reynolds Price.

Malan, Robin, comp. 1994. *Being Here: Modern Short Stories from Southern Africa.* Cape Town: David Philip.

These stories document many of the dramas surrounding nearly four decades of extraordinary changes in southern Africa characterized by cultural and political turmoil. Writers include Doris Lessing, Nadine Gordimer, Zoe Wicomb, and Alex la Guma of South Africa, as well as writers from Zimbabwe, Mozambique, and Botswana.

Sennett, Dorothy, and Anne D. Czamiecki, eds. 1991. *Vital Signs: International Stories on Aging.* St. Paul: Graywolf Press.

This book is a sequel to *Full Measure,* a collection of stories on aging by American authors, published by Graywolf Press in 1988. In this volume, as in the last, the editor has collected memorable portraits of older people that belie the stereotypes of age. Authors are drawn from Japan, China, Sweden, Australia, New Zealand, South Africa, Kenya, Egypt, Italy, and other countries.

Zahava, Irene, ed. 1989. *Finding Courage: Writings by Women.* Freedom, Calif.: Crossing Press.

This multicultural and international collection of fictional and autobiographical stories depicts acts of courage by women, not in a heroic sense but in ordinary contexts where the situation calls for them to overcome their fears. This collection provides examples of actions and reactions that take people forward rather than hold them back, giving it a liberatory value.

Note   1. A slender hardwood spear or light javelin usually tipped with iron and used in southern Africa.

IV Making Sense: The Experience of Metaphor

I think of metaphors as an . . . example of what chemists call hypergolic. You can take two substances, put them together, and produce something powerfully different (table salt), sometimes even explosive (nitroglycerine). The charm of language is that, though it's human-made, it can on rare occasions capture emotions and sensations which aren't.

Diane Ackerman, *A Natural History of the Senses*

Seeing and Hearing with the Imagination

The trick of reason is to get the imagination to seize the actual world—if only from time to time.

Annie Dillard, *An American Childhood*

Metaphors begin with experiences, not words. Indeed, we can see, hear, touch, taste, smell, and feel metaphors without using words at all. Words make them into a text that can evoke new experiences in others. Often the thrill of conceiving a metaphor comes at that moment when the experience crystallizes into words. Seeking metaphors in observations and experience is our human way of finding meaning in the world, what Annie Dillard (1987) calls "the trick of reason" (20). A master of both the sensory and the written metaphor, Dillard demonstrates on every page of her writing her deftness with this trick. She begins, always, by attuning herself to the world around her. The following passage from her essay "An Expedition to the Pole" shows how she imaginatively grasps the reality of a moth trying futilely to escape through a screen: "A paper wasp—*Polistes*—is fumbling at the stained-glass window on my right. I saw the same sight in the same spot last Sunday: Pssst! Idiot! Sweetheart! Go around by the door! I hope we seem as endearingly stupid to God—bumbling down into lamps, running half-wit across the floor, banging for days at the hinge of an opened door" (41).

Thus does the metaphorical mind find extended meanings in the configurations of concrete experience. To find these meanings, we need to be alert to patterns rather than parts, to the imaginary as well as the literal, and especially to the way direct experience transforms perceptions and thoughts. By being conscious of this transformation, we catch ourselves in the act of constructing what we know. Let's look at another example to see again how it works.

In a reflective memoir, Janet Malcolm (1990), an American journalist born in Czechoslovakia, describes a visual transformation she experienced during her first return to her native country since childhood. The scene was the Elbe River at twilight, where Malcolm was enjoying a moment of aesthetic solitude when she saw what she believed was a pile of paper litter on the bank. Shocked at first by this sight in "clean, orderly Prague," she then realized that she was actually looking at a white swan nesting on the bank below the promenade. Later that night, Malcolm returned to the same spot and saw the swan defending her nest against a gang of rats, a scene she compared to Czechoslovakia, a country she viewed at that time as small, surrounded, and constantly besieged. The next day she saw the swan a third time, now swimming serenely, and compared it to Vaclav Havel, the playwright who survived political persecution and imprisonment to become the nation's president.

In this sequence of transformations, we see Malcolm's metaphorical thinking develop from the perceptual to the conceptual. Her experience of seeing the swan, something so unexpected that at first she didn't recognize it, is heightened by her awareness of her native country's current moment in history. The metaphors develop from the combination of alert senses, past experience or knowledge, and the desire to seek deeper understanding.

Visual Metaphors

Children learn to see the world in terms of particular shapes and patterns characteristic of their social and physical environments. In Western urban society, the world appears to be largely linear, with certain geometric forms, especially those with angles, predominating. Even curved and circular shapes seem defined by line. We impart this linear perception into much of what we think and do: such concepts as order, progression, and sequence are examples. So compelling is our awareness of line that we often forget it is a construct of our own perception.

The shapes we behold, and the lines we conjure to define them, are repeated in so many phenomena that they surround us with visual metaphors. A rope is like a snake, and a monkey's tail is like a rope. All are curved or spiral forms long and narrow enough to suggest a line. What else could we add to this group? Perhaps braided hair, a hanging vine, or a river bed seen from an aerial view. If the connections we draw have meaning beyond visual likeness, the perceptual comparisons may suggest conceptual metaphors. In the story of Rapunzel, the captive woman's hair becomes a climbing rope that unites her with her lover and leads to her liberation—a metaphor of feminine power, perhaps.

A simple example of this phenomenon is cloud-watching. We "see" an identifiable object in a cloud mass and try to describe it so that a companion might see it too before the clouds shift into new forms. Another example might be the patterns that form in the foam of the surf as it spreads over the sand, which may resemble cloud forms, so that momentarily we see the sky at our feet.

Anyone who has toured a cave has observed that stalactites can copy the patterns of falling water. Cave guides are fond of pointing out numerous food metaphors for the formations: popcorn, bacon, and layer cake. The night skies are full of metaphors: the Big and Little Dippers, the Milky Way, and all the images of the zodiac. Fireflies in a field in July may look like tiny galaxies on the ground. The mind soars and returns, weaving a web of connections between the cosmic and the mundane, making the universe knowable.

Students do not need to be taught how to see visual metaphors, but they may be guided to bring this dimension of their imaginative awareness into the English classroom as a resource for understanding and expression.

Trying It Out

A Seeing Expedition

Nature is full of messages and information that are not verbal. People learn to perceive these meanings in the same way that they learn to read. Although students have been taught to emphasize linguistic and mathematical forms of meaning in schools, they have well-developed capacities for seeing and understanding such visual information as forms, patterns, textures, contrasts, colors, and so on. Participating in a seeing expedition, which can take place on school grounds, in the neighborhood, or anywhere else, reminds us of what we know about the designs of nature and of human construction and how these may have similar structures. The purpose of this activity is to guide your students in opening their eyes and their minds to the visual metaphors that surround them. To record their observations and ideas, students may use notepads or sketchpads and cameras if they are photographically inclined.

You might begin with a warm-up to awaken awareness of familiar shapes in the environment. These are some examples of common geometric figures discernible in ordinary observations:

Straight Lines

vertical lines in bark

horizontal lines in rock and cliff formations

horizontal and vertical lines in buildings and fences

Curved Lines

the horizon

outlines of leaves

drifted snow

Angular Lines

twigs joining branches or branches joining trunks

>   street corners
>   arms and legs joining torsos
>   Circular Lines and Shapes
>   sun and moon
>   fruits and flowers
>   seeds
>   seashells (spirals)
>   Radiating Lines
>   snowflakes
>   webs
>   starfish
>   patterns within leaves

Have students think of other common geometric shapes and lines, such as diagonals, rectangles, squares, spheres, and cubes, and record observations of objects that suggest these figures. Using their knowledge of geometry, drawing, and other subjects, they can think of as many terms as they can that are useful for alerting their eyes to their visual surroundings.

Trying It Out

Finding Like Structures and Correspondences

Every metaphor has an outer *structure* and internal *correspondences* within that structure. The structure refers to the general likeness. For example, we can say that the pattern on a leaf is like a tiny, leafless tree (see Figure 9.1). The correspondences refer to the details of that comparison. A leaf has a thick division going up the center, which is comparable to the trunk of a tree. There are finer veins branching out from the center, which are like branches of a tree. And these divide into finer veins, which are like the twigs growing from branches.

Have students come up with other comparisons of forms. The following examples in Figures 9.2, 9.3, and 9.4 may help them get started. They should also try to identify both the structure and the correspondences of their metaphors.

These are simple and obvious comparisons. Figure 9.4 is somewhat more complex in that it develops the *connotative* nature of metaphor. Feelings as well as structural likenesses are part of the correspondences.

Students can now be encouraged to look around them or remember places they have been to find more comparisons that can be developed into metaphors suggesting particular connotations.

Figure 9.1.
Comparison of Leaf and
Tree

Figure 9.2.
Comparison of Porcupine
and Cactus

Figure 9.3.
Comparison of Spiderweb
and Fishnet

Figure 9.4.
Comparison of Tears and
Raindrops

Here are more examples, which again seem obvious but may suggest connotations:

> A car in heavy traffic is a land turtle making its laborious way forward.
>
> A tree becomes an umbrella when you are caught in the rain.
>
> A boulder is a sleeping buffalo, suggesting the past.
>
> Bookcases are ladders to knowledge.
>
> A jet plane is a pencil drawing a white line across the sky.

Trying It Out

Finding Meaning in Forms

The metaphorical connotations of ordinary phenomena affect us constantly. In the following activities, ways are suggested for students to become conscious of the kinds of meanings they ascribe to objects seen daily.

Activity 1: Trees as Poems

Trees are eloquent forms in our lives, and almost without thinking we see them as expressing many different human emotions. The trees in Figure 9.5, which seem to express quite different feelings, can be used for discussion, after which students themselves can bring in pictures (drawings or photographs) of a tree they found expressive and use them as the basis for writing. Questions for discussion could include:

- What feelings or thoughts does each picture evoke in you?
- What stories do the trees suggest? Pick one and tell a story. (You may discover a story by relating a memory you have that involves a tree.)

Figure 9.5.
Comparison of Different
Trees

- If you were to pick a tree to represent you, which would it be? Why?
- Find a real tree (or any other natural object) that you think is the best representation or symbol for you, and make a drawing or take a photo. Orally or in writing, explain the structure and correspondences between yourself and the object you have chosen.

Activity 2: Vehicles as Metaphors

In some cities, downtown on Saturday night is the scene of a procession of vehicles that put their (mostly teenaged) drivers' personalities on parade. The 1970s classic *American Graffiti* (Universal Pictures 1973) revolves around this scene: the chromed and polished Chevrolet sedan, the chopped and souped-up Ford pickup, the Volkswagen "Bug," and the mysterious white Thunderbird were like characters themselves in the film. What do the vehicles in Figure 9.6 suggest about their owners?

Figure 9.6.
Different Types of Vehicles

**Activity 3:
Observing and
Recording**

Using their cameras, sketchpads, or journals, students can record descriptions of a number of vehicles that seem like metaphors for their owners or something else. For example, students might visit the parking lot of a school, shopping mall, business, or office building and speculate on the kinds of people they might encounter inside the establishment. Magazine features and advertising can be a source of vehicles, too. Look for the metaphors suggested by vehicles in magazines intended for different audiences, for example, *Time, Vogue, People,* the *New Yorker, Fortune,* etc.

Trying It Out

A Gallery of Visual Metaphors

Figure 9.7.
Images Showing
Combination of Human-
Made and Natural
Structures

**Activity 1:
Harmony in
Natural and
Human-Made
Structures**

What thoughts or feelings do these pictures evoke concerning the relationship between the natural and the human-made world? What contrasts can your students find among the pictures? What likenesses can they detect among some or all of them? What other metaphors of contrast or integration between the human-made and the natural world can they find in their environment? Students may be asked to sketch, photograph, or describe these.

Activity 2: Creating a Classroom Gallery

Invite your students to use a bulletin board or wall to create a gallery of visual metaphors, including excerpts from literature as well as art and photographs. They might also work with objects from the environment, both natural and humanly constructed, acting and pantomime (charades), special lighting effects, videos, shadow boxes, optical illusions, collages, murals, and any other arrangements or techniques that provoke unusual and interesting visual responses. Students may work on their contributions to this gallery individually or in small groups. In groups, some students may be more attuned to actual visual arrangements while others may focus on verbal representations of the metaphors involved. The following questions could help stimulate students' imaginations:

- What basic forms and repetitions do you notice in your environment?
- How does awareness of these shapes and patterns affect your experience of your surroundings?
- Humans are said to be visual creatures. In what sense does this hold true for you?
- What does it mean to say, "My eyes are my windows to the world"?

Hearing Metaphors

Have you ever thought that the whine of a mosquito coming close to your ear was like an approaching siren? Mosquitos and sirens have similar high-pitched sounds, so the metaphor is auditory, but it is conceptual too. Both convey warnings, coming from a direction that isn't clear. And when the sound stops, you feel suspense. Or you might think of the ticking of a clock as water dripping slowly, drop by drop. Time is leaking through a tiny crack in your life. Imagine someone sitting alone, in a strange neighborhood with no friends, listening to the ticking of a clock. This could be the beginning of a story.

Because of the emphasis our culture places upon seeing, we may not be as attuned to auditory metaphors as we are to visual ones. But for the same reason, the experiences we have with ordinary sound can be more intense once we start paying attention to them. Also, sounds can be evocative for the very reason that they don't have a visual image. What do these common sounds suggest to you? Think of a setting for each:

Car wheels spinning in the snow, mud, or sand.

The creak of a door swinging shut.

A long roll of thunder.

A person seated cozily in front of a fire during a snowstorm might hear the spinning wheels out in the street as a cry for help. What this person decides to do is the beginning of another story. Or suppose this person hears the creaking of a door swinging shut. This sound might be heard as the squeal of a small but threatening animal. A long roll of thunder could sound like an avalanche or a mountain falling.

Another kind of auditory metaphor is onomatopoeia, through which sensory experience may cross languages and cultures. In New Zealand, the kiwi bird is named for its song in the Maori language. Australian poet James Devaney tells the story of Dirrawan, the aboriginal song-maker, who changes his mind about hunting when he listens to "dirri dirri, the small bird, and deereeree, the wagtail" (in McDonald 1995b). Tumbarumba, a town in New South Wales, is called by the Aboriginal word for thunder because the ground in this area makes a hollow sound when stamped upon.

Infants accomplish the incredible feat of distinguishing words and syntax from the stream of sound around them in the speaking world until they have pieced together their mother tongue. They do this through a process of artful listening that may seem lost in later years but is only in abeyance. Sound remains the primary medium of language. One of the characteristics of aesthetic writing, as opposed to utilitarian writing, is its quality of sound. Even when read silently, poetry and a great deal of prose is meant to be heard in the mind's ear.

Trying It Out

Listening for Sound Metaphors

Many words in English refer to some aspect of sound. In the index of *Roget's International Thesaurus,* you will find not only the word *sound* but also *silence, faintness of sound, loudness, resonance, repeated sounds, explosive noise, sibilation, stridor, cry, call, animal sounds, discord, music,* and *harmonics,* not to mention related categories such as musicians and musical instruments.

The many words in any one of these categories show how suggestive of the actual sensory experience they can be. Under *stridor,* for example, are listed words for harsh or shrill sounds, such as *screech, squeak, creak, rasp, buzz, croak, twang,* and *chirr.* Ask your students to think of strident sounds they have experienced. Can they find metaphors in these sounds? For example, if they compare the rasp of a voice with the rasp of sandpaper on wood, they might come up with the phrase "a sandpaper voice." Or the buzz of a bee might be like the buzz of a power saw, producing "the bees hovered, sawing the air."

**Activity 1:
Tuning In**

Below are some examples from other categories in *Roget's Thesaurus*. You and your students can consult the thesaurus yourselves for many more.

Silence: *hush*   *shush*   *lull*   *mum*
    The fog *lulled* the city into sleep.

Faintness of sound: *murmur*   *rustle*   *swish*
    Her skirt *rustled* like autumn.

Loudness: *blare*   *boom*   *roar*   *clang*
    His words *boomed* with anger.

Resonance: *peal*   *toll*   *knell*   *rumble*
    Their voices *rumbled* in the auditorium like distant thunder.

Repeated sound: *staccato*   *ticktock*   *clackety*
    Spurning technology, the novelist spent a *staccato* morning with her old typewriter.

Sibilation: *hiss*   *sizzle*   *swish*   *zip*
    Her menacing whisper *zipped* the matter closed.

Discord: *jangle*   *clinker*   *clang*   *grate*
    As usual, our opinions met with a *jangle* and *clang*.

**Activity 2:
Capturing Sound
Effects**

For a certain period of time, say a day, students might keep an account of sounds that they notice. One way to do this is to block out a sheet of paper by hours of the day and jot down some of the sounds one notices each hour, leaving space on the paper to expand descriptions of any of these sounds later. Along with this, the class can be collecting interesting metaphors associated with sound that they find in their reading. Here are a few to start the collection:

The giggles hung in the air like melting clouds that were waiting to rain on me.

      Maya Angelou, *I Know Why the Caged Bird Sings* (1969, 5)

The birds have started singing in the valley. Their February squawks and naked chirps are fully fledged now, and long lyrics fly in the air. Birdsong catches in the mountains' rim and pools in the valley; it threads through forests, it slides down creeks.

      Annie Dillard, *Pilgrim at Tinker's Creek* (1974, 105)

The faint sibilation of insects was only as if, in the silence, you heard the sharp rays of the sun impinge on the earth.

      H. M. Tomlinson, *The Sea and the Jungle* ([1912] 1964, 127)

I listen for all the sounds I can hear from up and down the valley—a few tied-up dogs barking wretchedly, semi-trucks whining along Route 9W, a police siren from across the river (a noise designed to travel), car doors and front doors slamming in the hamlet, an airplane droning along in no particular direction, and underneath the rest, a vague white-noise roar punctuated with irregular thumping. It might be a steel mill heard across a lake, the kind of sound that touted the dynamism of America when I was a kid and is now a signal of pollution. This is the aural landscape of the Mid-Hudson Valley.

Jim Stapleton, "Listening to the Mid-Hudson" (1991, 157)

The river has come back to fit between its banks. . . . The sound of it at a distance is like wild horses in a canyon, going sure-footed away from the smell of a cougar come to them faintly in the wind.

Barry H. Lopez, *River Notes: The Dance of Herons* (1979, 81)

She wondered, at first, if the frogs had suddenly, for inexplicable reasons, gotten much louder, or whether the silence in the room was simply so intense that she'd pulled all the noise in closer to her, just to fill her mind.

Judith Freeman, "Going Out to Sea" (1988, 188)

Trying It Out

Synesthesia

Sound is associated with almost every other sense. A *sweet* melody or a *sour* note suggests taste. A *smooth* note or a *raspy* voice suggests texture or touch. A *choppy* rhythm evokes kinesthetic experience. An even static is called *white noise,* suggesting sight, as does *clear* tone. Synesthesia, or crossing over from one sensory realm to another, is common with auditory experiences.

Activity 1: Sound Collages

Sounds can be juxtaposed in such a way that they create interesting compositions or suggest stories, just as images can. Students can create sound collages on audio tapes, play their collages for each other, and record their impressions in words following whatever guidelines the creator of the collage provides. For example, they each can pick a spot—a room at home, a street corner, a corridor in school—and record different sounds that occur over a period of time, and then ask other students to visualize and describe a scene or event they imagine from hearing the sounds. Or they may concentrate on a theme, such as voices, asking classmates to imagine characters, relationships, or interactions. Other themes could be sounds in nature, machines, or media bombardment. By associating feelings and images with these sound collages, students will explore the ways in which one sensory experience—in this case, sound—can be metaphorical for other experiences.

**Activity 2: A
Classroom
Listening Gallery**

Although we usually associate visual art with a gallery and musical art with a stage, there is no reason to be constrained by the usual. Why not aim for the unusual and create a listening gallery, which would feature both performances and displays for visitor participation?

You and your students can bring in interesting sound effects from recordings, instruments, or any sound-producing objects. A group or the whole class can form an orchestra featuring non-musical instruments, using virtually anything that can be drummed, toned, or vibrated. A project of sounds and sound effects can be organized around a theme your class devises, such as "I Hear, Therefore I Am," or "If Eyes Are Windows, What Are Ears?"

The class can create an "aural salon" in which the primary experiences are auditory. The exhibits can include audio-tapings, sound displays that visitors can manipulate, literary metaphors based on sound (perhaps to be read aloud by visitors), and a tape recorder set up to record visitors' "voice prints" and vocal signatures.

Metaphors of Taste and Smell

. . . the currants and cloves and pomegranates, butter and sugar and dates, the nutmeg, ginger, musk and ambergris, Seville oranges and lemons, olives, capers and a cornucopious number of vegetables to be sauced, tansied, tarted, put into pastry "coffins" and used in "sallets." The grandeur, expense, the lavish generosity everywhere abundant in the cookbook conjured in Louisa's mind a sprawling manor with opulent gardens where, even in winter, the smell of boxwood floated on the fogs and crackling fires warmed every room in Lady Aylesbury's grand house.

Laura Kalpakian, "A Christmas Cordial"

Imagine life without the sensations of taste and smell. This unfortunate condition is the lot of a young man known to one of the authors, the result of a head injury in a motorcycle accident. Of all the life-changing consequences of that accident, he considers the loss of these senses the most tragic. Our conversations with him have given us pause to realize the importance of taste and smell to us and how much we take them for granted.

Gustatory Metaphors

"All your taste is in your mouth" is a common insult for people perceived to lack appreciation for the finer things in life. But this insults not only the person thus accused but also disparages the mouth itself, or the gustatory sense, as being more vulgar than the other senses, especially seeing and hearing. Wine tasting and gourmet cooking elevate the dignity of the palate somewhat, but to nothing like the status accorded to eyes looking at paintings or ears listening to symphonies.

Yet eating is so central to our being it is difficult to get it completely out of our minds. Therefore, the tastes that our tongues register provide some of our most intense experiences and memories. The twenty-seventh hexagram of the ancient Chinese text *I Ching; or, Book of Changes* (Baynes and Wilhelm 1967) has a solid line at the top and bottom and open lines in the center, which make an opening that symbolizes the mouth (see Figure 11.1). In the accompanying text, the mouth symbolizes nourishment and speech. Food goes into the mouth and words come out of it. The mouth is the portal through which one affects the world or is affected by it.

Figure 11.1.
The Twenty-Seventh
Hexagram from the *I Ching*

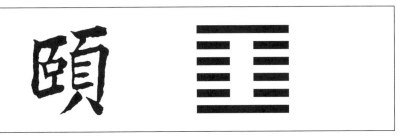

Trying It Out

Food as Metaphor

Because of the intimacy of our experiences with food, literature is full of gustatory images. Contemporary poet Gwendolyn Brooks (1971) uses food as a metaphor in her poem "My Dream, My Works Must Wait Till After Hell," which begins with the lines

> I hold my honey and I store my bread
> In little jars and cabinets of my will.
>
>   (50)

The poem's narrator goes on to tell that, although she is hungry, she must do other things before coming home to the "old purity" of what she has stored away. Different readers may find different meanings for the metaphors in this poem. After reading the entire piece, students may discuss the significance they find in the honey and bread, why she is always told to wait, and the hope she has that her taste will not turn insensitive. They may project themselves into her perspective as a woman and as an African American.

The intensity of taste of two quite different kinds of pears is also captured in the following descriptions by Eudora Welty and South African writer Zoe Wicomb:

> Again she thought of a pear—not the everyday gritty kind that hung on the tree in the backyard, but the fine kind sold on trains and at high prices, each pear with a paper cone wrapping it alone—beautiful, symmetrical, clean pears with thin skins and snow-white flesh so juicy and tender that to eat one baptized your whole face, and so delicate that while you urgently ate the first half, the second half was already beginning to turn brown. It's not the flowers that are fleeting, Nina thought, it's the fruits—it's the time when things are ready that they don't stay. (Welty 1947, 131)

> [Her mother] says that she managed to save some prickly pears. . . . She has slowed down the ripening by shading the fruit with castor-oil leaves, floppy hats on the warts of great bristling blades. The flesh

is nevertheless the colour of burnt earth, a searing sweetness that melts immediately so that the pips are left swirling like gravel in the mouth. (Wicomb 1987, 172)

In both passages, the experience of tasting is both direct and metaphorical. Eudora Welty's character, Nina, finds a general meaning in the transience of her ideal pear, and Zoe Wicomb's narrator finds a similar meaning in the brevity of the sweetness of the prickly pear in comparison to the duration of the grittiness that remains in the mouth after the taste is gone.

Activity 1: Kitchen Poetry

Because of their rich sensory associations, not only of taste but also of smell, shape, texture, and color, the names of foods carry their own strong images that can be captured in poetic expressions. Following are two recipes from *The Settlement Cookbook* (1954), first as originally given, then converted into poetic form:

Dandelion Wine, the recipe

1 gallon dandelion flowers
1 gallon boiling water
3 pounds sugar
3 oranges, cut in small pieces
3 lemons, cut in small pieces
1 ounce yeast

Pick dandelion flowers early in the morning, taking care not to have a particle of the bitter stem attached. Pour boiling water over the flowers and let stand 3 days. Strain and add the rest of the ingredients; let stand 3 weeks to ferment. Strain, bottle. (411)

Dandelion Wine, the poem

One: Gallon dandelion flowers
      Gallon boiling water
      Ounce of yeast

Three: Oranges
        Lemons
        Pounds of sugar

None: Even a particle of bitter stem.

Pick the first gallon
Pour the second gallon
Add the third one and the three threes
(Taking care, always, to avoid the particle of bitter stem)

Three again: Days to stand and strain
              Weeks to stand again and strain

Now bottle it!

(Pugh 1991)

Bunch of Grapes Salad, the recipe

8 canned pears
2 packages cream cheese
1/4 cup mayonnaise
1 or 2 bunches of green grapes
1 head lettuce

Drain pears well. Cover rounded side with cheese, mashed and moistened with mayonnaise. Cut grapes in halves, seed them; press grapes close together on the covered pears. Chill thoroughly. Serve on grape leaves or crisp lettuce leaves, with any desired dressing. (346)

Bunch of Grapes Salad, the poem

Cheese
Mashed and moistened with mayonnaise
Spread on the round sides of halved pears
Holding halved grapes
Seeded and pressed,
Chilled to be served on leaves of grape or crisp lettuce.
What would you call it?
Cheese?
Pears?
Salad?
Or a bunch of grapes or two?

(Pugh 1991)

Invite students to find or create recipes that can be converted into "kitchen poetry." Compile and name a class "cookbook" of poetic recipes, complete with tasting party, if you like.

Activity 2: Food for Thought

Everyone has a favorite food or memories of a favorite meal. Students can imagine what food they would choose to offer an alien from outer space who asked for a memorable sample of human cuisine. As a class they could construct a menu from which a whole spaceship of visitors could order their various meals, each item with both a direct and a metaphorical significance. The following examples may provide a beginning menu:

Garden Salad: You will enjoy a variety of textures and tastes that keep their individual identities while mixed together. This combination of difference and commonality is like our society, in which we have many kinds of people and cultures that keep their own identities while they join together. Salad, like human diversity, is a very healthy item.

French Bread: When fresh and warm, this bread is hard and chewy on the outside and very soft inside. It is like a person who first seems a stranger and then becomes a friend. A tough exterior encloses a soft interior.

Vanilla Ice Cream Cone: This scoop of creamy sweetness will chill your tongue and then melt in your mouth. It must be eaten quickly or it will melt in your hand instead, showing the need to be timely. Also, you can eat it while you are doing something else, another indication of the importance of time and efficiency to us humans. When the ice cream is gone, you may feel some regret, but you still have the crispy cone to chew on as a consolation.

Other food items that might appear on the menu include eggs, cereal, pizza, hamburgers, french fries, apples and other fresh fruits, and so on. Students with different ethnic backgrounds can contribute traditional foods representing their culture as a part of the great diversity of this society.

This activity could develop into other imaginative writing ventures, such as a story or play in which a metaphorical meal is served and shared, including conversation over the table and responses as new dishes are brought in.

Activity 3: Tip of the Tongue Memories

Biting into a madeleine (a kind of pastry) released a flood of memories in Proust (1922) that became a major literary event. Students can think of foods eaten in their early childhoods that they haven't had since but would, if tasted now, perhaps evoke those early days. In the spirit of Proust, a description of the food could be the opening to a memoir or story:

> When I was a child, a dime was hard to come by, so in choosing candy, I practiced a kind of economy that favored durability over luxury. Almost always, I would pass by a Hershey bar or Milky Way for a Bit-O-Honey, eight rectangles of hard golden taffy, each individually folded in a continuous strip of wax paper, or even better, a Big Hunk, a pure white taffy bar studded with bits of peanuts that was easily the longest selection in any display of candy bars. With either of these, I could savor each bite, first letting it soften in my mouth and then, almost regretfully, chewing it so that its sweet juice seemed to soak into my tongue.
>
> As far as I know, Big Hunks are no longer sold. But if by some miracle I were to have one in my hand today, I would still hold it wrapped for a while, feeling its substantiality, and then eat it slowly, savoring each bite. And surely I would find myself back on the pavement of my childhood, sitting on a curb in front of a brick apartment house, a set of clamp-on skates beside me, my knees scabbed or bandaged, suspended in time until I had swallowed the last bite of my candy. (Pugh n.d.)

Significant foods of childhood might include cereals, peanut butter, fast-food "fun meals," sweet drinks such as red pop or Kool-Aid, and food eaten at the movies such as popcorn or licorice ropes. Certain foods might also be associated with holidays or other special occasions such as picnics, birthdays, or visits to relatives. Students might even bring in samples of their memorable foods or drinks to accompany the writing in which they attempt to capture a mood of the past. The sampling may be even more effective during the drafting of such a piece, helping students to be more specific in their descriptions.

Olfactory Metaphors

Smell often catches us by surprise. Passing by a honeysuckle or lilac bush in bloom may make us stop and breathe deeply. The scent of a bakery blocks away may draw us in that direction. And even people who don't like to drink coffee often savor its aroma. We are quick to judge smells and find a bad one intolerable. Whole industries are built on our fears that we may smell bad to others. Indeed, it is hard to imagine any odor or fragrance to which we are neutral. Yet smell may be our most neglected sense, and the nose is an even more ignoble facial feature than the mouth.

Noses are sources of embarrassment. Think of famous noses: Pinocchio's, which grew longer every time he told a lie; Cyrano's, which prevented him from openly courting the woman he loved; and Jimmy Durante's, for which he was known as "the Schnoz." The feature of the face most likely to be altered through cosmetic surgery is the nose. It is also the feature most likely to be implicated in unpleasant behavior. Snobs "turn their noses up" at those they deem inferior. A grouchy person's "nose is out of joint." The nose is also the organ of intrusiveness, as when one "sticks one's nose" into the affairs of others. People who are "nosy" may be regarded as slipping a notch or two down from humanity, for animal, not human, noses are known for their skill and usefulness. After disparaging the human nose as an instrument of learning, the eighteenth-century naturalist Georges-Louis Leclerc (also known as the Comte de Buffon) characterized the noses of other animals by comparing them with the eye of humans as the supreme sense organ: "A universal of feeling, [the nose of an animal] is an eye that can see objects, not only where they are, but even where they have been; it is a taste organ by which the animal can savor not only what he can touch and seize upon, but even that which is far away and unattainable" (in Le Guerer 1992, 167).

But the common wisdom that our noses lack competence may not be doing justice to the importance that the sense of smell plays in our lives. In the following passage, for example, the narrator of Jean Rhys's novella *Voyage in the Dark* (1934), by recalling the fragrances associated with her childhood home in the Caribbean, finds that her memories become more real than her present environment:

—the smell of the streets and the smells of frangipani and lime juice and cinnamon and cloves, and sweets made of ginger and syrup, and incense after funerals or Corpus Christi processions, and the patients standing outside the surgery next door, and the smell of the sea-breeze and the different smell of the land-breeze.

Sometimes it was as if I were back there and as if England were a dream. (7)

Because of their vivid associations, smells are often metaphors themselves for places, people, and feelings. The metaphorical nature of smells is especially evident in the perfume industry, which markets different scents primarily by linking them with desirable images and experiences. No wonder the title character in Oscar Wilde's *Picture of Dorian Gray* ([1890] 1988) considered the study of perfumes to be the equivalent of a course in psychology:

He would now study perfumes, and the secrets of their manufacture, distilling heavily-scented oils, and burning odorous gums from the East. He saw that there was no mood of the mind that had not its counterpart in the sensuous life, and set himself to discover their true relations, wondering what there was in frankincense that made one mystical, and in ambergris that stirred one's passion, and in violets that woke the memory of dead romances, and in musk that troubled the brain, and in champak that stained the imagination; and seeking often to elaborate a real psychology of perfumes, to estimate the several influences of sweet-smelling roots, and scented pollen-laden flowers, of aromatic balms. . . . (103–4)

In a more recent novel, Patrick Suskind's *Perfume: The Story of a Murderer* (1986), a man with the defect of having no personal odor murders young women in order to extract their bodily scents as ingredients for concocting the perfect odor for himself:

[P]eople could close their eyes to greatness, to horrors, to beauty, and their ears to melodies or deceiving words. But they could not escape scent. For scent was a brother of breath. Together with breath it entered human beings, who could not defend themselves against it, not if they wanted to live. And scent entered into their very core, went directly to their hearts, and decided for good and all between affection and contempt, disgust and lust, love and hate. He who ruled scent ruled the hearts of men. (155)

The Power of Smell

Activity 1: What Your Nose Knows

Trying It Out

A good place to begin an investigation of the metaphorical/associational power of smell is with perfume ads, as the examples below show. Students can easily find examples of such metaphorical associations and critically examine the persuasive power of advertising at the same time.

Women's Perfumes

Opium: "Sheer sensuality"

Samsara: "A sense of serenity"

Le Parfum Lalique: "As sparkling and seductive as a sunlit garden"

Men's Perfumes

Versace L'Homme: "Virile e romantico" (note the easily translated terms in a "romance" language)

Egoiste: "Spicy. Woody. Sandalwood sparked with the impertinence of coriander." Further text actually associates this perfume with the wearer's character: "To assume he is uncaring or aloof is to misread him. He walks on the positive side of that fine line separating arrogance from an awareness of self-worth."

Students can collect many such examples from popular magazines and bring them in to analyze the verbal and pictorial associations with various scents, including the names of perfumes, other phrases associated with the perfume (what analogies are being implied), and pictures of people and scenes as well as of the perfume containers that suggest physical attractiveness, exotic experiences, elegance, and desirable personality and character traits.

Scratch-and-sniff pages can be collected for comparison with each other or for blind experiments to see what associations students themselves bring to particular scents without the influence of particular words or pictures. Students can also bring in samples of perfumes, lotions, or other scented cosmetics and respond with their own associations. It should be interesting to see how much commonality or variation there might be among different students' responses to the same scents. Students can record their sensory impressions in journals or contribute to a collective set of descriptions of each scent. Through additional writing and discussion, students can explore the individual connections they make with scents, perhaps branching off into stories, poems, or other literary productions.

Activity 2: Plants in Perfumery

The language of perfumes draws us into a poetry of the botanical world in which so many of the scents originate. Even by themselves, clusters of words can be highly evocative, as in the refrain "parsley, sage, rosemary, and thyme," from the Simon and Garfunkel song "Scarborough Fair." Students can compose their own chants along the same lines, capturing rhythms and sound reflections they design, such as

> Cinnamon, sandalwood, rosewood and wine
> Made out of orange blossoms, jasmine, and lime.

A partial list of plants used in perfumery, compiled by zoologist Michael Stoddart (1990, 154), is given in Figure 11.2. It should not be hard to extend the list in each category.

Figure 11.2.
Plants Used in Perfumery

Flowers	clove, hyacinth, mimosa (Acacia), jasmine, orange blossom, ylang ylang, boronia
Flowers & leaves	lavender, rosemary, peppermint, violet
Leaves & stems	geranium, patchouli, petigrain, verbena, cinnamon
Bark	canella (white cinnamon), cinnamon (bark oil), sandalwood, rosewood, cedarwood
Roots	angelica, sassafras, verivert
Fruits	bergamot, lemon, lime, orange
Seeds	bitter almond, anise (aniseed), fennel, nutmeg (muscat)

Activity 3: Aroma Therapy

Students can also use the language of perfumery to invent their own systems of "aroma therapy," such as was popular during the European plague as early as the fifteenth century. Enterprising pharmacists at the time concocted and sold sachets, dips, and incense containing various combinations of aromatic substances, as described by Annick Le Guerer (1992):

> Fragrant substances and antidotes frequently figure in prescriptions of the time. In addition to theriac, . . . deemed the "Queene of all the compounds vouchsafed by Heav'n to Man" and into which one dipped one's handkerchief, there were all sorts of other pleasant fragrances (incense, myrrh, violets, mint, melissa balm, rue, or a "cedar apple" made of storax, sandalwood, camphor and roses). One could also carry a citrus fruit, flowers, or a sweet-smelling plant. . . . Pills and electuaries were compounded of aloes, myrrh, saffron. . . . People drank and ate decoctions of flowers to dry out "poisonous humidities"; antitoxic plants like wild horseradish . . . ; waters of

melissa, rose, or scabious; or scorpion oil, which was made by boiling that dangerous creature in fifty-year-old olive oil. Perfumed sachets to be worn close to the heart to strengthen it were made of red roses, aloe wood, sandalwood, and coral. (73)

Aroma therapy still has practitioners today, who prescribe, for example, odors of lemons and oranges for depression; myrtle, mint, and sage to prevent an attack of epilepsy; neroli and lavender to relieve anxiety; and freesia and freshly cut hay for tension. More customized mixtures of essential oils may be prescribed for an individual's particular combination of problems (Engen 1991).

What "aroma therapy" might students prescribe to relieve such mental states as anxiety, tension, loneliness, sadness, or irritability? Alternatively, students can speculate on how certain aromas would affect their mood, such as those of fresh bread, crushed pine needles, popcorn, or a certain perfume. What smells comfort or repel? Do any aromas cause rather than relieve negative feelings? By exploring their own experiences with smells, students may discover greater richness in their olfactory world than they had previously imagined.

The Imagination of the Body: Movement and Touch

Art bids us touch and taste and hear and see the world, and shrinks from what Blake calls mathematic form, from every abstract thing, from all that is of brain only, from all that is not a fountain jetting from the entire hopes, memories, and sensations of the body.

William Butler Yeats, "The Thinking of the Body"

According to George Lakoff and Mark Johnson (1980), metaphors are grounded in our bodies and physical experiences. Our earliest learning is imitation, a kind of metaphorical response to the environment. Human inventions are also imitations of nature: roads are metaphors for rivers, airplanes are metaphors for birds, and computers are metaphors for brains. Susan Moon (1988), describing her feelings when her son was driving east from California to Harvard University, called his friend's car a "big fast fish in a dangerous river" (46). The narrator of Barbara Kingsolver's *Animal Dreams* (1990) compares her sister's breathing to the power of a tree growing: "Her breath expanded her chest against my arms, and I thought of the way a tree will keep on growing after a fence is wired around its trunk. The unbelievable force of that expansion. And I let her go" (33). Soon after the sisters' reluctant parting, they talk by telephone: "I just stood still for a minute," the narrator says, "giving Hallie's and my thoughts their last chance to run quietly over the wires, touching each other in secret signal as they passed, like a column of ants" (34).

Images of motion, pressure, speed, and other kinesthetic experiences can draw us in physically. Artistic forms of this expression are dance and pantomime. In games we have charades, statues, and hand-shadows. Kinesthetic metaphors can also be used to evoke certain behaviors or attitudes. *Run like a rabbit* might describe a sprint, while *run like a gazelle* suggests long-distance running. Being *quiet as a mouse* implies a state of alert and purposeful silence, while being *quiet as a pond* suggests a meditative state.

Metaphors of Movement

Activity 1: Walk This Way

One of the most famous visual jokes in movies follows the line "Walk this way," spoken by Marty Feldman after he has met Gene Wilder at the Transylvania train station in *Young Frankenstein* (20th Century Fox 1974). Bending low, Wilder starts out hobbling after the cloaked hunchback in front of him. Perhaps at some time or another we have all secretly imitated some individual or animal whose carriage we find interesting or admire, and even though the resemblance may be lost on an observer, within ourselves we feel, at least for the moment, that we have achieved a transformation.

Share the following passage with your students and ask them to reflect on individuals they have known or observed who were memorable for the way they moved or held themselves:

> "Walk like a Watutsi," Miss Carney often commanded when she thought her students were drooping. She never explained what she meant, but they understood that to walk like a Watutsi was to draw oneself up to a magnificent height, a gesture of the imagination intended to overcome the shortcomings of one's actual physical self. And Miss Carney, who of course was Miss Corney behind her back, would stretch her torso and without changing her actual dimensions, which were low and stout, become tall. But Jenny, although she understood the principle, would only contract her rubber self further as if to ward off, rather than take on, the life that lay ahead of her. (Pugh 1989b)

Have students talk or write about people whose carriage or locomotion enabled them somehow to transcend their ordinary appearance. Invite students to try the "walk this way" gag with any character they choose, such as a cheerleader, a basketball player (or any sports participant), a rock star, a cowboy, a Wall Street investment broker, or an American in a jungle (or any unusual place).

Activity 2: Body Capers

As actress Holly Hunter eloquently demonstrated in her role as a mute musician in the film *The Piano* (Miramax 1994), verbal language is only a part of communication, and nonverbal language—tone of voice, gestures, facial expression, body stance—will often speak more strongly than words. A good actor or liar is one who can make nonverbal and verbal expression coincide. Otherwise, we almost always know when someone is saying one thing and meaning another. Yet it is very easy to underestimate how much we communicate nonverbally and often unconsciously. The following activities, based on concepts developed in Nancy King's *Giving Form to Feeling* (1975), suggest ways to become aware of kinesthetic expressiveness:

Sculpturing. Statues can be made of a wide range of materials, including malleable substances such as clay or soap, stone materials such as marble or granite, and metals such as bronze or copper. Also, they can be made by various methods, such as molding, carving, or casting. Most statues are stationary, but those made of snow or ice will change form rapidly in warming temperatures, and mechanical sculptures, such as mobiles, may be made of moving parts. Because of their versatility, thinking about and imitating sculptures provide many possibilities for metaphorical exploration of experience. The following imitations will convey the feel of these different sculpting media:

- *Metaphor of development and transformation:* Imagine or act out changing from a hunk of clay to a molded form of anything you choose. Begin as an undifferentiated block of clay or marble and assume the form and dimensions of a sculpted object.

- *Metaphor of transitoriness or entropy:* Assume the form of a snow or ice sculpture and then melt.

- *Metaphor of aging, maturity, and change (both desirable and undesirable, with the passage of time):* Begin as a newly cast copper or bronze statue, polished and gleaming, and then slowly assume the changes of time as your surface becomes dull, corroded, perhaps covered with moss or vines.

Light and Heavy. Movement is dependent on gravity, and we are adapted to the particular pull of the earth's gravity, which is why weightlessness is both a mobility and a health problem for space scientists. Students can increase awareness of their own relationship to gravity and the nature of their own movement by projecting themselves imaginatively into objects of greater or lesser mass and weight:

- a balloon that has escaped from a hawker's collection
- a flower pot pushed from a second-story window sill
- a crumpled-up newspaper blown by the wind
- a pontoon boat on a choppy lake
- an anchor thrown overboard

A group of students can create a kinesthetically metaphorical scene featuring objects of different weights and porosity, for example, leaves blowing around the trunk of a tree or a gathering of small forest animals, such as birds, squirrels, rabbits, hedgehogs, and the like. The experience of each component of the scene could be written as part of a collective poem or story.

Talking Heads, Feet, Elbows, and Knees. A mime can convey a wide range of human emotions and attitudes without saying a word and, at the same time, convincingly convey actions, such as drinking tea or putting on a coat, without the objects or props. What the mime is doing is directly involving viewers in the enterprise of creating visuals and meaning.

Ask students to think of how they would convey particular emotions and attitudes through actions of different body parts rather than words. After practicing facial expressions, students can try for such representations as curious elbows, frightened feet, angry hands, or a shy head. Have them imagine and write about or act a scene in which people who don't speak each others' languages communicate in these alternative ways.

Mirrors. As *Alice Through the Looking Glass* (Carroll [1946] 1994) illustrates, a mirror is a powerful metaphor for looking at relationships between illusion and reality as well as such phenomena as symmetry, vanity, truth, and perspective. Why should breaking a mirror bring bad luck? What metaphor can students make for different kinds of mirrors, such as rearview mirrors, magnifying mirrors, two mirrors reflecting each other, fun-house mirrors, and mirror surfaces of objects such as windows and still ponds? Students can try the following demonstrations and then reflect on any concept or experience they wish in writing:

- With a partner, take turns being a mirror and the person, animal, or object it reflects.
- Imagine being reflected in mirrors of various size, beginning with a purse mirror, reflecting only one feature of your face, up to a full-size mirror that shows you from head to toe.
- Pretend to be moving from one fun-house mirror to another, each time changing the distortion you see in the mirror.

Interesting writing ventures might include the following:

- stories, essays, or poems on the theme of imitation as an element of learning and growth
- "reflections" on how people reflect each other in society
- responses to such questions as these: Can one be isolated from others without being isolated from oneself? What does it mean to put oneself in the position of another? Can you imagine or recall a time when you projected yourself into someone else's experience with interesting results?

Activity 3: Animal Kinetics

As pet owners know, body language is a principal form of expression for an animal. How does a cat express irritation, threat, hunger, contentment? How has the dog, as a species, earned the reputation of being "man's best friend"? In Betsy Byars's *Midnight Fox* (1968), a boy describes how the mysterious black-furred fox stands with her head cocked sideways and a front paw poised before she takes flight: "Suddenly her nose quivered. It was such a slight movement I almost didn't see it, and then her mouth opened and I could see the pink top of her tongue. She turned. She still was not afraid, but with a bound that was lighter than the wind—it was as if she was being blown away over the field—she was gone" (46).

Invite your students to imagine themselves changing into a string of animals as they walk the length of a city block: like a duck, like a cat, like a giraffe, like a porcupine, like a hippopotamus, like a chimpanzee, and like a tyrannosaur, or whatever sequence of animals they like. After this experiment, discuss how each way of walking affected their self-images. Did they particularly like or dislike any of them? Did they experience ways of walking they would like to cultivate as part of their personal styles?

Activity 4: Literary Moves

In his story "Where Pelham Fell," Bob Shacochis (1989) describes dogs who "barked and hopped into the air outside his door as if they sprang off trampolines" (55). Many writers have captured the kinesthetic feel of particular animals. Tennyson's "Eagle" watches over the "wrinkled sea," and then "like a thunderbolt he falls," lines which capture both the motionless vigil and the swift attack of a bird of prey (1976, 372). In her poem "Zebra," Isak Dinesen (1965) contrasts the eagle's shadow, which "runs along the plain," with the zebras' shadows, which "sit close between their delicate hoofs all day" (88). In his poem *"Toro,"* W. S. Merwin gives us "hooves detonating the dusk, under his rushing darkness" (in Briggs and Monaco 1990, 149). And one of the authors of this book, a dedicated cat owner, created these images in the poem "Reflection" after watching kittens play:

A
kitten
is a fist wrapped in fur
prancing on its
fingers

A
kitten
folds under like a glove
without a hand
in it

(Pugh n.d.)

Invite students to select any animal and describe its movement, using metaphors as appropriate, along with other images. This can be a particular animal, such as a pet, or a species, as in the poems about the eagle, the zebra, and the bull. Have students try to capture the animal's movement as an essential feature of its identity and character. They can also research and compile a collection of literary representations of their chosen species, either metaphorically described or used as a metaphor, as in Sandburg's image of fog coming "on little cat feet" (1950, 33) or Whitman's "noiseless patient spider" (in Hollander and Bloom 1961) that reminded him of his own soul, weaving its web in the unknowable space of the universe.

Writers frequently evoke the moods and experiences of the different seasons through kinesthetic imagery (often in combination with other imagery) that involves movement, touch, tension, and weight, as in e. e. cummings's poem comparing spring to a "perhaps hand" that moves a "perhaps fraction of flower" and "an inch of air" in its careful touch ("Spring is like a perhaps hand," in Whicher and Ahnebrink 1961, 161–62). In his elegy "Bells for John Whiteside's Daughter," John Crowe Ransom (1955) captures the feeling of summer in his description of geese,

> Dripping their snow on the green grass
> Tricking and stopping
>
> (10)

Philip Appleman (1976) describes how

> the big catalpa leaves
> float crippled down the slanting sun

in his poem "October Spring" (17). In "Thirteen Ways of Looking at a Blackbird," Wallace Stevens (1980) gives this image:

> The blackbird whirled in the autumn winds.
> It was a small part of the pantomime.
>
> (93)

One of the most memorable images of winter is Robert Frost's description of iced branches in "Birches" (1970), which "click upon themselves" and

> shed crystal shells
> Shattering and avalanching on the snow-crust.
>
> (92)

Trying It Out

Seasonal Motions

There are many aspects of seasonal images that you and your students may find to discuss, depending on students' interests and levels of maturity. Following are some ideas.

Activity 1: Seasons as I Know Them

Depending on locale, seasons may be highly defined or subtle. Not all regions have winters with glittering ice or enough snow to fill woods. Not all have autumns with gold, orange, and red trees, or springs with cherry blossoms. But people who have lived in an area have a sure feeling for each season, which is registered in all the senses. Students can find and compose imagery that captures the experiences of the seasons as they know them.

Activity 2: The Meanings of Seasons

Students interested in more abstract ideas may consider how the seasons exemplify the relationship between space and time. To have meaning, seasons must be situated both on the calendar and in a particular place. Seasons provide a key to capturing the mood as well as the physical attributes of a setting. A given place may well have a season with which it is particularly associated. Ask students what season they believe is most prominent where they live, and why. It will be interesting to see the extent to which they agree and experience the same setting in similar or different ways.

Activity 3: Introspections

Because seasons affect daily experience in so many ways, they provide a focus for reflection on one's perceptions, feelings, and beliefs. This kind of reflection is a pathway to the inner life and therefore a means of communicating with one's intuitive and imaginative ways of knowing, which are essential to both intellectual and emotional functioning.

Activity 4: Stories from Seasons

The seasons guide the rhythms of all life. They are also associated with periods of life, from infancy to old age, and with moods and emotions, from hope to resignation. Students themselves respond in many ways to the seasons, including how they dress, where they go, and what they do for fun. The changes that take place from one season to another, or across all the seasons in a year, can provide frameworks for stories. For example, imagine four scenes involving the same characters in the same setting over four seasons, such as a fast-food restaurant in which four friends have after-school jobs. The first scene could take place in autumn, when all are starting their senior year of high school and discussing their plans for what they will do when they graduate. The ensuing scenes could follow their various fortunes and final destinations in the summer.

In this story framework, the seasons not only advance the plot but are themselves metaphorical for the events and experiences of the characters. They begin in fall, the season when bulbs are planted, the harvest is stored, and other provisions are made for the future. In winter, immediate demands make us focus on the present. Hope arises in spring as one witnesses the materialization of the providence of autumn, and summer is the time of dispersion, as fruit ripens, seeds fly in the winds, and leaves get ready to fall in the next season.

**Activity 5:
Personalizing the
Seasons**

Students may personalize seasons metaphorically by choosing one they identify with most closely and feel represents them psychologically. This identification could be expressed in writing in any genre, and the genre itself might have a metaphorical connection with the season for the student, for example, poetry for spring, story for winter.

Kinesthetically oriented metaphors rarely exist without connection to other sensory images. The seasons themselves are experienced in multisensory, enveloping ways, and they are themselves profoundly metaphorical throughout our lives and in virtually every realm of experience.

Touch

Deprived of sight and hearing, Helen Keller moved from her prison of isolation into the social world of communication via her sense of touch. Her story of feeling first the cool water of a fountain and then the letters of the word traced in her palm has become a modern parable of learning. The story evokes awe in us as a testimony to the human mind's persistence in its quest for meaning. It also reminds us of the importance of our hands and skin as instruments of knowing.

Diane Ackerman (1990) has described human skin as "a kind of space suit in which we maneuver through an atmosphere of harsh gases, cosmic rays, radiation from the sun, and obstacles of all sorts" (67). Texture, temperature, pleasure, and pain are especially associated with the skin. The anthropologist Ashley Montagu (1971), who wrote an entire volume on skin, describes it as "the oldest and the most sensitive of our organs, our first medium of communication, and our most efficient protector," and touch as the "parent of our eyes, ears, nose, and mouth" (3).

Even when the images are primarily visual, our hands respond to such descriptions as the "russet braille" of peeling bark in Nancy Willard's poem "The Exodus of Peaches" (1992, 30) and Edna O'Brien's "shavings of dried paint curled on the wrought iron" (1991, 42) from her short story "The Cut." A different touch sensation is evoked by Alice Munro's description of satin laid over sheets: "Its broad, bright extent, its shining vulnerability, cast a hush over the whole house" (1992, 36). Touch is at least implicit in almost all experiences, and by cultivating their awareness of it, students can increase the authenticity and direct impact of their writing.

What Color Is Your Cat?

Our experiences with animals are significantly tactile, which is why we call those we own (or who own us) "pets." Although we may admire the visual beauty of our pets, we are often most engaged with their warm fur, wet noses, sharp claws, and nipping or gnawing teeth. It is much the same with the warmth, weight, moistness, poking, and grabbing of infants and toddlers. We know them through our hands and skin. Thinking and writing about these experiences can raise students' awareness of the importance of tactile experiences in their lives while developing in their writing the ability to evoke immediate physical response. The following passage describes one of the author's experience with cats. Students may write similar descriptions of their experiences with animals of their choosing.

What Color Is Your Cat?

A matter of great interest for any animal is its fur, and if you learn that someone has a pet, your first question is likely to be, what color is it? I have four cats who are all lion-colored. My oldest cat softens my lap with kneading paws for minutes before he settles down, drools with pleasure while I'm rubbing his head, and nips my hand when he's tired of it. The youngest is the most flexible, both physically and psychologically. He comes at a whistle and lies as limp as a mitten in my lap until he is ready to go, at which point he stiffens and pushes away like a rejecting hand. In between are my three-legged cat, muscular and husky from his undulating gait, who will always stop, roll over, and present a sheepskin stomach for rubbing, and my tiny fox-cat, quick and precise on the hunt, whose fine silky fur is touched appropriately with white. With their polished eyes of agate or jade, no wonder I call them my pride.

I once met a cat with a velcro underside. You had to peel him off your chest once you'd picked him up, and then he would reattach himself to your arm. He lived in a family composed predominantly of pets. The couple who owned him entertained their company by providing each guest with a cat to hold. We would sit, talking and petting, while the cats flexed, pawed, settled, snoozed, and eventually went their own ways. Mine, the velcro cat, would be with me much longer than anyone else's. (Pugh 1993)

Discussion questions could include:

- What do these metaphors convey to you: *lion-colored, softens my lap with kneading paws, pushes away like a rejecting hand, sheepskin stomach, velcro underside, fox-cat?*
- What if the family described gave everyone a hamster to hold while visiting? a monkey? a snake? any other animal? How might those experiences be described to highlight tactile experience?

- Even animals we don't actually touch, such as wild ones and most zoo animals, can evoke tactile responses. How would you describe your tactile responses to a leopard, an alligator, an anaconda, an elephant, a penguin, a wolf, or any other animals you think of?
- What other metaphorical significance might one attach to animals' fur?

The following continues the passage started above:

> Color and the other qualities of pelts are so wonderful that I must wonder why they have been construed so negatively among people. Maybe we need to start over, taking a lesson from our companion species, and all grow fur. Biogeneticists, let's see you get to work on that. Give us tiger stripes, ringed tails, blue points, silver tips, jet black velvet and Siamese silk, masks and mustaches, bibs and mittens, sleek calico flanks, plush white bellies, and feathery brindle backs. Make us as beautiful to touch as to see, our hands gloved, our feet silent in slippers with thick pads, our ears the eider points of crowns. Wouldn't we believe, then, in the beauty of diversity and only wish for more originality rather than less? Isn't that the way things ought to be?

To pursue the discussion further:

- Discuss the problem that is implied in the "solution" to the problems of the human race proposed by the author. What does it say about racial and ethnic prejudice? Why is this problem connected with the fate of the human race?
- Have students think about particular human problems and imaginative solutions. Or have them think about an extinct species, such as dinosaurs or the passenger pigeon, and how they might have been saved. A third variation might be to think of other favorite animal qualities or characteristics that might profitably be adopted by the human race, such as powerful jumping, like the kangaroo's, so that people wouldn't use so much fossil fuel, or prehensile tails that operated like a third arm. Encourage students to find their own themes and freewrite to find where their own imaginative flow takes them.

Just as animals' pelts evoke our tactile responses, the textures of human hair and skin are primary attributes in our images of people. In their extensive catalogue of comparisons found in literature, *Falser Than a Weeping Crocodile and Other Similes*, Elyse and Mike Sommer (1991) include references to hair that is "frizzy like an unravelled rope" (296), "like fuzz on a tennis ball" (298), and "thick and coarse as dune grass" (298). These similes suggest hair that is rough to the touch. The following, on the other hand, evoke quite different tactile responses, even if we may never have actually touched the object to which the comparison is being made: "like Persian lambs' fur"; "soft as milkweed silk" (298).

Description through Texture

Eyebrows are also important in our construction of human features. James Crumley has a character who raises "an eyebrow built like a wooly worm" (in Sommer and Sommer 1991, 211), suggesting a face quite different from that of Jean Stafford's character with "eyebrows like peaked black thread" (217). Even eyelashes evoke richly tactile responses, as evident in the contrasting impressions made by "lashes thick and furry as tarantula legs" and "eyelashes stiff as bird-tails" (217).

Have students think about features of appearance in which texture is an important attribute, such as hair, skin, and clothing. They can write short sketches in which they focus on these features in real or imagined characters. Following are descriptions of two women, each of which conveys a different image of old age:

> The old woman had aged delicately, her pale powdered face as finely lined as etched glass. Her scalp blushed through blue-tinted angel-hair, while her hands, pellucid and beautifully flawed as Nepalese paper, sparkled the air with old diamonds as they gestured in arabesques. (Pugh 1989a)

> The old woman's skin had the tone and subtle lustre of teak over her smooth brow and cheek bones, a magnificent contrast to the snow-white cotton of her hair. The lines deepening around her mouth and the cords emerging on her neck strengthened her features as if, in old age, her true self was coming out from behind the mask of her youth. (Pugh 1989a)

In their reading, students can find brief descriptions of characters who seem to convey a full picture through just a few strokes. Often these sketches draw strongly on one or two sensory responses, which are likely to activate memories and experiences with which readers complete the images suggested by the author. Have students find such thumbnail descriptions that seem to convey a great deal more than their literal meaning and reflect on how these quick descriptions can be so evocative. One reason is that the writer has succeeded in involving the reader in the constructive process by using concrete, suggestive imagery that almost inevitably connects with a strong personal association. Have students combine this reflective reading with their own efforts to achieve brief but sensorially rich descriptions of characters, actions, and settings. Following are further examples of how images that combine sensations of touch and movement can evoke visceral reactions:

> At rows of ferocious industrial sewing machines, pairs of sides were sewed together; huddled women peered into spots of light where their knobby tense hands guided the doubled leather along a single

curved edge stitched by a chattering needle. Then the two halves, nested together, shaped like open pods, were sewn into a single unit, at machines even more powerful. (Updike 1991, 211)

Corrie never just wiped the counters—she scoured them. Every move she made had the energy and concentration somebody would show when rowing a boat against the current, and every word she said was flung out as if against a high wind. When she wrung out the cleaning rag, she might have been wringing the neck of a chicken. (Munro 1994, 83)

For the first time, she felt the force of winter coming on. Snow, hard and fine as grains of sand, stung her face. The earth was warmer than the air now and the snow melted as it landed. Thick platters of mud built up on the soles of her shoes and weighted every step. (Freeman 1988, 195)

V Conclusion and References

Journey over all the universe in a map . . .

Miguel de Cervantes, *Don Quixote de la Mancha*

Conclusion

Language is a city, to the building of which every human being brings a stone.
Ralph Waldo Emerson

The globe reveals a larger world to us than the spot where our finger lands when we point to home. Our imaginations can take us beyond the multicolored artificial borders and longitudinal lines that have been superimposed on the globe—which is, after all, a representation of reality, and not everyone's reality. Borders and lines do not exist in the natural world. With our enhanced perception we are able to share and learn from different cultures. Our imaginations rise beyond our home base to explore diverse others. We are seeking not only a different understanding of ourselves in relation to others but also an expanded view of ourselves and to find a way through our writing to express that self.

Our desire is to share our renewed delight in the ways we express our thoughts and experience through literature with educators and English enthusiasts. Echoes of our language traditions will resound anew to those who listen.

With this book, we hope to have helped students find a voice that is relevant to themselves and to have helped the teacher facilitate the development of that voice. We, as educators, present the idea, image, or thought to launch students' unique discoveries and add to their understanding.

The imaginative transcendence of ordinary experience is at the heart of language arts learning. Literature in all its forms is an ongoing dialogue about who we are and how we connect with the world in which we live. Through expressive writing and deliberate acts of the imagination, students, too, can join the conversation.

References

Abrahamson, Richard F., and Betty Carter, eds., and the Committee on the Senior High School Booklist. 1988. *Books for You: A Booklist for Senior High Students.* 10th ed. Urbana, Ill.: NCTE.

Ackerman, Diane. 1990. *A Natural History of the Senses.* New York: Random House.

Adams, Jim. 1993. "City Took Moral Swipe at Mascots, but Few Seemed to Notice." *Louisville (Ky.) Courier-Journal,* 23 February, B1.

Allen, Michelle, and Lynn Burlbaw. 1987. "Making Meaning with a Metaphor." *Social Education* 51 (2): 142–43.

Allen, Paula Gunn, ed. 1989. *Spider Woman's Granddaughters: Traditional Tales and Contemporary Writing by Native American Women.* Boston: Beacon Press.

Aloian, David, ed. 1965. *Poems and Poets.* St. Louis: McGraw-Hill Book Company, Webster Division.

Alvarez, Julia. 1984. "Snow." *Northwest Review* 22 (1–2): 21–22.

Ammer, Christine. 1989a. *Fighting Words: From War, Rebellion, and Other Combative Capers.* New York: Paragon House.

———. 1989b. *It's Raining Cats and Dogs—and Other Beastly Expressions.* New York: Paragon House.

———. 1993. *Southpaws and Sunday Punches: And Other Sporting Expressions.* New York: Dutton.

Anaya, Rudolfo A., ed. 1987. *Voces: An Anthology of Nuevo Mexicano Writers.* Albuquerque: El Norte Publications.

Anderson, Charles W. 1987. "Strategic Teaching in Science." In *Strategic Teaching and Learning: Cognitive Instruction in the Content Areas,* edited by Beau Fly Jones. Alexandria, Va.: ASCD.

Anderson, Nick. 1991. Editorial cartoon. *Louisville (Ky.) Courier-Journal,* 2 September, A10.

Anderson, Philip M., and Bonnie S. Sunstein. 1987. "Teaching the Use of Metaphor in Science Writing." Paper read at annual meeting of the Conference on College Composition and Communication, at Atlanta, 19–21 March.

Angelou, Maya. 1969. *I Know Why the Caged Bird Sings.* New York: Random House.

Appleman, Philip. 1976. *Open Doorways: Poems.* New York: Norton.

Aprile, Dianne. 1994a. "Best of Times, Worst of Times." *Louisville (Ky.) Courier-Journal,* 30 October, H01.

———. 1994b. "Guns Don't Die, People Do." *Louisville (Ky.) Courier-Journal,* 4 September, H01.

Asante, Molefi Kete. 1991. *The Book of African Names.* Trenton, N.J.: Africa World Press.

Associated Press. 1994a. "French Exhibition Shut Down for Breaking Cruelty to Animals Law." *Bloomington (Ind.) Herald-Times,* 10 November, A7.

———. 1994b. "India's Plague Doesn't Stop Old Tradition of Rat Worship." *Bloomington (Ind.) Herald-Times,* 30 September, A1.

Barden, Jack, and Paul Boyer. 1993. "Ways of Knowing: Extending the Boundaries of Scholarship." *Tribal College: Journal of American Indian Higher Education* 4 (3): 12–15.

Barnhart, Clarence L., ed. 1954. *The New Century Cyclopedia of Names.* Vol. 2. New York: Appleton-Century-Crofts.

Bartlett, John. 1980. *Familiar Quotations: A Collection of Passages, Phrases, and Proverbs Traced to Their Sources in Ancient and Modern Literature.* 15th ed. Edited by E. M. Beck et al. Boston: Little, Brown.

Baynes, Cary F. (English translator), and Richard Wilhelm (German translator). 1967. *The I Ching; or, Book of Changes.* 3rd ed. Bollingen Series, no. 19. Princeton: Princeton University Press.

Beck, Emily Morrison, ed. 1968. *Familiar Quotations: A Collection of Passages, Phrases, and Proverbs Traced to Their Sources in Ancient and Modern Literature.* Boston: Little, Brown.

Beckwith, Martha Warren. 1970. *Jamaica Proverbs.* New York: Negro Universities Press.

Beeching, Cyril L. 1979. *A Dictionary of Eponyms.* London: Clive Bingley.

Belenky, Mary Field, Blythe McVicker Clinchy, Nancy Rule Goldberger, and Jill Mattuck Tarule. 1986. *Women's Ways of Knowing: The Development of Self, Voice and Mind.* New York: Basic Books.

Bellamy, Edward. 1968. *Looking Backward, 2000–1887.* New York: Lancer Books.

Bender, Steve. 1991. "Outdoors South: Navigators of the Night." *Southern Living,* July, 27.

Berry, Wendell. 1988. "People, Land and Community." In *Multicultural Literacy,* edited by R. Simonson and S. Walker. St. Paul: Graywolf Press.

Best, Judith A. 1984. "Teaching Political Theory: Meaning through Metaphor." *Improving College and University Teaching* 32 (4): 165–68.

Bethancourt, T. Ernesto. 1978. *Tune in Yesterday.* New York: Holiday House.

Bhengu, Vusi, Goodman Kivan, Nester Luthuli, Gladman "Mvukuzane" Ngubo, and November Marsata Shabalala. 1994. "The Man Who Could Fly." In *Being Here: Modern Short Stories from Southern Africa,* compiled by Robin Malan. Cape Town: David Philip.

Bierce, Ambrose. 1891. "An Occurrence at Owl Creek Bridge." In *Tales of Soldiers and Civilians*. San Francisco: E. L. G. Steele.

Big Eagle, Duane. 1983. "The Journey." In *Earth Power Coming: Short Fiction in Native American Literature*, edited by Simon J. Ortiz. Tsaile, Ariz.: Navajo Community College Press.

Bissoondath, Neil. 1990. *On the Eve of Uncertain Tomorrows*. New York: Clarkson Potter Publishers.

Blair, Cynthia. 1987. *Freedom to Dream*. New York: Fawcett Juniper Books.

Boreen, J. 1975. "Salmon Swims Up the River." *Yardbird Reader* 4: 34–39.

Borgmann, Dmitri A. 1967. *Beyond Language: Adventures in Word and Thought*. New York: Charles Scribner's Sons.

Borman, Kathryn M., and Patricia O'Reilly, eds. 1992. "Alternative Conceptualizations." *Educational Foundations* 6 (1): 85.

Boycott, Rosie. 1982. *Batty, Bloomers and Boycott: A Little Etymology of Eponymous Words*. London: Hutchinson.

Bridges, William. 1980. *Transitions: Making Sense of Life's Changes*. Reading, Mass.: Addison-Wesley.

Briggs, John, and Richard Monaco, comps. 1990. *Metaphor: The Logic of Poetry: A Handbook*. New York: Pace University Press.

Brooks, Gwendolyn. 1971. *The World of Gwendolyn Brooks*. New York: Harper and Row.

Brown, Dee. 1993. *When the Century Was Young*. Little Rock, Ark.: August House.

Brown, Karen McCarthy. 1991. *Mama Lola: A Vodou Priestess in Brooklyn*. Berkeley: University of California Press.

Brown, Phil. 1993. "When the Public Knows Better: Popular Epidemiology Challenges the System." *Environment* 35 (October): 16–20.

Brown, R. D., Thomas Kranidas, and Faith G. Norris, eds. 1959. *Oregon Signatures*. Corvallis: Oregon State College.

Bruchac, Joseph. 1992. *Turtle Meat and Other Stories*. Duluth, Minn.: Holy Cow! Press.

Bruner, Jerome S. 1990. *Acts of Meaning*. Cambridge: Harvard University Press.

Buckley, Christopher. 1995. "Doing the McNamara." *New Yorker*, 22 May, 100.

Bulfinch, Thomas. [1913] 1979. *Bulfinch's Mythology*. Reprint, New York: Crown Publishers.

Bunting, Eve. 1984. *The Man Who Could Call Down Owls*. New York: Macmillan.

Burroway, Janet. 1992. *Writing Fiction: A Guide to Narrative Craft*. 3rd ed. New York: HarperCollins.

Byars, Betsy. 1968. *The Midnight Fox.* New York: Scholastic.

Cahill, Susan, ed. 1975. *Women and Fiction: Short Stories by and about Women.* New York: New American Library.

Calkins, Lucy McCormick. 1991. *Living Between the Lines.* Portsmouth, N.H.: Heinemann.

Campbell, Joseph, with Bill Moyers. 1988. *The Power of Myth.* New York: Doubleday.

Carle, Eric. 1984. *The Mixed-Up Chameleon.* 2nd ed. New York: T.Y. Crowell Junior Books.

Carnes, Jim. 1994. "An Uncommon Language." *Teaching Tolerance* 3 (1): 56–63.

Carroll, Lewis. [1946] 1994. *Alice in Wonderland and Alice Through the Looking Glass.* Reprint, New York: Grosset and Dunlap.

Carson, Rachel. 1962. *Silent Spring.* Boston: Houghton Mifflin.

Chapman, Robert L., ed. 1987. *American Slang.* New York: HarperCollins.

Chen, Julie. 1996. Personal communication, 30 January.

Christenbury, Leila, ed., and the Committee on the Senior High School Booklist. 1995. *Books for You: An Annotated Booklist for Senior High Students.* Urbana, Ill.: NCTE.

Christensen, Jane, ed., and the Committee on the Junior High and Middle School Booklist of the National Council of Teachers of English. 1983. *Your Reading: A Booklist for Junior High and Middle School Students.* Urbana, Ill.: NCTE.

Cinnamond, Jeffrey. 1987. "Metaphors as Understanding: Recent Reform Reports on Education." Paper read at annual meeting of the Association for the Study of Higher Education, at San Diego.

Cirlot, J. E. 1971. *Dictionary of Symbols.* 2nd ed. New York: Philosophical Library.

Claiborne, Robert, and the American Heritage Dictionaries Editors, eds. 1986. *Word Mysteries and Histories: From Quiche to Humble Pie.* Boston: Houghton Mifflin.

Clausen, Christopher. 1994. "Language, Not Nationality, Should Distinguish the World's Literature." *Chronicle of Higher Education,* 22 June, A48.

Cohen, Hennig, and Tristram Potter Coffin. 1987. *The Folklore of American Holidays.* Detroit: Gale Research Press.

———. 1991. *America Celebrates! A Patchwork of Weird and Wonderful Holiday Lore.* Detroit: Visible Ink Press.

Cohen, Laura J. 1993. "The Therapeutic Use of Reading: A Qualitative Study." *Journal of Poetry Therapy* 7 (2): 73–83.

Coleman, Wanda. 1988. "The Seamstress." In *A War of Eyes and Other Stories.* Santa Rosa, Calif.: Black Sparrow Press.

Conley, Robert J. 1988. *The Witch of Goingsnake and Other Stories.* Norman: University of Oklahoma Press.

Cormier, Robert. 1977. *I Am the Cheese.* New York: Pantheon Books.

Cosman, Madeleine Pelner. 1976. *Fabulous Feasts: Medieval Cookery and Ceremony.* New York: George Braziller, Inc.

———. 1981. *Medieval Holidays and Festivals: A Calendar of Celebrations.* New York: Charles Scribner's Sons.

———. 1984. *The Medieval Baker's Daughter: A Bilingual Adventure in Medieval Life with Costumes, Banners, Music, Food, and a Mystery Play.* Tenafly, N.J.: Bard Hall Press.

Cresswell, Rosemary, ed. 1987. *Home and Away: Travel Stories.* Ringwood, Victoria: Penguin Books of Australia.

Crystal, David. 1995. *The Cambridge Encyclopedia of the English Language.* New York: Cambridge University Press.

Curtis, Helena, and N. Sue Barnes. 1985. *Invitation to Biology.* 4th ed. New York: Worth.

Cutler, Charles L. 1994. *O Brave New Words!: Native American Loanwords in Current English.* Norman: University of Oklahoma Press.

Darwin, Erasmus. [1791] 1973. *The Botanic Garden; a Poem, in Two Parts.* Reprint, Menston, Yorkshire, England: Scholar Press.

Davies, Paul. 1995. *About Time: Einstein's Unfinished Revolution.* New York: Simon and Schuster.

Davis, Marcia T. n.d. Unpublished journal.

———. 1995. Unpublished manuscript.

Dawkins, Richard. 1989. "Put Your Money on Evolution." *New York Times Book Review,* 9 April, 34.

Delaney, Sarah L., and A. Elizabeth Delaney with Amy Hill Hearth. 1993. *Having Our Say: The Delaney Sisters' First 100 Years.* New York: Kodansha International.

Dickson, Paul. 1986. *Names: A Collector's Compendium of Rare and Unusual, Bold and Beautiful, Odd and Whimsical Names.* New York: Delacorte Press.

Dillard, Annie. 1974. *Pilgrim at Tinker's Creek.* New York: HarperPerennial.

———. 1982. "An Expedition to the Pole." In *Teaching a Stone to Talk.* New York: Harper and Row.

———. 1987. *An American Childhood.* New York: Harper and Row.

Dillon, J. T. 1983. *Teaching and the Art of Questioning.* Phi Delta Kappa Fastback Series 194. Bloomington, Ind.: Phi Delta Kappa Educational Foundation.

Dinesen, Isak. 1965. "Zebra." In *The Golden Journey: Poems for Young People,* edited by L. Bogan and W. J. Smith. Chicago: Reilly and Lee.

Dunkling, Leslie. 1991. *The Guinness Book of Names.* Enfield, Middlesex, Great Britain: Guinness Publishing Ltd.

Dunning, Stephen, Edward Lueders, and Hugh Smith, eds. 1966. *Reflections on a Gift of Watermelon Pickle . . . and Other Modern Verse.* New York: Scholastic Book Services.

Eagar, Frances. 1976. *Time Tangle.* Nashville, Tenn.: Thomas Nelson.

Eiseley, Loren. 1957. "How Flowers Changed the World." In *The Immense Journey.* New York: Random House.

———. 1969. *The Unexpected Universe.* New York: Harcourt, Brace and World.

Eley, Mary M. 1996. *Chase's Calendar of Annual Events.* Chicago: Contemporary Books.

Elleman, Barbara. 1983. "Picture Books: More Than a Story." *Booklist* 80 (3): 292–94.

Ellison, Emily, and Jane B. Hill, eds. 1987. *Our Mutual Room: Modern Literary Portraits of the Opposite Sex.* Atlanta: Peachtree Publishers.

Emerson, Ralph Waldo. 1904. *Journals.* Vol. 4. Cambridge: Harvard University Press, Belknap Press.

Engen, Trygg. 1991. *Odor Sensation and Memory.* New York: Praeger.

Enser, A. G. S. 1987. *Filmed Books and Plays: A List of Books and Plays from Which Films Have Been Made, 1928–86.* Aldershot, Hampshire: Gower.

Erickson, Helen L. 1988. "Modeling and Role-Modeling: Ericksonian Techniques Applied to Physiological Problems." In *Developing Ericksonian Therapy: State of the Art*, edited by J. K. Zeig and S. Lankton. New York: Brunner/Mazel.

Espy, Willard R. 1978. *O Thou Improper, Thou Uncommon Noun: A Bobtailed, Generally Chronological Listing of Proper Names That Have Become Improper and Uncommonly Common; Together with a Smattering of Proper Names Commonly Used . . . and Certain Other Diversions.* New York: Clarkson N. Potter.

Ferris, Helen, ed. 1957. *Favorite Poems, Old and New.* Garden City, N.Y.: Doubleday.

Fischer, Janice, James Jeremias, and Jeffrey Boam. 1987. *The Lost Boys.* Burbank, Calif.: Warner Brothers Pictures.

Frazer, James G. [1894] 1981. *The Golden Bough: The Roots of Religion and Folklore.* Reprint, New York: Gramercy.

Freeman, Judith. 1988. "Going Out to Sea." In *Family Attractions.* New York: Viking Penguin.

Friend, Cliff, and Charlie Tobias. 1944. "Time Waits for No One." New York: Remick Music Corp.

Frost, Robert. 1970. "Birches." In *American Poetry and Prose*, edited by N. Foerster. Boston: Houghton Mifflin.

Fujioka, Mayumi. 1996. Personal communication, 30 January.

Gardner, Howard. 1983. *Frames of Mind: The Theory of Multiple Intelligences.* New York: Basic Books.

Gerard, R. W. 1952. "The Biological Basis of Imagination." In *The Creative Process: A Symposium,* edited by Brewster Ghiselin. Berkeley: University of California Press.

Ghiselin, Brewster, ed. 1952. *The Creative Process: A Symposium.* Berkeley: University of California Press.

Gibbs, Raymond W. 1994. *The Poetics of Mind: Figurative Thought, Language, and Understanding.* New York: Cambridge University Press.

Gilchrist, Ellen. 1981. *In the Land of Dreamy Dreams: Short Fiction.* Boston: Little, Brown.

———. 1984. *Victory over Japan: A Book of Stories.* Boston: Little, Brown.

Goodman, Ellen. 1995. "Hitlerian Language." *Louisville (Ky.) Courier-Journal,* 6 June, A7.

Goodspeed, Robert C. 1981. *From Greek to Graffiti: English Words That Survive and Thrive.* Smithtown, N.Y.: Exposition Press.

Grimm, The Brothers. 1966. "The Three Spinners." In *Folktales of Germany,* edited by K. Ranke. Chicago: University of Chicago Press.

Guralnik, David B., ed. 1970. *Webster's New World Dictionary of the American Language.* 2nd college ed. New York: Prentice-Hall.

Hall, Eric, Carol Hall, and Alison Leech. 1990. *Scripted Fantasy in the Classroom.* New York: Nichols Publishing Co.

Hall, Susan. 1990. *Using Picture Storybooks to Teach Literary Devices: Recommended Books for Children and Young Adults.* Phoenix: Oryx Press.

Hamilton, Sharon. 1995. *My Name's Not Susie.* Portsmouth, N.H.: Heinemann.

Hawking, Stephen W. 1988. *A Brief History of Time: From the Big Bang to Black Holes.* New York: Bantam.

Heartlands Fiction Collective. 1986. *These and Other Lands: Stories from the Heartland.* Loose Creek, Mo.: Westphalia Press.

Heilenman, Diane. 1995. Review of the Louisville Visual Art Association. *Louisville (Ky.) Courier-Journal,* 19 March, I4.

Heller, Louis G., Alexander Humez, and Malcah Dror. 1983. *The Private Lives of English Words.* London: Routledge and Kegan Paul.

Henisch, Bridget Ann. 1976. *Fast and Feast: Food in Medieval Society.* University Park: Pennsylvania State University Press.

Henley, Patricia. 1986. *Friday Night at Silver Star: Stories.* St. Paul: Graywolf Press.

Herron, Carol. 1982. "Foreign-Language Learning Approaches as Metaphor." *Modern Language Journal* 66 (Fall): 235–42.

Herzog, George. 1936. *Jabo Proverbs from Liberia: Maxims in the Life of a Native Tribe.* London: Oxford University Press.

Hicks, Jean Wolph. 1994. "The Dignifying Monkey." Unpublished manuscript.

———. 1995. "Guided Imagery." Unpublished manuscript.

Hilton, James. 1933. *The Lost Horizon.* New York: William Morrow.

Hirsch, E. D. 1987. *Cultural Literacy: What Every American Needs to Know.* Boston: Houghton Mifflin.

Hiura. 1986. *The Hawk's Well: A Collection of Japanese American Art and Literature.* San Jose, Calif.: Asian American Arts Projects.

Hoban, Russell. 1980. *Riddley Walker.* New York: Summit Books.

Hollander, John, and Harold Bloom, eds. 1961. *The Wind and the Rain: An Anthology of Poems for Young People.* New York: Doubleday.

Holmes, Oliver Wendell. 1895. *The Complete Poetical Works of Oliver Wendell Holmes.* Boston: Houghton Mifflin.

Holyoak, Keith, and Paul Thagard. 1995. *Mental Leaps: Analogy in Creative Thought.* Cambridge: MIT Press.

Honeck, Richard P., and Robert R. Hoffman, eds. 1980. *Cognition and Figurative Language.* Hillsdale, N.J.: Lawrence Erlbaum.

Hook, J. N. 1983. *The Book of Names.* New York: Franklin Watts.

Hope, Christopher. 1988. *White Boy Running.* New York: Farrar, Straus and Giroux.

Hsu, Kai-yu, and Helen Palubinskas, eds. 1972. *Asian-American Authors.* Boston: Houghton Mifflin.

Innocenti, Roberto, and Christophe Gallaz. 1985. *Rose Blanche.* New York: Stewart, Tabori and Chang.

Ison, Isaac, and Anna H. Ison. 1993. *A Whole 'Nother Language: Our Personal Collection of Appalachian Expressions.* Kentucky: Isaac and Anna H. Ison.

Iyer, Pico. 1993. "The Global Village Finally Arrives." *Time, Special Issue: The New Face of America,* Fall, 86–87.

Jacobson, John D. 1990. *Toposaurus: A Humorous Treasury of Toponyms.* New York: John Wiley and Sons.

Jarrell, Randall. 1969. *The Complete Poems.* New York: Farrar, Straus and Giroux.

Jaynes, Julian. 1976. *The Origin of Consciousness in the Breakdown of the Bicameral Mind.* Boston: Houghton Mifflin.

Jeans, Peter D. 1993. *Ship to Shore: A Dictionary of Everyday Words and Phrases Derived from the Sea.* Santa Barbara: ABC-CLIO.

Jensen, Julie M., and Nancy L. Roser, eds. 1993. *Adventuring with Books: A Booklist for Pre-K–Grade 6.* 10th ed. Urbana, Ill.: NCTE.

Johnson, Thomas, ed. 1960. *The Complete Poems of Emily Dickinson.* Boston: Back Bay Books.

John-Steiner, Vera. 1985. *Notebooks of the Mind: Explorations of Thinking.* Albuquerque: University of New Mexico Press.

Johnston, Peter H. 1993. "Assessment and Literate 'Development.'" *Reading Teacher* 46 (5): 428–29.

Kalpakian, Laura. 1989. "A Christmas Cordial." In *Dark Continent and Other Stories.* New York: Viking.

Kanwar, Asha, ed. 1993. *The Unforgetting Heart: An Anthology of Short Stories by African American Women (1859–1993).* San Francisco: Aunt Lute Books.

Kenyatta, Jomo. 1959. *Facing Mount Kenya: The Tribal Life of the Gikuyu.* London: Secker and Warburg.

King, Nancy. 1975. *Giving Form to Feeling.* New York: Drama Book Specialists.

Kingsolver, Barbara. 1990. *Animal Dreams: A Novel.* New York: HarperCollins.

Kohl, Judith, and Herbert Kohl. 1977. *The View from the Oak: The Private Worlds of Other Creatures.* San Francisco: Sierra Club Books; New York: Charles Scribner's Sons.

Kuhn, Jennifer. 1995. Unpublished manuscript.

Lahrson, Ann. 1995. "The Good, the Bad, and the Deadly of OBE." *Home Education* 12 (3): 36.

Lakoff, George. 1990. Lecture, 12 April, at Indiana University.

Lakoff, George, and Mark Johnson. 1980. *Metaphors We Live By.* Chicago: University of Chicago Press.

Landers, Ann. 1988. "There Is No Standard Timetable for Dealing with Grief." *Louisville (Ky.) Courier-Journal Scene,* 9 July, 16.

Lax, Roger, and Frederick Smith. 1984. *The Great Song Thesaurus.* New York: Oxford University Press.

Lazarus, Emma. 1965. "The New Colossus." In *Poems That Live Forever,* edited by H. Felleman. Garden City, N.Y.: Doubleday.

Lazebnik, Philip, and Joe Menosky. 1991. "Darmok." 202nd episode of *Star Trek: The Next Generation.* Paramount Pictures.

Leclerc, Georges-Louis (Comte de Buffon). [1753] 1969. "Histoire naturelle de animaux." In *Ouevres Completes.* Reprint, Paris: Gallimard.

Le Guerer, Annick. 1992. *Scent, the Mysterious and Essential Powers of Smell.* Translated by Richard Miller. New York: Turtle Bay Books.

Lee, Audrey. 1971. "Waiting for Her Train." In *What We Must See: Young Black Storytellers,* edited by Orde Coombs. New York: Dodd, Mead and Co.

Lee, Robert C. 1982. *Timequake.* Philadelphia: Westminster Press.

Lee, Virginia. 1972. "From: The House That Tai Ming Built." In *Asian-American Authors,* edited by Kai-yu Hsu and Helen Palubinskas. Boston: Houghton Mifflin.

L'Engle, Madeleine. 1962. *A Wrinkle in Time.* New York: Farrar, Straus and Giroux.

Leonard, Mike. 1994. "In Election Years, One Agency Thinks It Pays Not to Advertise." Bloomington (Ind.) *Herald Times,* 10 November, C4.

Lindsay, David. 1963. *A Voyage to Arcturus.* New York: Macmillan.

Lopate, Phillip. 1975. *Being with Children.* Garden City, N.Y.: Doubleday.

Lopez, Barry H. 1979. *River Notes: The Dance of Herons.* Kansas City, Kans.: Andrews and McMeel.

Luria, Salvador E. 1985. *A Slot Machine, a Broken Test Tube: An Autobiography.* New York: Harper Colophon Books.

Mahood, Wayne. 1984. "Using Metaphors to Teach Social Studies." *Social Science Record* 21 (2): 12–14.

Major, Clarence, ed. 1994. *Juba to Jive: A Dictionary of African-American Slang.* New York: Penguin Books.

Malan, Robin, comp. 1994. *Being Here: Modern Short Stories from Southern Africa.* Cape Town: David Philip.

Malcolm, Janet. 1990. "A Reporter at Large: Czechoslovakia." *New Yorker,* 19 November, 56–106.

Mallon, Thomas. 1984. *A Book of One's Own.* New York: Ticknor and Fields.

Marcus, Greil. 1993. "The Elvis Test." *San Francisco Examiner.* Image, 17 January, 8–11.

Markels, Alex. 1995. "Dreams Can Come True as Napping Eases into Workplace." *Louisville (Ky.) Courier-Journal,* 2 July, E6.

Markus, Hazel, and Paul Nurius. 1986. "Possible Selves." *American Psychologist* 41 (9): 954–69.

Marshall, Helen Lowrie. 1969. "The Wonder of It All." In *A Gift So Rare.* Kansas City, Mo.: Hallmark Editions.

Martin, Bill, Jr., and John Archambault. 1987. *Knots on a Counting Rope.* New York: Henry Holt.

Martin, Judith. 1982. *Miss Manners' Guide to Excruciatingly Correct Behavior.* New York: Atheneum.

———. 1984. *Miss Manners' Guide to Rearing Perfect Children.* New York: Penguin Books.

Mason, Bobbie Ann. 1982. *Shiloh and Other Stories.* New York: Harper and Row.

May, Wanda T. 1993. "Teaching as a Work of Art in the Medium of Curriculum." *Theory into Practice* 32 (4): 210–18.

McBride, William G., ed., and the Committee to Revise *High Interest–Easy Reading.* 1990. *High Interest–Easy Reading: A Booklist for Junior and Senior High School Students.* 6th ed. Urbana, Ill.: NCTE.

McCrum, Robert, William Cran, and Robert MacNeil. 1986. *The Story of English.* New York: Viking.

McDonald, Donald S. 1994. Personal correspondence, 20 October.

———. 1995a. Personal correspondence, 4 March.

———. 1995b. Personal correspondence, 25 June.

McDonald, James C. 1992. "Student Metaphors for Themselves as Writers." *English Journal* 81 (4): 60–64.

McKnight, Reginald. 1988. *Moustapha's Eclipse.* Pittsburgh: University of Pittsburgh Press.

McNamara, Shelley G. 1984. "Children Respond to Satire in Picture Books." *Reading Improvement* 21 (Winter): 303–23.

Mead Johnson. 1989. *Names for Boys and Girls.* Evansville, Ind: Bristol-Myers.

Melville, Herman. [1853] 1990. "Bartleby the Scrivener." In *Bartleby; and, Benito Cereno,* edited by S. Appelbaum. Reprint, New York: Dover.

Menken, Alan, and Stephen Schwartz. 1995. *Colors of the Wind.* New York: Hyperion.

Mills, Joyce C., and Richard J. Crowley in collaboration with Margaret O. Ryan. 1986. *Therapeutic Metaphors for Children and the Child Within.* New York: Brunner/Mazel.

Minnesota Humanities Commission. 1991. *Braided Lives: An Anthology of Multicultural American Writing.* St. Paul: Minnesota Humanities Commission and Minnesota Council of Teachers of English.

Mitchell, Emerson Blackhorse, with T. D. Allen. 1967. *Miracle Hill: The Story of a Navajo Boy.* Norman: University of Oklahoma Press.

Molner, Miklos. 1990. Classroom presentation at Indiana University, April.

Montagu, Ashley. 1971. *Touching: The Human Significance of the Skin.* New York: Columbia University Press.

Moon, Susan. 1988. "Sons and Mothers." *Ms.,* October, 46–47.

Moore, F. C. T. 1982. "On Taking Metaphor Literally." In *Metaphor: Problems and Perspectives,* edited by D. S. Miall. Brighton, Sussex, England: Harvester Press.

Morrison, Toni. 1977. *Song of Solomon.* New York: Alfred A. Knopf.

Munro, Alice. 1992. "A Real Life." *New Yorker,* 10 February, 30–40.

———. 1994. "Hired Girl." *New Yorker,* 11 April, 82–88.

Muscari, Paul G. 1988. "The Metaphor in Science and in the Science Classroom." *Science Education* 72 (4): 423–31.

Naisbitt, John. 1982. *Megatrends: Ten New Directions for Transforming Our Lives.* New York: Warner Books.

Naisbitt, John, and Patricia Aburdene. 1990. *Megatrends 2000: Ten New Directions for the 1990s.* New York: William Morrow.

Narayan, R. K. 1985. "Like the Sun." In *Under the Banyan Tree and Other Stories.* New York: Viking.

Nash, Walter. 1993. *Jargon: Its Uses and Abuses.* Cambridge, Mass.: Blackwell.

Nilsen, Alleen Pace, ed., and the Committee on the Junior High and Middle School Booklist. 1991. *Your Reading: A Booklist for Junior High and Middle School Students.* 8th ed. Urbana, Ill.: NCTE.

Nilsen, Alleen Pace, and Kenneth L. Donelson. 1993. *Literature for Today's Young Adults.* 4th ed. New York: HarperCollins.

Norman, Gurney. 1977. "The Dance." *Yardbird Reader* 1 (1): 115–16.

Nugent, Susan Monroe. 1993. "Stories Told in a Different Voice: Women Students as Developing Writers." ERIC 361042.

O'Brien, Edna. 1991. "The Cut." *New Yorker,* 4 November, 40–50.

Okada, Rokuo. 1963. *Japanese Proverbs and Proverbial Phrases.* Vol. 20. Tokyo: Japanese Travel Bureau.

Omar, Noritah. 1996. Personal communication, 1 March.

Opie, Iona, and Moira Tatem. 1989. *A Dictionary of Superstitions.* New York: Oxford University Press.

Ortman, Patricia E. 1993. "A Feminist Approach to Teaching Learning Theory with Educational Applications." *Teaching of Psychology* 20 (1): 38–40.

Ortony, Andrew, et al. 1983. "Theoretical and Methodological Issues in the Empirical Study of Metaphor [and] Implications and Suggestions for Teachers." Reading Education Report 38. Urbana, Ill.: Center for the Study of Reading.

Pace, David, and Sharon L. Pugh. 1996. *Studying for History.* New York: HarperCollins College Publishers.

Partridge, Eric. 1950. *Name into Word: A Discursive Dictionary.* New York: Macmillan.

———. 1958. *Origins: A Short Etymological Dictionary of the English Language.* New York: Macmillan.

Pascal, Francine. 1977. *Hangin' Out with Cici.* New York: Viking.

Paul, Richard. 1985. "Dialectical Reasoning." In *Developing Minds: A Resource Book for Teaching Thinking,* edited by A. Costa. Alexandria, Va.: ASCD.

Peck, Richard. 1989. *Voices after Midnight.* New York: Delacorte Press.

Peelle, Howard A. 1984. *Computer Metaphors: Approaches to Computer Literacy for Educators.* Eugene, Oreg.: International Council for Computers in Education.

Perkins, David. 1988. "Taking Stock after Thirty Years." In *Teaching Literature: What Is Needed Now,* edited by J. Engell and D. Perkins. Cambridge: Harvard University Press.

Peters, Arno. 1990. *Peters Atlas of the World.* New York: Harper and Row.

Phelan, Patricia, ed., and the Committee to Revise *High Interest—Easy Reading.* 1996. *High Interest—Easy Reading: An Annotated Booklist for Middle School and Senior High School.* 7th ed. Urbana, Ill.: NCTE.

Phillips, D. C., and Jonas F. Soltis. 1985. *Perspectives on Learning*. New York: Teachers College Press.

Plante, David. 1983. *Difficult Women: A Memoir of Three.* New York: E. P. Dutton.

Poey, Delia, and Virgil Suarez, eds. 1992. *Iguana Dreams: New Latino Fiction.* New York: HarperPerennial.

Pollio, H. R., et al. 1977. "Psychology and the Poetics of Growth: Figurative Language in Psychology, Psychotherapy, and Education." In *Metaphor and Cognition: A Survey of Recent Publications,* edited by F. Nuessel. Hillsdale, N.J.: Lawrence Erlbaum.

Proust, Marcel. 1922. *Swann's Way.* Translated by C. K. Scott-Moncrieff. New York: Holt.

Pugh, Sharon L. n.d. "Reflection." In unpublished manuscript.

———. n.d. Unpublished journal.

———. 1985. Unpublished journal.

———. 1986. Unpublished journal.

———. 1989a. Unpublished manuscript.

———. 1989b. "Walk Like a Watusi." In unpublished manuscript.

———. 1990. Unpublished manuscript.

———. 1993. "What Color Is Your Cat?" In unpublished manuscript.

Pugh, Sharon L., Jean Wolph Hicks, Marcia Davis, and Tonya Venstra. 1992. *Bridging: A Teacher's Guide to Metaphorical Thinking.* Urbana, Ill.: NCTE.

Qoyawayma, Polingaysi [Elizabeth Q. White], with Vada F. Carlson. 1964. *No Turning Back: A True Account of a Hopi Indian Girl's Struggle to Bridge the Gap between the World of Her People and the World of the White Man.* Albuquerque: University of New Mexico Press.

Ransom, John Crowe. 1955. *Poems and Essays.* New York: Vintage Books.

Reed, Arthea J. S. 1994. *Reaching Adolescents: The Young Adult Book and the School.* New York: Merrill.

Reed, Ishmael, Kathryn Trueblood, and Shawn Wong, eds. 1992. *The Before Columbus Foundation Fiction Anthology: Selections from the American Book Awards, 1980–1990.* New York: W. W. Norton.

Reissman, Rose. 1994. "Reading through Sound Effects: A Radio Writing Approach to Teaching Reading." *Notes Plus* 12 (1): 8–10.

Rheingold, Howard. 1988. *They Have a Word for It: A Lighthearted Lexicon of Untranslatable Words and Phrases.* New York: St. Martin's Press.

Rhys, Jean. 1934. *Voyage in the Dark.* London: Constable.

Rodriguez, Stephanie. 1993. *Time to Stop Pretending.* Middlebury, Vt.: Paul S. Eriksson.

Root, Waverly, and Richard de Rochemont. 1976. *Eating in America: A History.* New York: William Morrow.

Rosengarten, Jim. 1994. "The Mood Museum." *Notes Plus* 12 (1): 10.

Rosenthal, Peggy, and George Dardess. 1987. *Every Cliché in the Book.* New York: William Morrow.

Ross, David, ed. 1970. *The Illustrated Treasury of Poetry for Children.* New York: Grosset and Dunlap.

Roth, Kathleen J. 1985a. *Food for Plants: Teacher's Guide.* East Lansing: Michigan State University Institute for Research on Teaching.

———. 1985b. "Conceptual Change: Learning and Student Processing of Science Texts." Paper read at annual meeting of the American Education Research Association, April, at Chicago. ED 267980.

Roth, Kathleen J., and Charles W. Anderson. 1987. *The Power Plant: Teacher's Guide to Photosynthesis.* East Lansing: Michigan State University Institute for Research on Teaching.

Samuels, Barbara G., and G. Kylene Beers, eds., and the Committee on the Middle School and Junior High Booklist. 1996. *Your Reading: An Annotated Booklist for Middle School and Junior High.* 1995–96 ed. Urbana, Ill.: NCTE.

Sandburg, Carl. 1950. *Complete Poems.* New York: Harcourt, Brace and World.

Santino, Jack. 1994. *All Around the Year: Holidays and Celebrations in American Life.* Urbana: University of Illinois Press.

Santos, Bienvenido N. 1979. *Scent of Apples: A Collection of Stories.* Seattle: University of Washington Press.

Sapir, J. David, and J. Christopher Crocker, eds. 1977. *The Social Use of Metaphor: Essays on the Anthropology of Rhetoric.* Philadelphia: University of Pennsylvania Press.

Schotter, Roni. 1981. *A Matter of Time.* New York: Learning Corp. of America.

Seattle, Chief. [1855] 1978. "All Things Are Connected (Letter to President Franklin Pierce)." In *Native American Testimony: An Anthology of Indian and White Relations,* edited by P. Nabokov. Reprint, New York: Thomas Y. Crowell.

Seldes, George, ed. 1983. *The Great Quotations.* Secaucus, N.J.: Citadel Press.

Sennett, Dorothy, and Anne D. Czamiecki, eds. 1991. *Vital Signs: International Stories on Aging.* St. Paul: Graywolf Press.

The Settlement Cookbook. 1954. New York: Simon and Schuster.

Shacochis, Bob. 1989. "Where Pelham Fell." In *The Next New World.* New York: Crown Publishers.

Sharma, Bhupender K. 1996. Personal communication, 30 January.

Sharma, Sue, and William Gargan. 1988. *Find That Tune: An Index to Rock, Folk-Rock, Disco and Soul in Collections.* 2nd ed. New York: Neal Schuman Publishers.

Sharp, Peggy Agnostino. 1984. "Teaching with Picture Books throughout the Curriculum." *Reading Teacher* 38 (2): 132–37.

Silverstein, Shel. 1974. *Where the Sidewalk Ends: The Poems and Drawings of Shel Silverstein.* New York: HarperCollins.

Simpson, James B., ed. 1988. *Simpson's Contemporary Quotations.* Boston: Houghton Mifflin.

Slagle, Patti. 1994. "Visual Essay." *Notes Plus* 12 (1): 7–8.

Smith, Arthur H. [1914] 1965. *Proverbs and Common Sayings from the Chinese.* Reprint, New York: Paragon Book Reprint Corp.

Sommer, Elyse, and Mike Sommer. 1991. *Falser Than a Weeping Crocodile and Other Similes.* Detroit: Visible Ink Press.

Sommer, Elyse, with Dorrie Weiss, eds. 1995. *Metaphors Dictionary.* Detroit: Gale Research Press.

Spurlin, William J. 1990. "Theorizing Signifyin(g) and the Role of the Reader: Possible Directions for African-American Literary Criticism." *College English* 52 (7): 732–42.

Stambler, Irwin. 1989. *The Encyclopedia of Pop, Rock and Soul.* Rev. ed. New York: St. Martin's Press.

Stanglin, Douglas. 1991. "The Commonwealth to Be Built on the Ruins of Empire." *U.S. News and World Report* 111 (27): 47.

Stannard, Russell. 1990. *The Time and Space of Uncle Albert.* New York: Henry Holt.

Stapleton, Jim. 1991. "Listening to the Mid-Hudson." *North Dakota Quarterly* 59 (2): 156–57.

Sternberg, Robert J. 1990. *Metaphors of Mind: Conceptions of the Nature of Intelligence.* Cambridge: Cambridge University Press.

Stevens, Wallace. 1980. *The Collected Poems of Wallace Stevens.* New York: Alfred A. Knopf.

Stevenson, Burton Egbert, ed. 1953. *The Home Book of Modern Verse: An Extension of The Home Book of Verse.* 2nd ed. New York: Holt, Rinehart and Winston.

———. 1958. *Home Book of Quotations.* New York: Dodd, Mead.

Stoddart, D. Michael. 1990. *The Scented Ape: The Biology and Culture of Human Odour.* Cambridge: Cambridge University Press.

Suhor, Charles. 1991. *Semiotics and the English Language Arts.* Bloomington, Ind.: ERIC Clearinghouse on Reading and Communication Skills.

Suskind, Patrick. 1986. *Perfume: The Story of a Murderer.* Translated by John E. Woods. New York: Alfred A. Knopf.

Sutton, Wendy K., ed. 1997. *Adventuring with Books: An Annotated Booklist for Pre-K–Grade 6.* Urbana, Ill.: NCTE.

Tapahonso, Luci. 1993. "The Kaw River Rushes Westward." In *A Circle of Nations: Voices and Visions of American Indians,* edited by J. Gattuso. Hillsboro, Oreg.: Beyond Words Publishing.

Tennyson, Alfred Lord. 1976. "The Eagle." In *Poems by Alfred Tennyson.* London: The Scolar Press.

Thomas, James, and Denise Thomas, eds. 1990. *The Best of the West 3: New Short Stories from the Wide Side of the Missouri.* Salt Lake City: Peregrine Smith Books.

Tiempo-Torrevillas, Rowena. 1980. *Upon the Willows and Other Stories.* Quezon City, Philippines: New Day Publishers.

Tomlinson, H. M. [1912] 1964. *The Sea and the Jungle.* Reprint, New York: Time.

Trousdale, Ann M., and Violet J. Harris. 1993. "Missing Links in Literary Response: Group Interpretation of Literature." *Children's Literature in Education* 24 (3): 195–207.

Tuleja, Tad. 1987. *Curious Customs: The Stories behind 296 Popular American Rituals.* New York: Harmony Books.

Turner, Barbara K. 1991. *Baby Names for the '90s.* New York: Berkley Books.

Updike, John. 1991. "The Football Factory." In *The Sound of Writing,* edited by A. Cheuse and C. Marshall. New York: Anchor Books.

Urdang, Laurence, Walter W. Hunsinger, and Nancy LaRoche. 1991. *A Fine Kettle of Fish and Other Figurative Phrases.* Detroit: Visible Ink Press.

Wakatsuki-Houston, Jeanne, and James Houston. 1974. *Farewell to Manzanar.* New York: Bantam.

Waldrop, Judith. 1990. "You'll Know It's the 21st Century When . . ." *American Demographics* 12 (December): 22–27.

Ward, Joe. 1995. "Book Details 'Rice-Paper Ceiling' of Japan Firms." *Louisville (Ky.) Courier-Journal,* 17 April, B7–8.

Warnock, Mary. 1994. *Imagination and Time.* Oxford, U.K.: Blackwell.

Watson, Jerry J. 1978. "Picture Books for Young Adolescents." *Clearing House* 51 (5): 8–12.

Watterson, Bill. 1989. "Calvin and Hobbes." Universal Press Syndicate. 31 October.

Webb, C. Anne, ed., and the Committee on the Junior High and Middle School Booklist. 1993. *Your Reading: A Booklist for Junior High and Middle School.* 9th ed. Urbana, Ill.: NCTE.

Wells, H. G. [1895] 1990. *The Time Machine.* Adapted by Les Martin. New York: Random House.

Welty, Eudora. 1947. "Moon Lake." In *The Golden Apples.* New York: Harcourt, Brace and World.

Wendt, Albert. 1986. *The Birth and Death of the Miracle Man.* Middlesex, U.K.: Viking.

Whicher, Stephen E., and Lars Ahnebrink, eds. 1961. *Twelve American Poets.* New York: Oxford University Press.

White, Alana. 1990. *Come Next Spring.* New York: Clarion Books.

Wicomb, Zoe. 1987. *You Can't Get Lost in Cape Town.* New York: Pantheon Books.

Wilde, Oscar. [1890] 1988. *Picture of Dorian Gray and Other Stories.* Reprint, Philadelphia: Lippencott.

Willard, Nancy. 1992. "The Exodus of Peaches." *New Yorker,* 27 July, 30.

Willinsky, John. 1984. *The Well-Tempered Tongue: The Politics of Standard English in the High School.* New York: P. Lang.

———. 1990. *The New Literacy: Redefining Reading and Writing in the School.* New York: Routledge.

Winegrad, Dilys Pegler. 1987. "The Flying Coffin: Memories of a Wartime Childhood." *American Voice* 6 (Spring): 64–76.

Wolf, Dennie Palmer. 1992. "Becoming Knowledge: The Evolution of Art Education Curriculum." In *Handbook of Research on Curriculum: A Project of the American Education Research Association,* edited by P. W. Jackson. New York: Macmillan.

Wolfson, Evelyn. 1986. *Growing Up Indian.* New York: Walker and Company.

Wong, Jade Snow. 1972. "A Measure of Freedom." In *Asian-American Authors,* edited by Kai-yu Hsu and Helen Palubinskas. Boston: Houghton Mifflin.

Wurth, Shirley, ed., and the Committee on the Senior High School Booklist. 1992. *Books for You: A Booklist for Senior High Students.* 11th ed. Urbana, Ill.: NCTE.

Yolen, Jane. 1988. *The Devil's Arithmetic.* New York: Viking.

Zahava, Irene, ed. 1989. *Finding Courage: Writings by Women.* Freedom, Calif.: Crossing Press.

Zemelman, Steven, and Harvey Daniels. 1988. *A Community of Writers: Teaching Writing in the Junior and Senior High School.* Portsmouth, N.H.: Heinemann.

Permissions Acknowledgments

Index

A. H. (abbreviation), 108
A. M. (abbreviation), 108
Abrahamson, Richard F., 53
Aburdene, Patricia, 96, 102
Ackerman, Diane, 155, 187
Adams, Jim, 26
Advertising, 78, 177
Africa, 143–44
African Americans, 171
Ahnebrink, Lars, 185
Alice Through the Looking Glass
    (Carroll), 183
All Quiet on the Western Front
    (Remarque), 37
Allen, Michelle, 18
Allen, Paula Gunn, 149–50
Aloian, David, 56
Alvarez, Julia, 147
Ammer, Christine, 139–40
Ampere, Andre Marie, 137
Anaya, Rudolfo, 150
Anderson, Charles, 37, 39
Anderson, Nick, 30–31
Anderson, Philip, 18
Angelou, Maya, 167
Animal rights, 81–82
Appleman, Philip, 185
Aprile, Dianne, 25, 87
Archambault, John, 18, 63
Argument, 25–33
Aristotle, 34
Armistice Day, 115
Aroma therapy, 179
Asante, Molefi Kete, 60
Audience, 32–33
Australian English, 130

Back to the Future, Part III, 104
Baldwin, Billy, 93
Barden, Jack, 34
Barnes, N. Sue, 21
Barnhart, Clarence, 47
Bartlett, John, 96, 97
Battered women, 49–50
Baynes, Cary F., 170
Beaton, Cecil, 92

Beckwith, Martha Warren, 126
Beeching, Cyril L., 137
Beers, G. Kylene, 53
Belenky, Mary Field, 35
Bellamy, Edward
    Looking Backward, 106
Bender, Steve
    "Outdoors South: Navigators of
        the Night," 24
Berry, Wendell, 27, 87
Best, Judith, 14, 40
Bethancourt, T. Ernesto
    Tune in Yesterday, 106
Bhengu, Vusi, 142
Bierce, Ambrose
    "An Occurrence at Owl Creek
        Bridge," 106
Big Eagle, Duane, 147
Bionics, 75–77
Birthdays, 111–12
Bissoondath, Neil, 150
Blair, Cynthia
    Freedom to Dream, 106
Bloom, Harold, 185
Blum, Stella, 94
Boam, Jeffrey, 57
Boreen, J., 70
Borgmann, Dmitri A., 130
Borman, Kathryn, 34
Boycott, Rosie, 137, 138
Boyer, Paul, 34
Bridges, William, 85
Bris, 122
Brooks, Gwendolyn, 171
Brown, D., 101
Brown, Karen McCarthy, 99
Brown, P., 34
Bruchac, Joseph, 150
Bruner, Jerome, 6
Buckley, Christopher, 138
Bulfinch, Thomas, 112
Bulletin-board anthologies, 46
Bunting, Eve, 18
Burke, Edmund, 84
Burlbaw, Lynn, 18
Burns, Robert, 84
Burroway, Janet, 15

Byars, Betsy, 183

Cahill, Susan, 152
Calendars, 104–5, 108, 112, 119, 122
Calkins, Lucy, 56
Campbell, Joseph, 78, 109, 119
Carle, Eric
    Mixed-Up Chameleon, 4–5
Carnes, Jim, 129
Carroll, Lewis, 183
Carson, Rachel, 85
Carter, Betty, 53
Cartoons, 30–32
Casey, Helen, 25
Celtic new year, 109
Ceremonies, 110–12. *See also* Ritual
    Bris, 122
Cervantes, Miguel de, 193
Change, 84–94
    attitudes and, 90
    conceptual, 37–40
    superstitions and, 87–92
Chapman, Robert, 13
Chargaff, Erwin, 85
Chen, Julie, 60
Christenbury, Leila, 53
Christensen, Jane, 53
Christianity, 109
Chu, Stephen, 84
Church and state, 109
Cinnamond, Jeffrey, 26
Cirlot, J. E., 15
Claiborne, Robert, 135
Classroom galleries, 165, 169
Clausen, Christopher, 142
Clinchy, Blythe McVicker, 35
Clinton, Bill, 78–79
Coffin, Tristram Potter, 113, 115, 116
Cohen, Hennig, 113, 115, 116
Cohen, Laura J., 52
Coleman, Wanda, 147
Come Next Spring (White), 52
Comparisons
    leaf and tree, 161, 162–63
    porcupine and cactus, 161
    spiderweb and fishnet, 161

tears and raindrops, 162
vehicles, 163
Compton-Burnett, Ivy, 99
Conceptual change, 37–40
Conley, Robert J., 150
Content areas, 21–25
Cosman, Madeleine Pelner, 113, 118, 120
Cousteau, Jacques, 85
Cran, William, 129
Cresswell, Rosemary, 153
Crocker, J. Christopher, 13
Crowley, Richard, 4
Crumley, James, 190
Crystal, David, 134
Cultural literacy, 41
Cultural perspectives, 8
Cultural traditions, 109–26. *See also*
    Multiple perspectives; Ritual
    book list about, 112–14
    comparisons, 118–19
    food and, 130–32
    resources for multicultural
        literature, 147–53
    rites of passage, 124
    transformations and, 121–24
cummings, e. e., 185
Curtis, Helena, 21
Cutler, Charles L., 140
Czamiecki, Anne D., 153

Dances with Wolves, 63
Daniels, Harvey, 56
Dardess, George, 13, 15
Darwin, Erasmus, 23
    Botanic Garden, The, 20
    Economy of Vegetation, The, 19–20
Davies, Paul
    *About Time: Einstein's Unfinished
        Revolution*, 95, 97
Davis, Marcia, 23–24
Dawkins, Richard, 21, 27
Delaney, A. Elizabeth
    *Having Our Say: The Delaney
        Sisters' First 100 Years*, 106
Delaney, Sarah L.
    *Having Our Say: The Delaney
        Sisters' First 100 Years*, 106
"Depth perception," 70
Devaney, James, 166
Dialogical reasoning, 8, 80–83
Dickinson, Emily
    "Bat Is Dun with Wrinkled

Wings, The," 20
Dickson, Paul, 138
"Dignifying Monkey, The," 45–46
Dillard, Annie, 157, 167
Dillon, J. T., 144–46
Dinesen, Isak, 184
Donelson, Kenneth L., 53
Dunbar, John, 63
Dunkling, Leslie, 57, 58

Eager, Frances
    Time Tangle, 106
Earth Day, 115
Eiseley, Loren, 3
Eley, Mary M., 113
Elleman, Barbara, 17
Ellison, Emily, 153
Emerson, Ralph Waldo, 101, 195
Empathy, 8
Engen, Trygg, 179
English, 129–41. *See also* Etymology
    Australian, 130
    books on metaphorical roots of,
        139–41
    dialects and, 129
    imperialism and, 129
    onomatopoeic aspects of, 130
English Only movement, 129
Enkido, 47
Environment, 5, 27, 85–87
Eponyms, 136–37
    books on, 138–39
Epsy, Willard R., 139
Erickson, Helen, 51
Esu, 45
Etymology
    dictionaries of, 134
    disputed origins of words, 136–37
    food names, 130–32
    from people's names, 137–38
    place names, 133
    travel and word change, 134–36
    unrelated similar words, 135

False memories, 50
Fashion, 92–94
Feature story, 24
Feldman, Marty, 181
Fischer, Janice, 57
Food, 130–32, 170–75
Fortune cookies, 126
Franklin, Benjamin, 101

Frazer, James G., 114, 121
Freeman, Judith, 168, 191
Friend, Cliff, 98
Frost, Robert, 185
    "Road Not Taken, The," 56
Fujioka, Mayumi, 60

Gallaz, Christophe, 18
Games, 37
Gardner, Howard
    *Frames of Mind: The Theory of
        Multiple Intelligences*, 35–37
Gargan, William, 104
Geometric figures, 159–60
Gerard, R. W., 6
Gernreich, Rudi, 94
Gibbs, Raymond W., 4, 127
Gilbert, W. S., 95
Gilgamesh, 47
Goldberger, Nancy Rule, 35
Goodman, Ellen, 29
Goodspeed, Robert C., 130
Gregorian calendar, 104–5
Grimm, The Brothers, 4
Guided imagery, 53–56
Guralnik, David B., 60

Hall, Susan
    *Using Picture Storybooks to Teach
        Literary Devices*, 17
Hamilton, Sharon
    My Name's Not Suzie, 49
Harmony, 27
Harris, Violet, 36
Havel, Vaclav, 158
Hawking, Stephen
    Brief History of Time, 97
Hearth, Amy Hill
    *Having Our Say: The Delaney
        Sisters' First 100 Years*, 106
Heilenman, Diane, 123
Hemingway, Margaux, 58
Henisch, Bridget Ann, 114
Herbert, George, 97
Herron, Carol, 29
Herzog, George, 125, 126
Hicks, Jean Wolph, 43, 55
Hill, Jane B., 153
Hilton, James
    The Lost Horizon, 106
Hindu mythology, 80–81
Hirsch, E. D., 41

History, 22. *See also* Etymology
    oral, 88–89
Hiura, 151
Hoffman, Robert, 21
Holidays, 110–11. *See also* Ritual
    book list about, 112–14
    history of, 117–18
    recent, 115
Hollander, John, 185
Holmes, Oliver Wendell
    "Our Banker," 97–98
Holocaust Museum, 25
Holyoak, Keith, 3
Honeck, Richard, 21
Hook, J. N., 60
Hope, Christopher, 48
Houston, James, 143, 148
Hsu, Kai-yu, 151
Huang Yon Ping, 81–82
Hungary, 26
Hunsinger, Walter W., 15, 141
Hunter, Holly, 181

I Ching, 170–71
Iliad, The, 42
Image (*San Francisco Examiner*'s
    magazine), 78
India, 80–81
Indigenous Peoples Day, 110
Innocenti, Roberto, 18
Ison, Anna H., 140
Ison, Isaac, 140

Jackson, Holbrook, 96
Jacobson, John D., 140
Japanese-Americans, 143–44
Jarrell, Randall
    "Bats," 23–24
Jeans, Peter D., 141
Jensen, Julie M., 53
Jeremias, James, 57
Joan of Arc, 80
Johnson, Mark, 20, 180
Johnson, Mead, 60
Johnston, Peter H., 3
Journal writing, 52, 64
    quote of the day, 98

Kalpakian, Laura, 170
Kanwar, Asha, 151
Karp, Miriam, 123

Keller, Helen, 187
Kenyatta, Jomo, 143–44
Kinesthetic awareness. *See* Movement
King, Nancy, 181
Kingsolver, Barbara, 180
Kitchen poetry, 172–73
Kivan, Goodman, 142
Knots on a Counting Rope (Martin &
    Archambault), 18, 63
Kohl, Herbert, 75–76
Kohl, Judith, 75–76
Kopp, Rochelle, 28
Krakatau, 85
Kuhn, Jennifer, 4–5
Kwanzaa, 115

Lahrson, Ann, 28
Lakoff, George, 20, 180
Lamm, Robert William, 104
Language
    imagination and, 3–10
    thought and, 3–10
    used by Nazis, 29–30
LaRoche, Nancy, 15, 141
Lax, Roger, 97
Lazarus, Emma, 80
Lazebnik, Philip, 40
Le Guerer, Annick, 175, 178
Learning, 34–47
    conceptual change, 37–40
    gender and, 35
    multiple ways of knowing, 42–47
Lee, Audrey, 148
Lee, Bruce, 84
Lee, Hannah, 58
Lee, Robert C.
    Timequake, 106
Leighton, Louise, 97
L'Engle, Madeleine
    A Wrinkle in Time, 107
Leonard, Michael, 78
Lindsay, David
    Voyage to Arcturus, 77
Linnaeus, Carl, 20
Literary devices, 17–18
Literature, 51–53, 70–75
    metaphors of time in, 97
    resources for multicultural
        literature, 147–53
    world, 142–53
    writing and, 146
Loisy, Jean de, 82

Lopez, Barry H., 168
Lost Boy, The (Warner Brothers), 57
Luria, Salvador, 21
Luthuli, Nester, 142

MacNeil, Robert, 129
Mahood, Wayne, 21
Major, Clarence, 141
Malan, Robin, 153
Malcolm, Janet, 157–58
Mallon, Thomas, 64
Man Who Could Call Down Owls, The
    (Bunting), 18
"Man Who Could Fly, The," 142
Man Who Loved Cat Dancing, The, 63
Mann, Thomas
    Magic Mountain, The, 95
Maps, 6–7, 133, 193
Marcus, Greil, 78
Markels, Alex, 95
Markus, Hazel, 48
Marshall, Helen Lowrie, 84
Martin, Bill, Jr., 18, 63
Martin, Judith, 114
Martin Luther King Day, 115
May, Wanda, 36
May Day, 120
McBride, William G., 53
McCrum, Robert, 129
McDonald, Donald S., 7, 130
McDonald, James C., 166
    English Journal, 51
McKnight, Reginald, 151
McNamara, Shelley, 17
Meaning, 8, 13–33
Melville, Herman, 4
Memory, 174–75
Menken, Alan, 69
Menosky, Joe, 40
Mercator Map, 7
Merwin, W. S., 184
Metaphor
    aging and, 182
    argument and, 25–33
    change and, 182
    children and, 4
    comparison theory of, 14
    connotations of, 26, 160
    constructing meaning and, 8,
        13–33
    content areas and, 21–25
    conventional versus imaginative
        use of, 14

development and, 182
entropy and, 182
as heuristic, 18–21
interaction theory of, 14
learning and, 11, 34–47
maturity and, 182
mixed, 29
ritual and, 109–26
of senses
    hearing, 165–69
    movement and touch, 180–91
    olfactory, 175–79
    taste, 170–75
    visual, 158–65
structure and correspondences,
    160–62
substitution theory of, 14
symbol-making and, 8, 14–18
therapy and, 4
time and, 97–104
transformation and, 120–24, 182
transitoriness and, 182
types of
    animals, 82–83, 91, 183–84,
        188–89
    bridge, 6
    chameleon, 4–5
    domino effect, 18
    English as metaphor, 129–41
    food, 170–75
    laying an egg, 15
    map, 6–7
    mirrors, 183
    nut, 119
    people, 77–80, 137–38
    sack, 13
    salad, 131
    seasonal images, 86, 185–87
    shrinking globe, 119
    water images, 86
    weather images, 86
Metaphorical thinking, 3–4
Metonymy, 4
Meynell, Sir Francis, 97
Mills, Joyce, 4
Minnesota Humanities Commission,
    151
Molner, Miklos, 26
Montagu, Ashley, 187
Moon, Susan, 180
Moore, F. C. T., 13
Morrison, Toni, 4
Movement, 180–91

kinetics of animals, 183–84
light versus heavy, 182
walk, 181
Moyers, Bill, 78, 109, 119
Multiple perspectives, 69–83
    culture and, 109–26
    dialogical thinking, 80–83
    English and, 129–41
    persona and, 70–75
    proverbs, 124–26
    superstitions in other cultures, 91
    time and, 105
    world literature and, 141–53
Multiplicity of reality, 8
Munro, Alice, 187, 191
Muscari, Paul, 20, 67

Naisbitt, John, 96
    Megatrends, 101, 102
Names, 56–64
    Chinese tradition, 58
    female, 60, 62
    free association and, 58
    male, 59, 61
    Native American traditions, 63
    puns and, 64
    stories of, 57–58
Narayan, R. K., 146
Native Americans, 27, 34, 63, 110, 133
Nature. See Environment
Nazi language, 29–30
NCTE booklist series, 53
Newspapers, 30–31
Ngubo, Gladman "Mvukuzane," 142
Nilsen, Alleen Pace, 53
Norman, Gurney, 148
Nose, 175
Number, 122
Nurius, Paul, 48

O'Brien, Edna, 187
Observation, 164
Okada, Rokuo, 124, 125, 126
Omar, Noritah, 60
Onomatopoeia, 130, 166
Opie, Iona, 88
O'Reilly, Patricia, 34
Ortony, Andrew, 13
Orwell, George
    1984, 99, 108
O'Shaughnessy, Arthur, 101

Pace, David, 22
Palubinskas, Helen, 151
Partridge, Eric, 134, 139
Pascal, Francine
    Hangin' Out with Cici, 107
Paul, Richard, 70
Peck, Richard
    Voices after Midnight, 107
Peelle, Howard, 11, 19
Performance-based assessment, 36
Perfume, 177–78
Perkins, David, 42
Persona writing, 69–75
    literature and, 70–75
Peters, Arno, 7
Phelan, Patricia, 53
Photosynthesis, 37
Piano, The, 181
Plante, David, 50
Poetry, 185
    kitchen poetry, 172–73
    tree poetry, 162–63
Poey, Delia, 152
Political cartoons, 30–32
Political correctness, 26
Political slogans, 28
Pollio, H. R., 49
Polynesia, 143–44
Power of Myth, The (Campbell), 78,
    109
Presley, Elvis, 78–79, 116
Projection, 70
Proust, Marcel, 174
Proverbs, 124–26
    east versus west, 124–25
    fortune cookies, 126
    opposite, 126
Public health, 34
Pugh, Sharon L., 3, 22, 65–66, 172–73,
    184, 188, 190
Puns, 64

Qoyawayma, Polingaysi, 144

Ransom, John Crowe, 185
Reading, 51–53
    therapeutic, 52
Recording, 164
Reed, Arthea J. S., 53
Reed, Ishmael, 152
Reflection, 44

Reissman, Rose, 37
Representation, 123
Research, 44
Rhys, Jean, 50, 175
Rites of passage, 124
Ritual, 109–26. *See also* Multiple
     perspectives
     birthday, 111–12
     book list about, 112–14
     in college towns, 116
     evolving, 115
     regional, 115–16
     sports and, 116–17
     symbols in, 122
Rochemont, Richard de, 114
Rodriguez, Stephanie
     Time to Stop Pretending, 49
Roget's Thesaurus, 167
Romeo and Juliet (Shakespeare), 56
Root, Waverly, 114
Rose Blanche (Innocenti & Gallaz), 18
Rosengarten, Jim, 37
Rosenthal, Peggy, 13, 15
Roser, Nancy L., 53
Roth, Kathleen, 38
Roy, Amita, 81
Rubinstein, Helena, 94

Saint Lucia Day, 121
"Salmon Swims Up the River," 70–75
Samhain, 109
Samuels, Barbara G., 53
Sandburg, Carl, 184
Santino, Jack, 114, 116
Santos, Bienvenido, 152
Sapir, J. David, 13
Scapegoat, 120
Schema, 37
Schotter, Roni
     A Matter of Time, 107
Schwartz, Delmore, 97
Schwartz, Stephen, 69
Science, 24–25, 37, 76–77, 85
Science Frontiers, 50
Sculpturing, 182
Seasons, 122, 185–87
Seattle, Chief, 27
Seldes, George, 28
Self, 48–66, 119–20
     battered women and, 49–50
     names and, 56–64
     personal transformations and,
        123–24

writers and, 50–51
Semiotics, 15
Sennett, Dorothy, 153
Shabalala, November Marsata, 142
Shacochis, Bob, 184
Shakespeare, William, 56, 94
Shape of the World, The (PBS series), 7
Sharma, Bhupender K., 60
Sharma, Sue, 104
Signified, 13
Signifier, 13
Silence, 146, 149
Silverstein, Shel, 4
Simpson, James B., 85, 92, 93
Skin, 187
Slagle, Patti, 37
Smell. *See* Metaphor, of senses
Smith, Arthur H., 125, 126
Smith, Frederick, 97
Sommer, Elyse, 189, 190
Sommer, Mike, 189, 190
Sound bites, 28
Sound collages, 168
Sports, 116–17
Spurlin, William, 45
Stafford, Jean, 190
Stannard, Russell
     The Time and Space of Uncle Albert,
        107
Stapleton, Jim, 168
Star Trek, 40–42
Star Wars, 78
Stevens, Wallace, 185
Stevenson, Burton Egbert, 96, 97, 100
Stoddart, Michael, 178
Strauss, Levi, 94
Structure
     correspondences and, 160–62
     human-made, 164
     natural, 164
Student-centered classroom, 144–46
Suarez, Virgil, 152
Suhor, Charles, 15
Sullivan, Arthur, 95
Sunstein, Bonnie, 18
Superstitions, 87–92
Surtees, Robert Smith, 136
Suskind, Patrick, 176
Sutton, Wendy K., 53
Symbol, 8, 14–18, 122
     definition of, 15
     emotions and, 16
     shoes as, 25

stories for, 17
Synecdoche, 120
Synesthesia, 168

Tapahonso, Luci, 34
Tarule, Jill Mattuck, 35
Tatem, Moira, 88
Teacher-centered classroom, 144–46
Tennyson, Alfred Lord, 184
Texture, 190–91
Thagard, Paul, 3
Thanksgiving, 110
Thompson, Francis, 85
Time, 8, 95–108
     cultural differences and, 105
     future and, 99
     metaphor and, 97–104
     microscope versus telescope view
        of, 76
     turn of the century, 96, 99, 101–4
     universality of, 105
Tobias, Charlie, 98
Tomlinson, H. M., 167
Touch, 180–91
Traditions. *See* Multiple perspectives;
     Ritual
Transactive writing, 46
Transmediation, 37
Trees, 161, 162–63
Trousdale, Ann, 36
Trueblood, Kathryn, 152
Tuleja, Tad, 109, 114
Turner, Barbara K., 60

University of Louisville, 24
Updike, John, 191
Urdang, Laurence, 15, 141

Valentine's Day, 117–18
Veteran's Day, 115
View from the Oak, The (Kohl), 75–76

Wakatsuki-Houston, Jeanne, 143, 148
Waldrop, Judith, 102
Walter Hays School, 110
Ward, Joe, 28
Watson, Jerry, 17
Watterson, Bill
     "Calvin and Hobbes," 22

Webb, C. Anne, 53
Wells, H. G., 99
    The Time Machine, 107, 108
Welty, Eudora, 171–72
Wendt, Albert, 143
Whicher, Stephen E., 185
White, Alana, 52
Whitman, Walt, 184
Wicomb, Zoe, 171–72
Wilde, Oscar, 176
Wilder, Gene, 181
Wilder, Thornton, 98
Wilhelm, Richard, 170

Wilkie, Wendell, 28
Willard, Nancy, 187
Williams, Tennessee, 98
Willinsky, John, 129
Winegrad, Dilys Pegler, 143
Wodehouse, P. G., 97
Wolf, Dennie Palmer, 34
Wolfson, Evelyn, 63
Women's Ways of Knowing (Belenky,
    Clinchy, Goldberger & Tarule), 35
Wong, Jade Snow, 149
Wong, Shawn, 152
Wrinkle in Time, A (L'Engle), 37

Writing
    literature and, 70–75, 146
    persona writing, 69–75
Wurth, Shirley, 53

Yeats, William Butler, 180
Yolen, Jane
    The Devil's Arithmetic, 107
Young Frankenstein, 181

Zahava, Irene, 153
Zemelman, Steven, 56

Authors

Sharon L. Pugh is an associate professor of language education and director of the Student Academic Center at Indiana University. She was director of the Young Authors Program in the Indianapolis Public Schools and has published short fiction in several literary magazines. She teaches and does research in critical reading and recently co-authored a text on reading and studying history as part of the HarperCollins College Series. Another ongoing focus of her work concerns the use of multicultural tradebooks in language arts teaching.

Jean Wolph Hicks is a language education doctoral candidate at Indiana University. She is a secondary education instructor at the University of Louisville, where she works with the Louisville Writing Project. She also has worked with Southern Indiana schools committed to systemic reform through the Harmony School Education Center of Bloomington. She has taught preservice education courses at the University of Louisville and Indiana University since 1987 and works with student and intern teachers. Previously she taught language arts and journalism at the middle and high school levels in Oldham and Jefferson Counties, Kentucky.

Marcia Davis is currently doing graduate work in language education at Indiana University. She is co–vice president of the Bloomington chapter of the International Reading Association and has taught middle school language arts, science, and drama in Michigan, California, New Jersey, and Indiana. She has also coached students in Olympics of the Mind, a program for imaginative thinking. Her professional writing includes short stories, literature reviews, and computer games, as well as editing.

This book was typeset in Palatino and Avant Garde Demi by Electronic Imaging.
The typeface used on the cover was Bernhard Modern.
The book was printed on 50 lb. Finch by Capital City Press.